PSYCHOPATHOLOGY

Contemporary Jungian Perspectives

Andrew Samuels

PSYCHOPATHOLOGY
Contemporary Jungian Perspectives

Edited and with an Introduction by
Andrew Samuels

THE GUILFORD PRESS
New York   London

Printed in the United States of America

This book is printed on acid-free paper

Last digit is print number   9 8 7 6 5 4 3 2 1

Library of Congress Cataloging-in-Publication Data

Psychopathology : contemporary Jungian perspectives / edited and with
   an introduction by Andrew Samuels
      p.   cm.
   Reprint. Originally published: London: Karnac Books, 1989.
   Includes bibliographical references and index.
   ISBN 0-89862-765-6 (hard.) — ISBN 0-89862-473-8 (pbk.)
   1. Mental illness.   2. Psychiatry—Philosophy.   3. Jung, C. G.
   (Carl Gustav), 1879–1961.   I. Samuels, Andrew.
   [DNLM: 1. Jungian Theory.   2. Mental Disorders.   3. Psychoanalytic
   Theory.   4. Psychoanalytic Therapy.   WM 469 P9784 1989a]
RC 454.4.P797   1991
616.89—dc20
DNLM/DLC
for Library of Congress   91-12646
                                                                CIP

CONTENTS

ACKNOWLEDGEMENTS

I am grateful to the following for their helpful comments on an early draft of the Introduction or for their support in other ways; responsibility for the ideas expressed in the Introduction, the introductory remarks before each paper, and the selection of papers is, of course, mine: Coline Covington, Miranda Davies, Hugh Gee, Rosemary Gordon, Rosie Parker, Corinna Peterson, Fred Plaut, Arthur Sherman, and Barbara Wharton. Roger Hobdell was the Series Editor for the volume, and I have appreciated his advice and encouragement.

In addition, the work done on the papers by successive Editors of *The Journal of Analytical Psychology* deserves acknowledgement: Michael Fordham, Fred Plaut, Judith Hubback and Rosemary Gordon.

Finally, I want to express heartfelt thanks to the authors for reading, revising, and approving the short introductions that precede their papers. This has made the production of the book a truly international and collaborative venture.

Acknowledgements and bibliographical details for each paper are given at the start of that paper.

Acknowledgements are due to Routledge, London, and Princeton University Press, Princeton, NJ, for permission to quote from the *Collected Works of C. G. Jung*.

NOTES ON BIBLIOGRAPHY AND CONVENTIONS

Citations of the works of C. G. Jung

Except where indicated, reference to Jung's writings is by volume and paragraph number of the *Collected Works of C. G. Jung*, published by Routledge, London, and Princeton University Press, Princeton, NJ (edited by H. Read, M. Fordham, G. Adler and W. McGuire; translated mainly by R. Hull).

Note on spelling

The convention has evolved, especially in Britain, of using the spelling 'phantasy' as opposed to 'fantasy' when it is intended to refer to whatever activity lies under and behind thought and feeling. 'Fantasy' is restricted to daydreaming and mental activity of a similar nature of which the subject is aware. The contributors to this book, coming, as they do, from diverse backgrounds, do not display a uniformity of style. Editorial policy has been to let each writer retain his/her original usage. The Editor's present personal preference is to use 'fantasy' in all circumstances, relying on context to make the meaning clear.

CONTRIBUTORS

Gustav Dreifuss, Ph.D. Diploma in Analytical Psychology, C.G. Jung Institute, Zürich. Training Analyst and former President, Israel Association of Analytical Psychology. Lecturer, Psychotherapy, Psychiatric Department, Rambam Hospital, Haifa. Author, *Collected Papers 1965–1984* and *Bild und Seele* (with Martin Kinz). In practice in Haifa.

Alan Edwards, M.D., M.R.C.P., F.R.C.Psych. Training Analyst, Society of Analytical Psychology. Former Medical Director, C. G. Jung Clinic, London. Former Consultant Psychiatrist, Watford General and Napsbury Hospitals. In practice near London.

Michael Fordham, B.A., M.D., F.R.C.Psych., Hon.F.B.P.S. Training Analyst, Society of Analytical Psychology. Co-editor of the *Collected Works of C. G. Jung*. Founding editor, *The Journal of Analytical Psychology*. Author of numerous books, including *Children as Individuals, The Self and Autism, Explorations into the Self*. In practice near London.

C. T. Frey-Wehrlin, Dr.Phil. Professional Member, Society of Analytical Psychology. Training Analyst, C. G. Jung Institute, Zürich. Initiator, co-founder and former Director of Psychotherapy, Zürichberg Clinic (Clinic and Research Centre for Jungian Psychology). In practice in Zürich.

Rosemary Gordon, Ph.D., F.B.P.S., Fell. Anthrop. Soc. Training Analyst, Society of Analytical Psychology. Editor, *The Journal of Analytical Psychology*. Author of *Dying and Creating: a Search for Meaning*. In practice in London.

Judith Hubback, M.A. Training Analyst, Society of Analytical Psychology. Former Editor, *The Journal of Analytical Psychology*. Author, *Wives Who Went to College* and *People Who Do Things to Each Other: Essays in Analytical Psychology*. In practice in London.

Peer Hultberg, Dr.Phil. Diploma in Analytical Psychology, C. G. Jung Institute, Zürich. Training Analyst, C. G. Jung Institute, Zürich. In practice in Hamburg.

Mario Jacoby, Ph.D. Diploma in Analytical Psychology, C. G. Jung Institute, Zürich. Training Analyst, C. G. Jung Institute, Zürich. Author, *The Analytic Encounter: Transference and Human Relationship, Longing for Paradise: Psychological Perspectives on an Archetype, Individuation and Narcissism* (forthcoming). Co-author, *Das Böse im Märchen*. In practice near Zürich.

Thomas Kirsch, M.D. Member of the Society of Jungian Analysts of Northern California. First Vice-President, International Association of Analytical Psychology. Co-editor, Jungian section, *International Encyclopaedia of Psychiatry, Psychoanalysis, Psychology, and Neurology*. In practice in Palo Alto, California.

Rushi Ledermann, Cert. Ment. Health. Training Analyst, Society of Analytical Psychology and British Association of Psychotherapists. Formerly psychotherapist, Lady Chichester Hospital, Hove, Sussex. In practice in Hove, Sussex.

Fred Plaut, B.Ch., D.P.M., M.B., F.R.C.Psych. Training Analyst, Society of Analytical Psychology and German Society for Analytical Psychology. Former editor, *The Journal of Analytical Psychology*. Co-author, *A Critical Dictionary of Jungian Analysis*. Author, *Analysis Analysed* (forthcoming). In practice in Berlin.

Joseph Redfearn, M.A., M.D.(Cantab.), M.D. (Johns Hopkins), M.R.C.Psych. Training Analyst, Society of Analytical Psychology. Author, *My Self, My Many Selves*. In practice in London.

Andrew Samuels, Dip. Soc. Admin., Dip. Soc. Wrk. Studs. Training Analyst, Society of Analytical Psychology and British Association of Psychotherapists. Author, *Jung and the Post-Jungians* and *The Plural Psyche: Personality, Morality, and the Father*. Co-author, *A Critical Dictionary of Jungian Analysis*. Editor, *The Father: Contemporary Jungian Perspectives*. In practice in London.

Nathan Schwartz-Salant, Ph.D. Diploma in Analytical Psychology, C. G. Jung Institute, Zürich. Member and Training Analyst, New York Association for Analytical Psychology. Author, *Narcissism and Character Transformation: the Psychology of Narcissistic Character Disorders* and *The Borderline Personality: Vision and Healing*. Co-editor of the *Chiron Clinical Series*. In practice in New York.

Eva Seligman, Dip. Ment. Health., Cert. Soc. Sci. Training Analyst, Society of Analytical Psychology. Former senior staff member, Institute of Marital Studies, Tavistock Centre. Co-author, *Marriage: Studies in Emotional Conflict and Growth*. In practice in London.

Anthony Storr, M.B., B.Chir., M.A., D.P.M.., F.R.C.Psych., F.R.C.P. Honorary Consulting Psychiatrist, Oxford Health Authority. Author of numerous books, including *The Integrity of the Personality, The Dynamics of Creation, Jung, The Art of Psychotherapy, The School of Genius*.

Mary Williams, Cert. Ment. Health. Training Analyst, Society of Analytical Psychology. Former tutor in marital therapy, Tavistock Clinic.

Luigi Zoja, Ph.D. Diploma in Analytical Psychology, C. G. Jung Institute, Zürich. Training Analyst of C. G. Jung Institute, Zürich and Centro Italiano di Psicologia Analitica. Author, *Drugs, Addiction, and Initiation.* Co-author, *Incontri con la morte.* In practice in Milan.

INTRODUCTION

Andrew Samuels

... the loss of manifest psychopathology may or may not be desirable, for there is a positive aspect of mental disorder.
[Fordham, 1978, p. 8]

The psyche does not exist without pathologising.
[Hillman, 1975, p. 70]

I am simply a psychiatrist. ... Everything else is secondary for me. ... I am merely thinking within the framework of a special task laid upon me: to be a proper psychiatrist, a healer of the soul. That is what I have discovered myself to be and this is how I function as a member of society.
[C. G. Jung, in Adler, 1974, pp. 70–71]

The Background

Since its inception in 1955, *The Journal of Analytical Psychology* has stood for the clinical dimension of analytical psychology. Jungian analysts, like their counterparts in psychoanalysis, have found it necessary to expound their

1

refinement of thinking and technique in a professionally public arena. The *Journal* has been edited and staffed by members of the Society of Analytical Psychology, London, and hence has shown a marked, though by no means exclusive, orientation towards what I have called the developmental school of analytical psychology (Samuels, 1985). I use that term rather than a phrase like 'the London school' because developmental analytical psychology is now a world-wide enterprise, and it would be foolish to impose a geographical limitation where one no longer exists. At one time, the appellation 'London' made sense, particularly in apposition or opposition to 'the Zürich school'; 'Zürich', too, is an overly geographical tag. It is far better to refer to the classical school of analytical psychology.

In fact, the reader will find some papers in this volume which emanate from classically oriented analytical psychologists. What is more, the influence of the archetypal school, with its emphasis on impersonal, mythopoeic depth, will also be apparent. Two papers—those on borderline personality disorder and on marital dysfunction—were not published in the *Journal*; they have been included to make the scope of the book as comprehensive as possible.

It may be asked why it has been thought fruitful to produce a volume of papers on psychopathology, most of which have already been published in the same organ. There are two reasons: first, to meet a very real need for a resource book for analysts and psychotherapists which deals in turn with the more commonly encountered psychological conditions, helping the clinician to sharpen her or his thinking in respect of the problem the patient is bringing. Such a need has been put to the editor on numerous occasions by trainees and by more experienced practitioners. The second reason for producing the book arose, in true Jungian fashion, after it had been decided to go ahead on the basis of the first reason! It became apparent that the papers assembled for the book contained a wealth of clinical knowledge—pragmatic, flexible, disposable, but, above all, rooted in what actually happens in analysis. What is more, although these papers speak to discrete pathologies, it is my contention that the writers have, as a group, achieved a difficult balancing act between the claims of the individual, the soul and the imagination—and the claims of the typical, the professional and the clinical task of healing. I shall return to this topic in due course.

The knowledge to which I have been referring deserves an airing beyond the Jungian community, which this book is intended to provide. Psychoanalysis itself is an exemplar of pluralistic diversity: classical, ego-psychology, self-psychology, Kleinian etc. But if we were to extend the field and call it depth psychology (or dynamic psychology), then analytical psychology takes its place as one strand of the diversity. Not that analytical psychology and psychoanalysis are the same—rather, they are complementary, sibling disciplines.

The Jungian heritage

To this end, it may be helpful to outline a few features of the common Jungian background of these authors, for there are some areas of theory and practice in which Jung's can now reasonably be regarded as a pioneering voice. He seems to have anticipated, sometimes by 25 years or more, what would become accepted as mainstream in psychoanalysis. Of course, Jung often did not go on to develop his initial insights and intuitions, but giving a flavour of some of them will serve as a useful orientation.

For example, the contribution of analytical psychology to the general area of countertransference reflects Jung's prescience. As early as 1929, Jung was saying that 'You can exert no influence if you are not susceptible to influence. ... The patient influences [the analyst] unconsciously. ... One of the best-known symptoms of this kind is the countertransference evoked by the transference' (CW 16, para. 163). And in the same paper Jung refers to countertransference as a 'highly important organ of information'. This can be compared with Freud's early negative evaluation of countertransference as neurotic and suggestive of the analyst's resistance. In sum, Jung's conception of analysis is of a 'dialectical process'. By this, he means that there are two fully involved persons present, there is a two-way interaction between them, and they are to be conceived of as 'equals' (CW 16, para. 289). What Jung means by 'equality' resembles the more modern word 'mutuality'. It follows that Jung emphasized what is nowadays called the 'real relationship' or 'treatment alliance' alongside the transference relationship.

Regarding psychopathology, from his early days as a psychiatrist, Jung was interested in schizophrenia (then known as *dementia praecox*). As he developed his concept of the collective unconscious and the theory of archetypes, he moved to the position that psychosis could be understood as an overwhelming of the ego by the contents of the collective unconscious (hence the fantastical imagery), and as demonstrating the domination of the personality by a split-off complex or complexes.

The crucial implication of this position was that schizophrenic utterance and behaviour could be seen as meaningful, if only it were possible to work out what the meaning might be. This was where the technique of word association was first used and, later, amplification as a method of seeing the clinical material in conjunction with religious and cultural motifs. This led, firmly and finally, to Jung's break with Freud, which occurred with the publication of the volume later known as *Symbols of Transformation* (*CW* 5).

But what of the aetiology of schizophrenia and psychosis? The evolution of Jung's thought reveals some uncertainty. He is clear that psychosis is a psychosomatic disorder, that changes in body chemistry and personality distortions are somehow intertwined. The issue was which of these should be regarded as primary. Jung's superior, Bleuler, thought that some kind of toxin or poison was developed by the body, which then led to psychological disturbance. Jung's contribution was to reverse the elements: psychological activity may lead to somatic changes (*CW* 3, para. 318). Jung did attempt to combine his ideas with those of Bleuler, by means of an ingenious formula. While the mysterious toxin might well exist in all of us, it would only have its devastating effect if psychological circumstances were favourable to this. Alternatively, a person might be genetically predisposed to develop the toxin, and this would lead to psychosis if the psychological circumstances were so inclined.

That psychosis was anything other an an innate, neurological abnormality was, in its time, revolutionary. That its causation was psychogenic within a psychosomatic framework (Jung's final position—*CW* 3, paras. 553ff.) enabled him to propose that psychological treatment might be appropriate. The decoding of schizophrenic communication and its treatment within a therapeutic milieu are central stands in the existential–analytic approaches developed by Binswanger (1945) and Laing (1967) and are, to an extent, recognizable in contemporary psychiatric endeavours.

When psychotic material is florid, it can resemble the phenomena of creative inspiration and religious conversion. However, the psychotic lacks a container of sufficient strength (such as mother, or work of art, or religious ritual) for stability and a sense of purpose to be maintained until individual balance is restored and meaning becomes apparent.

Concluding this brief survey of some pertinent aspects of Jung's thought, there is a sense in which his is an object relations psychology. Jung was among the first to spell out the primary importance of the relationship of mother and infant in terms recognizable today. This has to be compared with Freud's insistence that it was the oedipal triangle that imposed its vicissitudes on later relationships (*CW* 8, para. 723, written in 1927). In the same paper, Jung stressed the centrality of the need to separate from the mother. In his view, clinicians have to accept that, throughout maturation, there will be regression, that separation from the mother involves a struggle, and that nutritional functions are of central psychologial importance.

Jung gave descriptions of psychological processes, some of which he applied to infantile states, all of which anticipate object relations theory. One such process is splitting, which is usually seen in Kleinian theory as an early defence involving control of the object by dividing it into a good and a bad part-object. Similarly, the ego is also divided into good and bad. Jung refers to splitting in relation to the mother—or, to be more precise, the image of the mother. He wrote of the 'dual mother' (in 1912), and this phrase can be understood on several levels: as the duality between the personal mother and pre-personal psychological patterning of the mother archetype, or as the duality between good and bad images of the mother (*CW* 5, paras. 111 and 352).

A second process is delineated by Jung as 'primary identity'. By this he means an experiential likeness based on an original non-differentiation of subject and object. Such identity, as experienced by a baby in relation to the mother, for instance, is unconscious and 'characteristic of the mental state of early infancy' (*CW* 6, paras. 741–742). Already in 1921 Jung had depicted a stage of development similar to Balint's 'area of creation' or Mahler's 'normal autistic stage'.

Then there is Jung's use of a special kind of identity for which he employs the term *participation mystique*. This is a phrase borrowed from Lévy-Bruhl, the anthropologist. In anthropology this refers to a form of relationship with a thing; in this relationship, the person involved cannot distinguish him- or herself from the thing in question—be it cult object, holy artifact or spirit. Jung used the term from 1912 onward to refer to a state of affairs between people in which the subject, or a part of the subject, attains influence over the other, or vice versa, so that the two become indistinguishable to the subject's ego. Translated into psychoanalytic language, Jung is really describing projective identification in which a part of the personality is projected into the object, and the object is experienced as if it were the projected content.

Jung was wont to claim that his approach to analysis subsumed and transcended those of Freud and Adler (CW 16, paras. 114–174). To some extent, this claim does little more than illuminate Jung's leadership complex and power urges. But, in quieter vein, it is possible to see in many of these papers how the Jungian 'bit' sits firmly on or in a psychoanalytic grounding, whilst retaining its distinctiveness. The integration of analytical psychology with many aspects of contemporary psychoanalysis has been an absolute necessity as and when Jungians faced up to the deficiencies in Jung's clinical teaching. In my view, many of the criticisms of analytical psychology that were valid in, say, 1945 have been addressed by this integration. So the debt to psychoanalysis is acknowledged to be immense. However, it is fair to say that the contribution made by analytical psychology has not always been duly recognized (see Samuels, 1985, pp. 9–11, 270–271). In the short introductory passages that precede each paper I try to pick out the Jungian heritage and highlight it, thus facilitating the use of the book by psychoanalytic and eclectic practitioners.

Attitudes to psychopathology

Psychopathology is a quest for the meaning of the soul's suffering. At its worst, as Hillman says, it can involve the soul's suffering of meaning (1975, p. 71). There is a general ambivalence towards psychopathology within depth psychology, though hardly ever a total turning away from the fascinating task of trying to say something definite, even for a moment, about the shifting grounds of mental pain. Even those who loathe conventional psychopathology will sometimes find themselves using it. But what about this ambivalence? What is the problem with psychopathology?

There seem to be at least seven main objections to the project of psychopathology:

1. By the patient being labelled, her or his individuality is lost. When aping a medical doctor, the soul doctor deprives himself of his best medicine—an intuitive, attentive connection to the internal world of the individual before him.
2. There is an epistemological objection. The categories of psychopathology do not describe anything in the patient, for they are mere constructs. Rather, diagnostic categories imported unnecessarily from descriptive psychiatry primarily reveal the clinician's state of mind.
3. Psychopathology is sometimes regarded as 'unpsychological'— an insult and affront to the psyche itself.
4. Psychopathology fails to see through itself, fails to notice how *relative* its findings are—normality for women is different from normality for men; last century's madness is not this century's; Italian and British stereotypes of behaviour are different; no two psychiatrists can agree on a diagnosis.
5. The use of psychopathology plays into the modern tendency to overvalue expertise and professionalism. The problem here is that the expert pathologist may be a poor therapist. Moreover, part of the appeal of psychotherapy in a dark, technocratic age is that there are no obvious tools of the trade other than the self or selves involved. Psychopathologizing throws this treasure away.
6. Notwithstanding struggles to avoid moralizing, psychopathology cannot avoid contamination from ethical hierarchy, whether this is on a collective basis or contained in the analyst's own prejudices and problems (see Samuels, 1989, pp. 11–13).
7. There is a political angle to psychopathology in that segments of the population are marginalized.

Clearly, there is some substance to each of these objections. However, rather than defend psychopathology, it occurred to me that it might be possible to scan the list for a possible

enantiodromia. This term, which Jung borrowed from Hera-
kleitos, means that sooner or later everything turns into, or is
seen to be identical with, its opposite (*CW* 6, para. 708). Psychopathology is apparently inimical to any therapy based on depth
psychology. It is apparently hostile to the development of the
individual. It is apparently moralistic. How could this undeniably
flawed enterprise possibly contain something of the highest value
for psychotherapists?

At the outset, we need an anatomy of psychopathology; the
blanket term is really of use only in dinner-party debates.
Following Rosenbaum (in Rosenbaum & Beebe, 1975, pp.
273–275), it is possible to see many different uses of the term. For
example, we distinguish a label for a symptom or syndrome (such
as 'obsessional neurosis') from one that refers to a whole
character or personality (such as 'anal character'). Then there are
labels that refer to specific disorders (such as 'narcissistic
personality disorder'). A fourth category is that of 'organ system'
labels, designed to cover psychosomatics (such as when a peptic
ulcer develops at a time of personal difficulty and we refer to a
'psychophysiological gastrointestinal disorder'). This is different
from a label that is used to depict a current situation (such as
'adjusting to adult life') or a life-stage label ('adolescence').
Behavioural traits may also acquire labels (such as 'perversion' or
'addiction').

Rosenbaum mentions one particular kind of label that is of
importance for analysts and therapists. Aetiological labels imply
some kind of causation or at least foundation for the psychopathology in question. These can be of two kinds: 'statements of
early life experiences suggesting predisposition toward the
current symptomatology' (such as 'early oral deprivation'), or
'assessment of current threats to harmony' (such as leaving
home). The themes of aetiology and causation are discussed in
greater detail towards the end of the introduction.

The careful sub-division of the notion of psychopathology may
help the clinician to be more aware of the implications of the
language he is using, whether to the patient, to himself, or to
colleagues. A word like 'depression' may be played through all or
any of the variants of psychopathology that have been listed.

Another advantage of breaking up the ideogram 'psychopathology' is that light may be shed on what we mean by 'normal'.

As Joseph (1982) pointed out, the use of the word 'normal' by psychoanalysts is not synonymous with 'regular', 'standard', 'natural' or 'typical', as the dictionary seems to suggest. Rather, what is normal is determined by subjective evaluation. Freud (1937) had talked of normality as an 'ideal fiction', and so, Joseph concluded, Freud equated normality with analysability and with the outcome of a successful analysis. Jones (1931) proposed that normality could be assessed in terms of 'happiness', 'efficiency', and 'adaptation to reality'. Klein (1960), in a similar vein, wrote of normality as involving the harmonious interaction of several aspects of mental life such as emotional maturity, strength of character, capacity to deal with conflicting emotions, a reciprocal balance between internal and external worlds, and, finally, a welding of the parts of the personality leading to an integrated self-concept.

The term in analytical psychology that corresponds most happily to this specifically psychoanalytic idea of normality is *individuation*. If we consider Klein's suggestions, we can see striking similarities with Jung's idea of individuation: a person's becoming her- or himself, whole, indivisible, and distinct from other people or collective psychology (though in relation to these). Each kind of psychopathology represents a verbalization of a different kind of threat to what psychoanalysts seem to call 'normality' and analytical psychologists call 'individuation'.

The kind of psychopathology to which I have been referring occupies one end of a spectrum. The spectrum stretches from what might be called a *professional* approach to psychopathology to a *poetic* approach. Making diagnoses such as 'narcissistic personality disorder' or 'anal character', or discussing normality and abnormality, represent the professional dimension. However, there is also the poetic style of pathologizing to consider. Before doing that, I would like to make a few comments about the spectrum, itself a creative falsehood, offered for its heuristic value. Of course, the spectrum does not really exist, for there is no reason for the poles to stay in permanent opposition (though they certainly are, on one level at least, opposed to one another). What is more, no one analyst will occupy one pole exclusively; indeed, many analysts will claim that they make explicit use of the whole spectrum in their work. There may even be a level on which the two poles turn out to be identical: the poesy of consummate professionalism and the professional cutting edge of an acute poetic imagination. My view is that a linking of analysis-as-science and analysis-as-art may be regarded as an ideal at which to aim. But in the everyday sense, there is a professional–poetic split in the attitudes to psychopathology held by analysts.

What of the poetic end of the spectrum?

Hillman (1975, p. 58) places pathology at the core of the psyche. Provided we do not get seduced by cheap professionalism, and provided we do not attempt an artificial division between normal and abnormal, then, according to Hillman, the study of psychopathology is an absolute necessity. Of course, Hillman means something different from what Rosenbaum means by psychopathology, but the central point remains: the individual case, or symptom, contains the person, or culture, or God. The part contains the whole. So, working towards the whole implies a working on the parts. And, what is more, Hillman suggests that we do not abandon the familiar medical jargon, but merely use it so imaginatively that it starts to function once again as psyche's language, psyche's words, psyche-ology. The problem with Hillman's approach is in its denial of its own professionalism, its own importation of jargon and its own dogmatic distinction between an acceptable and unacceptable use of psychopathology (abnormal psychopathology?).

The idea I want to advance is that there is one way in which the creative and careful use of psychopathology by workaday analysts may, through *enantiodromia,* subvert the contemporary tendency to see everything as susceptible to psychological therapy, a tendency that casts the therapist in a falsely powerful and censorious position. The way in which the study of psychopathology serves this subversive end has to do with what has been called *analysability*. Stripped down, this means: whom do I turn away when they ask for analysis?—those I cannot help rather than those I can.

Analysability and the wounded healer

Returning to the professional end of the professional–poetic spectrum, in 1983 Edwards, a psychiatrist and analytical psychologist, proposed a list of criteria on which suitability for treatment might be based. These were:

1. the strength, flexibility, and integration of the ego, and the quality of ego consciousness;
2. the capacity of the ego to maintain boundaries between inner and outer, and between phantasy and reality;
3. the degree of differentiation and disidentification of the ego from the self and the archetypal level, and the extent to which the representations in the ego were possessed or permeated by archetypal images, whether of a positive or a negative nature;
4. the degree of splitting of personal self- and object-representations in the ego, and the resultant effects on identity and the perception of the external world;
5. the nature of the defences that predominated and whether these were of a primitive type;
6. the kinds of anxiety and their intensity: panic, fears of annihilation and disintegration, or hypochondriacal, persecutory, phobic, or depressive anxieties;
7. the extent of controlling behaviour, linked, as it often is, with omnipotence, compulsive needs for narcissistic self-objects, or the control of bad persecutory objects;
8. narcissistic vulnerability, with feelings of being easily wounded or humiliated in response to criticism or disapproval, or with shame reactions and loss of self-esteem;
9. The presence of depression and whether it is empty, hopeless or despairing; or combined with guilt, remorse or self-accusation;
10. the presence of psychosomatic illness with liabilities to exacerbation triggered by emotional stress; early developmental levels are usually involved with splitting defences firmly established and resisting therapy;
11. poor or threatened control of instinctive impulses and primitive affects, with the chance of breakthroughs of unpredictable aggression, self-destructive acts, impulsive or perverse sexuality;
12. motivation for, and type of resistance to, therapy;
13. capacities for humour, imagination, insight, and the use of symbols. [p. 310]

Edwards's final comment on the subject of analysability concerns the matching of the patient with the 'right' analyst.

Here, intuition plays its part. We could extend this last point to coin a term like *dialectical psychopathology*; for is it not the case that each of Edwards's criteria or desiderata may be applied to the *analyst* as well as to the patient? It would follow that the analyst's knowledge of her or his own psychopathology, or assessment of that of a colleague in supervision, would also lie at the heart of analysability. Turning a patient away is reframed as a creative and altruistic act. What is more, now that the analyst's use of self has come to occupy a central place in reflection upon the patient's dynamics, psychopathology and the use of counter-transference go together (see Samuels, 1989, pp. 143–174). Psychopathology, the archprofessional activity of analysts, undermines that very professionalism, leading to a reining-in of clinical omnipotence and to psychology assuming a modest place in cultural consciousness (and, hence, becoming more credible). Edwards ends with Jung's words: 'Not everything can and must be cured' (*CW* 16, para. 463).

Just as psychopathology illumines the weaknesses of the analyst, so it can point up the strengths of the patient. Here, I am thinking not only of the value of symptoms as indicators of the patient's psychological destiny, but also of the intimate connections between wounds and health. This is exemplified by the image of the wounded healer, which, as Guggenbühl-Craig (1971) has pointed out, is an image that our culture tends to split. As far as the individual is concerned, the wounded and the healthy/ healing parts of the personality are split off from each other. When that happens, health is seen as being confined to the analyst, and the patient is seen as the only wounded one. If the patient is to develop her or his healthy potentials, the analyst must contribute her or his wounds to the process—wounds that may have led to the choice of profession in the first place. In psychoanalysis, a similar argument has been advanced by Searles (1975) in a paper called 'The patient as therapist to his analyst'. Briefly summarized, Searles's view is that it is an inalienable part of being human to be a 'therapist'—that is, to want to help others and to be able to do so. In a neurotic or a psychotic, the potential to be a therapist is also damaged. It follows that the healing of mentally ill persons requires that the patients work on and improve their capacity to be therapists. Searles suggested that the patient must develop the capacity to be a therapist by practicing on the one person available for this—namely, the analyst (see Samuels, 1985, pp. 187–191, for a fuller discussion).

The tendency of psychopathology to provide an absolutist account of the patient is another feature which, when the angle of vision alters, may turn out to have quite different implications. For, in the formulation of a diagnosis concerning the patient, a pluralistic process is hopefully in train. One needs to hold the tension between 'this is what I think' (a unified view) and 'maybe there are other possibilities' (a diverse view). The introduction of other possibilities suggests a tension within the analyst, and this, too, is a characteristically pluralistic endeavour. Is it too fanciful to suggest that any psychopathological label results from intense bargaining within the analyst between the various interest groups represented by the various diagnostic labels?

I am working towards a suggestion that there is a sense in which psychopathology may have an *individualizing,* in addition to a generalizing, effect upon analysis. To the degree that analytic understanding alters analytic technique, and to the degree that analytic understanding employs some aspect of psychopathology, then it is psychopathology that makes a central contribution to the analyst's attempts to meet the patient as an individual. As Greenson says: 'Clinical experience has taught us that certain diagnostic entities make use of special types of defence and therefore that particular resistances will predominate during the course of the analysis' (1967, p. 93). In other words, the kind of pathology involved will directly affect the course of the analysis. In particular, the patient's response to interpretations will be markedly different, and the analyst will be reminded that not all patients are the same. *Judicious employment of what is known to be generally true may protect what is sensed to be unique.*

Jung and psychopathology

So far, I have been reflecting on the ambivalence towards psychopathology and making some suggestions about a reframing of our understanding of the subject. At this point, it may be interesting to look in greater detail at how Jung came to terms with the same ambivalence, this split between professionalism and poesy. In *Memories, Dreams, Reflections* (1963), Jung wrote that though 'clinical diagnoses are important, since they give the doctor a certain orientation ... they do not help the patient. The crucial thing is the story' (p. 145). We may well wonder how it is possible to help the doctor without helping the patient! Later on, Jung says that he does not have a particular method and that 'psychotherapy and analysis are as varied as are human individuals' (p. 152). Yet, an analyst 'must be familiar with the so-called "methods"' (p. 153). There is a discrepancy, or at least an ambiguity, here. McCurdy (1982) also notes this and understands it in terms of Jung's tendency to 'find answers in the tensions between opposites'. If this is so, then the opposites that McCurdy discerns as being relevant to Jung's ambivalence concerning psychopathology and diagnosis may repay study because they could speak for the general ambivalence we have been negotiating.

McCurdy (1982) understands these opposites as being

> the clinical responsibility of the analyst to be well trained in the fundamentals of depth psychology and psychopathology; to understand and be able to apply insights from the basic schools of psychological thought; and, above all, to have had experience in these ways of diagnosing and working with people. [p. 48]

The other opposite concerns

> the ability and responsibility to 'forget' all of this information and to orient him- or herself to the person in analysis as an individual. It is much like the artist, who, after great efforts and much time spent in mastering the fundamentals of a medium, can produce art without 'thinking' of fundamentals. [p. 49]

McCurdy concludes that it is a matter of 'letting go' and 'holding on' at the same time.

But there is a problem with this formulation, surely an ideal one for the average analyst, when we come to apply it to Jung. For Jung's 'letting go' tends to receive more attention than his 'holding on'. Indeed, Jung is often accused of letting things go so far that his work is not really analytic at all (cf. Goodheart, 1984)! But, throughout this introduction, I have been illustrating how Jung also held on to his role as a psychiatrist and analyst, writing like a professional on the stock-in-trade of his profession: neurosis, psychosis and depression.

Modes of psychopathology

Reading and re-reading the papers in this book, it occurred to me that psychopathology signals its presence in differing modes. It may, for instance, be manifest in an *affective mode*. The patient may be conscious of problematic emotions, unwanted feelings and fantasies, and so forth. Or the analyst may, by scanning the countertransference, be alerted to a disturbance or incongruence of affect.

A second psychopathological mode reflects a preoccupation with *psychic structure*. Hence, disturbance is verbalized in terms of imbalances and unresolvable conflicts between parts of the personality, or invasive behaviour by one part towards the other. Thus, confused sexual identity may be understood as stemming from an inflation of animus or anima to the point where the personality as a whole is flooded.

The third mode I can identify operates on a model of *deficit*. I would include the notion of excess here because to have too much of something is implicitly a form of deprivation (stuffing mothers are as problematic as withholding ones). When analytic writers mention deficits, they refer either to something deficient in parental handling or to some constitutional (inborn) lack/excess (such as instinctual aggression), or to a combination of these.

Cutting across these modes of psychopathology, all of which are represented in the book, there is an axis of understanding ranging from the *phenomenological* to the *aetiological*. What I am getting at can be depicted diagrammatically (Figure 1).

As I mentioned previously, an aetiological approach has a crucial place in a great deal of thinking about psychopathology. Does this have to be the case? In analytical psychology, there is a long tradition of questioning seriously whether experiences in early life do have the determining effect on adult personality that has been claimed. And there has been a more recent counter-movement stressing the importance of early experiences which to some eyes, including this writer's, can be excessively determinis-

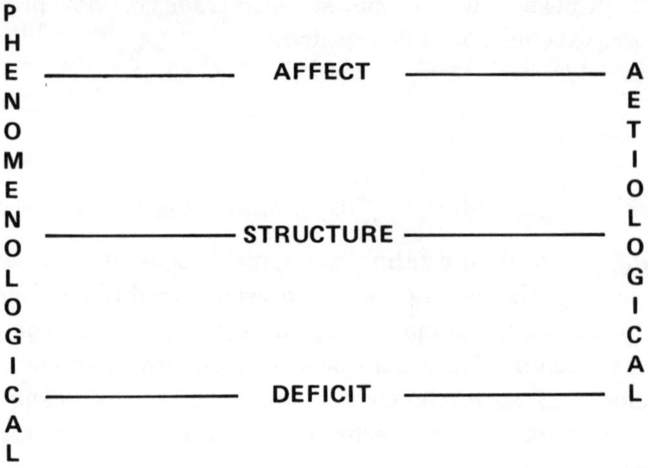

FIGURE 1

tic and literal-minded. Storr (1979, pp. 148–149) confronts this issue. He states that his approach to psychopathology is 'primarily descriptive', rather than being concerned with causes (though he is careful not to rule out the effects of early experiences on adult personality altogether). He goes on:

> partial explanations of adult character in terms of possible childhood influences ... are not essential in understanding. ... When Freud began the practice of analysis, he was ... concerned to trace the origin of particular symptoms; to discover their cause in some traumatic event occurring at an identifiable time. However appropriate this way of proceeding may be in the case of traumatic neurosis or certain kinds of hysterical symptom, it is not, in my view, important in understanding most of the difficulties which patients seeking psychotherapy present us today.

This still leaves those deficits due to adverse inborn imbalances of instinctual energy or activity, and it is to the credit of analytical psychology that it attempts therapy in the full consciousness that what is being addressed is nothing less than the fateful disposition of character that is the individual's inheritance. It is *much* easier to work knowing or claiming to know *why* your patient is as he/she is, but it may not be as honest or profound an approach.

Jung's synthetic method

The objection may be made that sophisticated analysts do not deal in anything so crude as 'causes'—rather, the concern is for pattern and repetition. While the desire to escape the charge of being mechanistic is understandable, the current tendency to speak of 'patterns' of adult psychological performance which originate in childhood is still deterministic, if not outright causalistic. So, even when reference is made to spiral models of development in which the earlier elements appear later in transmogrified form, the venture still sits firmly within the deterministic–causalistic camp.

Actually, there is nothing wrong with being causalistic. Jung's approach was happily causal, though, for him, it was Aristotle's *causae finales* (final causes) that were of central importance. This teleological viewpoint (from *telos,* meaning goal), or prospective approach, is characteristic of classical analytical psychology. It involves considering a psychological phenomenon from the standpoint of what it is for, where it is leading, for the 'sake' of what it is happening. All these were more interesting to Jung than the effects on the situation of causes located in the chronological past (Aristotle's *causae efficientes*). The search for causes in the past, which characterized psychoanalysis as Jung knew it, was regarded by Jung as 'reductive'; his own method was termed 'synthetic', with the implication that it was what *emerged* from the starting point that was of primary significance.

Jung's emphasis on teleology led him to propose that symptoms, and, indeed, mental illness itself, may often signify something of great psychological value for the individual. For example, Jung saw depression as a damming up of energy, which, when released, may take on a more positive direction. Energy is trapped because of a neurotic or psychotic problem but, if freed, actually helps in the overcoming of the problem. A state of depression is one that should be entered into as fully as possible, according to Jung, so that the feelings involved may be clarified. Such clarification represents a conversion of a vague feeling into a more precise idea or image to which the depressed person can refer. Depression is connected to regression in its regenerative and enriching aspects. In particular, it may take the form of 'the empty stillness which precedes creative work' (*CW* 16, para. 373).

In such circumstances, what has happened is that the new development, already active unconsciously, has siphoned off energy from consciousness, leading to depression.

Jung pointed out that the synthetic method is taken for granted in everyday life, where we tend to disregard the strictly causal factor. For example, if a person has an opinion and expresses it, we want to know what she or he means, what is being got at, rather than the origins of the remark. Use of the synthetic method in analysis means considering psychological phenomena such as symptoms *as if* they had intention and purpose—i.e. in terms of goal-orientedness or teleology. Jung grants to the unconscious a kind of knowledge or even fore-knowledge (*CW* 8, para. 175).

It must be emphasized that Jung never eschewed the analysis of infancy and childhood as such. Rather, he regarded this as essential in some cases though unavoidably limiting (*CW* 16, paras. 140–148). My own feeling is that there is much to be gained even from a highly mechanistic, deterministic and causalistic approach—provided that this is balanced by the simultaneous use of a non-linear, metaphorical and teleological approach to the development of personality. Paradoxically, the existence and use in parallel of two competing perspectives guarantees that neither will dominate the mind of the practitioner. Then, as I have tried to show elsewhere (Samuels, 1989, pp. 48–65), *diachronic* models of personality development, with images of an unfolding of personality over time in a causally connected way, battle creatively with *synchronic* models, which attempt to embrace the all-at-oneness of the personality with an accent on what is eternal therein. Moreover, the pluralistic sparks that fly from such competitiveness prevent decay into either therapy-by-numbers or therapy-as-fortune-telling—the respective ultimate dangers of the reductive and synthetic methods.

Psychopathology and culture

Jungian analysts often hear during their training that 'when you treat the patient, you treat the culture'. The slogan can be understood in two ways. The patient is an individual expression of the *Zeitgeist,* positive and negative; an analysis of any depth must include an analysis of the patient's portion of collective consciousness. Then there is another, more subtle sense in which treating the patient means treating the culture. Treatment of an individual's malaise is a contribution to a psychological therapy of a cultural malaise. The analysed individual may become a 'change agent', or the influencing may be less direct and more mysterious.

These remarks are intended to explain the presence in a book on psychopathology of papers on the Holocaust and on old age. These cultural phenomena, both of them collective though rather different in kind, display psychological characteristics that are met in the consulting room, In Britain, in recent years, an interest in the psychological aspects of mass disasters has arisen. The focus has been on the consequences for both survivors and mourners. There was a fire at a football stadium, a ferryboat capsized, a madman with a gun killed many people in a small town, an oil platform went up in flames with heavy loss of life, an airliner crashed on a small town. When Dreifuss wrote his paper, this current interest would have been unfamiliar, yet the paper has a striking relevance. Similarly, demographic revelations about aging populations in Western countries add a piquancy to Zoja's thinking on the subject.

Concluding remarks

In this introduction, I have tried to give the background to the book and to say for whom it is intended. The general ambivalence in depth psychology concerning psychopathology is to be found *par excellence* in the Jungian world. However, if we are careful not to use 'psychopathology' in an all-inclusive manner, and if we nurture the tension between the professional and poetic nuances of the theme, psychopathology may lead creatively to the patient's being seen as an individual to whom health, potency and a sense of enablement can be returned. The play of opposites between a professional and a poetic standpoint makes *in itself* a fruitful contribution to analysis as well as to personal psychological reflection.

Jung's ambivalence concerning psychopathology is illuminated when one considers the specific contributions he makes concerning clinical practice and psychopathology—whilst, at the same time, his professionalism is itself undermined by the poetic assumption of clinical humility.

Psychopathology need not be wedded to reductive *or* to synthetic analysis. Rather, its straddling of the professional–poetic spectrum facilitates movement between these orientations. Similarly, psychopathology provides one bridge between an analysis of the individual and an analysis of culture.

REFERENCES

Adler, G. (ed.) (1974). *C. G. Jung, Letters*. Vol. 2. London: Routledge and Kegan Paul.

Binswanger, L. (1945). Insanity as life historical phenomenon and as mental disease: the case of Ilse. In R. May, E. Angel & H. Ellenberger (eds.), *Existence*. New York: Basic Books (1958).

Edwards, A. (1983). Research studies in the problems of assessment. *Journal of Analytical Psychology* 28:4.

Fordham, M. (1978). *Jungian Psychotherapy: a Study in Analytical Psychology*. Chichester: Wiley. [Reprinted 1986, London: Maresfield Library.]

Freud, S. (1937). Analysis terminable and interminable. *Standard Edition* 23. London: Hogarth.

Goodheart, W. (1984). C. G. Jung's first 'patient': on the seminal emergence of Jung's thought. *Journal of Analytical Psychology* 29:1.

Greenson, R. (1967). *The Technique and Practice of Psychoanalysis*. London: Hogarth.

Guggenbühl-Craig, A. (1971). *Power in the Helping Professions*. New York: Spring Publications.

Hillman, J. (1975). *Revisioning Psychology*. New York: Harper & Row.

Jones, E. (1931). The concept of the normal mind. *International Journal of Psycho-Analysis* 23.

Joseph, E. (1982). Normal in psychoanalysis. *International Journal of Psycho-Analysis* 63:1.

Jung, C. G. References are to the *Collected Works* (*CW*) and by volume and paragraph number, except as below. Edited by H. Read, M. Fordham, G. Adler & W. McGuire, Trans. in the main by R. Hull.

London: Routledge and Kegan Paul; Princeton: Princeton University Press.

———— (1963). *Memories, Dreams, Reflections*. London: Collins and Routledge and Kegan Paul; Fontana (1972).

Klein, M. (1960). On mental health. *British Journal of Medical Psychology* 33.

Laing, R. (1967). *The Politics of Experience*. Harmondsworth, Middlesex: Penguin.

McCurdy, A. (1982). Establishing and maintaining the analytical structure. In M. Stein (ed.), *Jungian Analysis*. La Salle: Open Court.

Perry, J. (1962). Reconstitutive processes in the psychopathology of the self. *Annals of the New York Academy of Sciences*, Vol. 96, article 3.

Rosenbaum, C., & Beebe, J. (1975). *Psychiatric Treatment: Crisis/Clinic/ Consultation*. New York and London: McGraw-Hill.

Samuels, A. (1985). *Jung and the Post-Jungians*. London and Boston: Routledge and Kegan Paul.

————. (1989). *The Plural Psyche: Personality, Morality, and the Father*. London and New York: Routledge.

Searles, H. (1975). The patient as therapist to his analyst. In *Countertransference and Related Subjects: Selected Papers*. New York: International Universities Press (1979).

Storr, A. (1979). *The Art of Psychotherapy*. London: Secker and Warburg/Heinemann.

CHAPTER ONE

Depressed patients and the *coniunctio*

Judith Hubback

Hubback's paper is of interest because of her express intention of using both 'archetypal structuralist concepts' and 'the findings of developmental research'; the former is represented in the paper by a tracking of the dynamics of the coniunctio oppositorum, *the patterns within a person of integration and unintegration, harmony and dissonance, and the latter by a study of the part played in her patients' depression by their having had a depressed mother. Where experience of parental imagos of a depressed kind has led to splitting defences, this has injured the innate capacity of the person for* coniunctio. *What is more, when the parental marriage is experienced as divisive, weak or non-existent, a further injury is done to the prospect of internal marriage within the patient.*

This is the background for Hubback's noting a special clinical phenomenon in relation to her group of depressed patients: the

---

First published in *The Journal of Analytical Psychology* 28:4, in 1983. Reprinted in *People Who Do Things to Each Other: Essays in Analytical Psychology*, by Judith Hubback (Wilmette, IL: Chiron Publications, 1988). Published here by kind permission of the author and the Society of Analytical Psychology.

necessity of analysing the patient's 'phantasies about his mother's inner life'. The interactive focus naturally falls on the inner life of the analyst in general and on her countertransference in particular. Thus the analyst's participation in the patient's process is explicitly noticed—and compared by Hubback to the vital presence of the soror, *the alchemist's assistant, in the alchemical process—a Jungian metaphor for analysis itself.*

A.S.

Introduction and theme

There are six particular people—patients—whose lives and therapies are at the empirical core of this paper. What they have in common is that their mothers were each of them seriously depressed during their son's or daughter's infancy and childhood. The other thing they have in common is that they had their analytical therapy with the particular analyst that I am, and that over the years I have had a growing interest in trying to find out more about what it is that enables someone effectively to emerge from long-term depressions. I would like to isolate one particular factor from those, often explored and discussed, concerning the nature, the manifestations and the treatment of depression. I am thinking of a factor whose absence could be a great disadvantage, but whose presence can enable a patient to become, in the course of therapy and time, less depressed, less frequently so, and less paralysingly; such a factor might also help the person to be less aggressive towards others and facilitate the development of a truly viable sense of self.

Depression as a form of feeling ill, and as a clinical syndrome or illness, has been known for thousands of years and described from the earliest days onwards both by sufferers and by their doctors. A precise or short definition cannot be offered here, particularly as I am not a psychiatrist and because all authorities agree that there is a wide spectrum of symptoms and indications. At one end of that spectrum, depression is a natural reaction to painful emotional experiences, to bereavement and loneliness, to physical ill-health or the approach of death—all features of the human condition. At the extreme melancholic or pathological end of the spectrum the mood change is extreme and persistent. If more of us had time to read (rather than occasionally dip into) Robert Burton's *The Anatomy of Melancholy,* first published in 1621, as well as to study modern psychiatric textbooks, we would appreciate even more widely than we do from introspection and as Jungian psychotherapists the many aspects of the whole depressive picture. Its main attributes are: (1) alteration in mood to sadness, apathy and loneliness; (2) a negative or otherwise self-attacking self-concept, with self-reproaches and self-blame; (3) regressive wishes, the desire to escape, to deny, to hide, to die; (4) crying, irritability, insomnia, loss of sexual appetite; (5) a low level of general activity, loss of decisiveness and of other ego capacities, sometimes a heightened level of inappropriate anxiety, fear or agitation. In this paper there is no possibility of describing or accurately naming in psychiatric terms just which kind of depression afflicted the mothers of the patients about whom I am writing, e.g. whether these were basically endogenous depressions reactivated during their son's or daughter's infancy; the more important common feature was that the mothers had suffered a serious personal loss, a bereavement from which it appeared they had not recovered. None of them was hospitalized; the patients each had a far clearer impression of the depressed moods than of any intervening manic ones that there may have been; and the suicide of one of the mothers undoubtedly affected her daughter's life most deeply. The manifestations of depression in the patients themselves will emerge, I think, in the course of the paper.

The following thoughts have become the theme of this paper: too many and too strong negative archetypal images are absorbed by an infant or young child from a depressed mother, most particularly if she is a bereaved woman who is still caught up in her anger and sadness, so that she cannot direct herself towards the baby and genuinely smile into its eyes. Not enough validation of its lovableness is offered to such an infant at the stage in life when that experience is essential for a healthy self-belief to develop, which will be based on enough internal feeling that there is more growth than destructiveness both in himself and in his environment. To alter the attitudes stemming from those early inner and outer pathological experiences, an analytical therapist makes herself available for a relationship to grow within which a number of *coniunctiones* can occur: if, at the level of the objective psyche as manifested in the analyst, there is a well-established *coniunctio* of internal images, and if the patient is able to identify with that inner healer—whose outer scars may still be evident—then what is happening is that both archetypal structuralist concepts and the findings of developmental research are confirmed.

I am not speaking simply about the patient's need to (I quote Jung) 'kill the symbolic representative of the unconscious, i.e., his own *participation mystique* with animal nature ... the Terrible Mother who devours and destroys, and thus symbolises death itself' (*CW* 5, paras. 504–506). The patient with a depressed mother does need to emerge from an unconscious identification with his mother because of the killing quality of her depression and needs to cease participating in her anger and sadness. After the passage quoted above, Jung added in brackets:

> I remember the case of a mother who kept her children tied to her with unnatural love and devotion. At the time of the climacteric she fell into a depressive psychosis and had delirious states in which she saw herself as an animal, especially as a wolf or pig. ... In her psychosis she had herself become the symbol of an all-devouring mother.

And, following that clinical vignette, he went on:

> Interpretation in terms of the parents is, however, simply a *façon de parler*. In reality the whole drama takes place in the individual's own psyche, where the 'parents' are not the parents at all but only their imagos: they are representations which have arisen from the conjunction of parental peculiarities with the individual disposition of the child. [ibid., para. 505]

If for the term *participation mystique* we substitute the words and concepts *unconscious identification,* then I can go along with the way Jung used Lévy Bruhl's term. Many writers since Jung have used the concept of *participation mystique* in a more simplistic manner than he in fact did, at least in the passage quoted. And it is regrettable that the anthropologist Lévy-Bruhl should have had his phrase over-used and distorted, when the perhaps rival psychological concepts of projection, introjection, identification and the transcendent function really serve us better. Identifying with those structures in the analyst which have developed as a result of her working on instinctual 'animal nature' in herself can and does happen within the therapeutic relationship; projections and introjections can be discerned and described. I think they are marvellous, but not mystical.

The patient with a depressed mother is suffering from a serious narcissistic wound. I develop in this paper the theme that such patients benefit greatly—perhaps essentially—from the analyst using to the full a combination of developmental observations and her own internal search for harmony, for *coniunctio*.

From the following brief descriptions of the patients (with fictitious names) it can be seen that the character and quality of their mothers' depressive reactions to the loss of either their husbands or an earlier child ran the whole spectrum of possibilities: paranoid, manic, animus-ridden, schizoid, closed, sulky, aggressive, obsessional and suicidal. Some of these patients made images, or allowed the images to make themselves, easily and early on in their analyses, others with difficulty and only much later. They also varied in their ability to fantasize in the transference, and to dream. Each of them suffered from internal impoverishment.

Anthony

A's father abandoned A's mother when he was very young; the precise age is unknown. This unsupported woman suffered all the rest of her life from a depressive and persecutory reaction to that loss. In addition to having to try to learn to live with such a mother, A (who became my patient in middle age) had certainly inherited some of his father's capacity to opt out of emotional commitments. He was evacuated at the age of six from a large city, with his school, for the duration of World War II, and billeted with several different families, who treated and ill-treated him in various ways. His parental imagos were of course very confused.

He related to other people in as distant a way as possible. Virtually the whole gamut of possibilities reappeared in the transference, from delusional idealization, via distancing cold- ness, to destructive hatred. Trust and self-confidence grew only slowly, through many discouraging phases.

Belinda

B's father disappeared even earlier in his child's life than did Anthony's; she thinks he was not told she had been born, and he may even not have known she had been conceived. All through her childhood her mother suffered from that, to her, crucial object-loss; it came after other similar losses. As a mother she seems to have been unable to emerge enough from her own narcissistic wounds to offer her daughter (my patient) a reliable self-feeling as a reflector of the child's potential belief in herself. The mother's long-drawn-out self-attacks, sulky depressions and obsessional cleanliness were partly introjected by her daughter and partly defended against; the defensive manoeuvre was fairly successful, perhaps as a result of the daughter having inherited from the father what may have been a self-protective ability to push 'the woman' to one side. But analysis, as it progressed, revealed how very powerful the damaged and damaging mother still was.

Christine

C was the younger of two children and was in her fourth year when her parents' marriage broke down in violence, and her mother never forgave her father for the loss not only of economic support but, more dangerously, of personal happiness. While the mother saw herself as the injured and wronged one, the father also had in fact been deeply hurt and deprived of his children. My patient C grew up with an aggressively depressed mother and an absent, rarely mentionable, unmourned father, for whom all the same she hankered. C's depression had, for a time, a paranoid quality to it. In her, the defences of the self (Fordham, 1974) were obstinately structured, and early in her analysis she was blocked against using her imaginative or symbolizing capacities.

Dominic

D's mother had lost her first son when he was aged about eight months, before D was born, and although there was no factual evidence that he was a mere 'replacement baby', his insistent conviction of hardly having his own real identity was tenaciously held on to for many years. His mother's depression was so thoroughly introjected that it acquired a most powerful melancholic grip on him. He knew a great deal about the losses of other significant males in his mother's and his maternal grandmother's lives, each of those males having either died suddenly or been killed in various wars. In analysis the transference projections were intense, violent, cold, envious and haunting; the counter-transference affect was inescapable. But, as in the cases of A and B, he had internal warmth, which, however strenuously he used his splitting defences to ward it off, always came back sooner or later.

Erica

E's mother had had to leave her country of birth and childhood when, as a teenager, her parents became refugees. This woman apparently never fully accepted the loss of her mother country: she gave all her children, E and her brothers and sisters, names that were clearly foreign in the country of *their* birth, which was in the Antipodes. E could not identify with a mother who was still mourning, everlastingly yearning for the impossible. She came to England. She developed moderate anorexia nervosa; in spite of the somatization of her mother complex she made a fair beginning in analytical therapy. But the shadow of her mother's depression came between her and all attempted relationships with men or women. And my offer of intensifying her analysis, which would have taken it a stage forward, into a deeper commitment, and would have involved the underlying archetypal structures, led to her abrupt flight to the place where her parents still lived, as far away from me as possible: the other side of the world.

Freddie

F was the first of three children of his mother's second marriage: before that she had twin sons in a marriage which had broken down in a way or from a cause which F never heard mentioned. Her intensely erotic relationship with F when he was a baby and a child, her grousing attitude to life, her constant denigration both of the twins and of F's father and a number of physical ills probably indicate a long-term depression. There was a mysterious or glamorous other man between the two marriages. She does not seem to have mourned the failure of her first relationship, nor the disappointment over the mystery man, but moaned about her marriage. F was very closely bound to her and decided one day early in puberty that he was a homosexual. He would not move from that decision: it meant to him that he was not an ordinary or banal man like his father, he was going to be extraordinary, his mother's lover. He himself was not a depressed man, but his psychic development was held up by the bond to a mother who had—as far as I could tell—not been able to mourn losses which occurred before F's birth.

In the interests of analytic theory it would be satisfying if it were possible to point to some factor in these people which seems to have made them especially liable to identify with their mothers, and to receive the projection of the mother's damaged self. For example, the stage of the patient's life at which the mothers were bereaved might be significant: but it was not the same for all, e.g. the first year of life, or one of the later developmental stages, such as the oedipal one, when the incest archetype dominates. Then, another possible factor would be personality type; they were all certainly more introverted than extraverted, but in terms of the classical Jungian typology of the four functions I can discern no categorical significance.

Another possibility, to which I incline, but it is a speculative one, is that the characterological feature of both the mother and the father by which each of them was both victim and victimizer had been inherited by the son or daughter, and the component of aggression–passivity led the child to identify with the available parent, namely the mother, in whom the victim/victimizer syndrome had led to depression. That factor would be a somewhat subtle version of the well-known defence of identifying with the aggressor. The theme of identification needs more examination than is possible here, and contributions from several angles, with clinical examples.

Self-feeling, narcissistic deprivation and depression

Many analytical psychologists have studied both the self in the sense that Jung used the term, and the patient's sense of himself, self-feeling, or self-experience. Moreover, the originally psychoanalytic (Freudian) term, narcissism, is currently used more frequently in studies relating to the Jungian self and the primal self by analytical psychologists than in Jung's own writings. (See, for example, Ledermann, 1982; Gordon, 1980; Humbert, 1980; Schwartz-Salant, 1982; Kalsched, 1980; and Jacoby, 1981). The study of narcissistic personality disorder is proceeding apace, within a current Jungian frame of reference. Jungians are also making use of Kohut's and Kernberg's post-Freudian observations. My impression, derived from depressed patients in analysis, is that the relation between narcissistic unsatisfaction in infancy and depression in adulthood is extremely close. Further analytical studies of different groups of depressed adults may, if they are undertaken, lead to deeper understanding of exactly how the two kinds of suffering are related.

The depressed patient, whose mother was *not* subject to depression, brings to his analyst pathological material which is principally his own. The one whose mother is known to have been seriously depressed when he was very young will be listened to by an analyst with her ear ready to try to extricate the mother's bad internal self-view from the patient's phantasies about it. There are cross-currents of identifications which can be navigated successfully, if slowly, through the patient's transference manifestations and the analyst's countertransference self-analysis. We are concerned with more than the familiar process of enabling the patient to separate out from his mother and to develop firm (but not rigid) boundaries between himself and every later representative of the first object, that first partner. Rather, our focus is on the task of analysing his phantasies about his mother's inner life. They cannot be assumed to be totally fantastic, or 'merely' subjective. The analyst's familiarity with her own inner life and willingness to use it indirectly in her work will be a major factor in analysing the patient effectively. She has to be bold, and enough *in* her own residual depression, or depressive phases, and at the same time to have good enough boundaries, to distance herself enough from her depressive tendencies so that the patient can use them in the transference—symbolically.

The symbolic attitude and approach (Hubback, 1969) to the patient whose mother was depressed brings together the understanding of environmental influence, of developmental studies and of archetypal disposition. Jung has written that the 'appearance of the mother-image at any given time cannot be deduced from the mother archetype alone but depends on innumerable other factors' (*CW* 9i, para. 155). Jung also insisted that 'the archetype in itself is empty and purely formal ... a possibility of representation ... the representations themselves are not inherited, only the forms, and in that respect they correspond in every way to the instincts, which are also determined in form only.' The ethologists' theory of internal release mechanisms is in line with that formulation. In another passage Jung wrote: '. . . *the contents of the child's abnormal fantasies* can be referred to the personal mother only in part, since they often contain clear and unmistakable allusions which could not possibly have reference to human beings' (*CW* 9i, para. 159, emphasis added).

We can also observe normal infants when they are in the grip, early on, of desperate hungry anxiety, infants who gradually grow less anxious and angry when there have been repeated experiences of someone responding to their hungry, demanding and envious attacks. Working for many months or even years may be necessary with patients who despair of ever becoming free from hatefulness. They feel over-full of hate against the apparently ungiving mother analyst, and over-full of terror that she will hate them for hating her.

The phantasies that such patients have are very extremist. On two separate occasions, with two different patients, I took marginally longer than usual to answer the door-bell when they arrived. One, a woman, said she had, in those instants, imagined me lying on the floor of my room, dead from a heart attack. The other, a man, phantasied that my husband had been killed in a motor accident and I had been called away. On another occasion, a man patient phantasied dying then and there while lying on the couch, of heart failure, which would give me, he hoped, the most difficult situation I had ever had to deal with. That was the day after he had voiced both a grossly idealized description of me, and his miserable envy, saying, 'You have a really good, balanced, internal self-feeling, you believe in yourself. I don't.' I told him I saw the imagined 'heart attack' in the present session as a suicidal phantasy of self-punishment following the envious attack on me of the day before, but that he was also telling me that he was very much alive, to be able to go at me like that, with such attacking hunger. His response was, 'Yes! I'll attack, and attack, and attack again! I'm very hungry!' The following week, the atmosphere between us changed. The feeling arose in him that there was a 'we', and he remembered some of the earlier positive phases of the analysis. He smiled on arrival, ruefully, he grew gentler. And he even managed a joke.

In therapies with such patients it was never any use to skimp on the long process of working through the experiences of unsatisfied narcissism or the images associated with them. Time and again the transference and countertransference projections, when elucidated, showed how the lack of outgoing and positive response of the personal mother had contributed in a major way to the patient having not only a consciously poor self view and an unconsciously grandiose and arrogant one, but an actively negative one. It was when that self-attacking view was in the ascendant that the structures in-forming the analysis were put to the greatest strain. The patients I am talking about were all either extremely sensitive to even the minutest alteration in externals, such as my appearance or the contents of the room, or they defended themselves against their sensitivity being apparent. Each of them in his or her own particular way would make use of whatever came to hand to try to demonstrate how inadequately they considered I was treating them and how impossible was any change. Things were as bad as they could be, always had been and always would be. There was no time any more, only timeless hell. Their very present despair could only be reached with the help of accumulated experiences in the analysis, from which they gradually discovered that change, time and development do exist. They began to recognize the alternation of hell and heaven. Then, in time, those extremes were modified.

Both patient and analyst have their own personal and actual selves which stem from primal body-experiences of psychosomatic unity. The self is a concept which is the best possible way of referring to the sense of selfhood that each person needs if he is to use, rather than be misled by, what he gets from other people—identifications. He needs to have boundaries, and a sense of those boundaries, before he can identify healthily. If the actual mother fails to grant the infant boundaries, otherness, individuality and aloneness, as she has not detached herself from the image of another person to whom she was ambivalently over-attached, then she ties the infant in a false closeness based on her unconsciously identifying with her own abandoned self that she has projected into the infant. That infant is then grossly over-burdened. His mother's angry depression is experienced by him in infancy and childhood as though it were his own capacity to attack, to defeat and to be defeated. Each of us in our original undifferentiated libido has the potential to direct it positively or negatively (experiencing the world as giving us nourishing food or destructive poison, love or hate, life or death, and so on), but the infant whose mother is depressed over-develops his negative potential. The infant's need to discover the difference between despairing loneliness and positive separateness is not met by a mother who has not achieved it herself. Such a mother offers the infant a model of much more bad than good, as compared with a model (or image) of a person who discovers that the self contains both, and that the loving, constructive, forces can defeat the destructive ones.

Questions connected with technique and countertransference

The problem of where the most powerful force of pathology lies for any particular patient may or may not affect the course of the analysis. How much does it matter whether the analyst gives great weight (in the reflections she does not communicate directly to the patient) to the presumed influence of the mother's unworked-through mourning, or adopts the other course of paying major attention to the patient's autonomous imagery? How much difference does it make to the healing process, to the development of reconciling and integrating forces, to the patient's potential for continued self-analysis and further improvement of personal relationships after he has separated from the analyst, if there has been concentration on one approach to the problem and neglect of the other? Or, is the wisest course to work with no framework of theory at all, no model associated with any group or school?

Only tentative answers can be offered here. Several of the patients produced images of quite exceptional force. But the transference projections were very powerful, whether there was much or little imagery. The mother's unworked-through mourning seemed to me to be still exerting a pathological influence, so that I consider attending to the images on their own is not enough. I observed that the introjected image of a depressed mother became more amenable to analysis at times when I myself either was, or was believed by the patient to be, depressed. The analysis became more stressful. It was important then that I should try to understand what losses or personal failings I had not yet faced, mourned and accepted. It would be defensive idealization to see myself as fully individuated, or so free from ever being disturbed by personal emotions that no affect leaked from me to a patient.

Integration of all kinds of shadow material proceeded when I was able to use a combination of intuition, memory and well-tried theoretical concepts to come to something I hoped could be dignified with the name understanding. That is where acquaintance with, and reflection on, other schools of analysis and other arts and sciences can be of great help.

Granting full acknowledgement to powerlessness is very necessary if the analyst is to avoid getting enmeshed in the patient's projective identification. The illusion of omnipotence must be dissolved. Being myself a parent, I find that unhappy or anxious affects in relation to one or other of my children can on occasion intrude and cause me to associate (privately) to a patient's perhaps similar experiences. Usefully, however, I find that they tend to see my professional persona as giving them a convenient experience of me being a sort of father to them. None of those I am speaking about had an effective father—he was either physically or psychologically not available to them. With most of these patients, the father transference has been frequent, necessarily negative at first, gradually or intermittently becoming positive, and useful in both ways. The evidence of dreams and phantasies has, however, accumulated and attacks on the father-whom-the-mother-had-come-to-hate could be convincingly detected via attacks on me or self-attacks. A male patient's self-attacking actions make me feel angry with myself, as I believe a father does, when he worries about whether he is being a good-enough father to his son.

As a mother in the transference, I find that the countertransference affect, perhaps more frequently experienced than anger, is that of a nearly despairing kind, with predominance of a defensive splitting of affect. One patient in particular had received a great deal of despair projected from her mother, who seems to have been oblivious of her own pathological attitudes. In the mother and the daughter the negative animus was very powerful. In the countertransference, I had phases of losing self-confidence, and at times felt that I was not the right analyst for her.

An adequately functioning partnership within the analyst of libido both from the self and from the ego structures is necessary for treating a patient who is defending against ego-development by blanking, which can represent total destruction. I remember the dream of one of my patients: she looked in a mirror and saw no one, nothing. Some time later, she was feeling upset and was talking about my approaching holiday: she described how I 'vanish into thin air' when she knows I am away from home. If she cannot make an image of me being in a particular and familiar place, she is imageless. She cannot reconcile terror and hope. The parental imagos are, in her, not so much negative (e.g. hated or feared or despised) but more dangerously they disappear completely at difficult junctures. I do not know whether they have an existence of their own, so that their disappearance happens *to* her, or whether she has an as-yet fully known anger against them so that unconsciously it is she who *makes* them disappear.

From the point of view of the day-to-day work with that patient, my experience is that if I interpret that she is actively blanking and destroying, that feeds her capacity to develop on the ego side and to begin emerging from the dangers attendant upon such imagos. The central criterion I use is to try to speak within the transference in such a way as to foster her potential for experiencing herself as an individual, subject to certain forces but not entirely at their mercy.

When a patient begins to feel sure of being an individual, he will credit the other person with individuality. When the healing process is at work and the old imago of *mater dolorosa* is less in power and the introjection of her is less strangling, then a reconciling symbol appears in a dream or a phantasy. For example:

> The dreamer was mixing a drink at a party, for his sister, his wife and his daughters; the drink was made up of milk and of semen. Also at the party, in a communicating room, were his professional colleagues.

Some months later I came across the following in 'Transformation symbolism in the Mass', in which Jung is explaining a passage in an alchemical text of Simon Magus, who was quoting Hippolytus' *Elenchos*:

> It [the divine pneuma] is the very ground of existence, the procreative urge, which is of fiery origin. Fire is related to blood, which is 'fashioned warm and ruddy like fire'. Blood turns into semen in men, and in woman into milk. ... The operative principle in semen and milk turns into mother and father. [*CW* 11, para. 359]

The dreamer had not read the book.

His dream shows, first, a patient's use of body imagery; second, his desire to reconcile himself and get back into harmony with certain closely related females who usually received various anima projections from him; and third, the desire that there should be a better internal communication than previously in his feelings about himself as the son of his parents, as a family man and as a worker. There were transference and countertransference features at the time which contributed significantly to the dream and the combination of those with the symbols in it heralded a new phase of development.

The purposive nature of instincts releases healing and creative symbols since, in the analytical treatment, the patient has been put in touch with his capacity to connect the conscious mind with growth processes from the unconscious. It is *his* own capacity: the analyst is the assistant, similar to the alchemical *soror*.

Attacks of envy and envious attacks

The flow of reconciling symbols is often held up by renewed envious attacks on the analyst. The stage of hungry envy (Hubback, 1972) is followed by the second stage of denigratory envy. Sarcasm, scorn and cynicism are the consulting-room versions of the emotions belonging to the stage at which 'the infant in the patient' is trying to emerge from its deep-seated fears of another abandonment.

So it happens that there is a new envious attack in a phantasy or a dream just when it seemed possible that real progress had been achieved. For example, the absence of my car from its usual place in the street outside was said to 'mean' that I had gone off to enjoy myself with someone I found more attractive than the patient. Another patient dreamed that he met me on the doorstep of my house as I departed, most elegantly dressed, with a high-and-mighty Afghan hound which bared its teeth fiercely while I took no notice of him.

The patient who has been enviously attacking the analyst as the present representative of the once-powerful mother gradually comes to recognize the character of the images in such dreams and phantasies and discovers how to reconcile the warring emotions. Where work with such a patient is concerned, there is an optimistic passage in Jung's paper entitled, 'Concerning the archetypes with special reference to the anima concept': 'The projection ceases the moment it becomes conscious, that is to say when it is seen as belonging to the subject'—but a footnote to that runs as follows:

> There are, of course, cases where, in spite of the patient's seemingly sufficient insight, the reactive effect of the projection does not cease, and the expected liberation does not take place. I have often observed that in such cases meaningful but unconscious contents are still bound up with the projection carrier. It is these contents that keep up the effect of the

projection, although it has apparently been seen through. [*CW* 9i, paras. 121 and 121n]

Conclusion:
Mysterium Coniunctionis

The dissociation between spirit and matter, of which Jung wrote a great deal in the last chapter of *Mysterium Coniunctionis,* is comparable—in the inner world of some of the patients described here—to the dissociation between the imagos of each of the two parents. Other patients could not make contact with any image of loving parents, and less despondent images about life emerged only gradually during their analyses. Early in the paper I used the concept of *coniunctio* to refer to the kind of healed split which I think the therapist of depressed patients should—if possible—be able to offer. My thesis is that, via the transference/countertransference, there can be a carry-over of the psychological possibility of *coniunctio* from the analyst to the patient. The theme can be worded in the fully Jungian form of granting *coniunctio* archetypal status, so that the constellation of that archetype can be postulated to activate in the patient the capacity to move from dissociation to internal harmony, or integration—the integration of the father and mother imagos. The analogy of Jung's concern with spirit and matter in *Mysterium Coniunctionis* seems to me to be one which can validly be used, and other writings of his, e.g., 'Transformation symbolism in the Mass' and 'The transcendent function', also give the background and basis for this theme.

Much work has to be done before the depth and extent of the dissociation is well enough appreciated, which lends weight to Jung's statement that 'a *conscious* situation of distress is needed in order to activate the archetype of unity' (*CW* 14, para. 772). Then, in the 'Epilogue', he enquires whether the psychologist can throw out the antagonistic forces, or whether he had not better 'admit their existence ... bring them into harmony and, out of the multitude of contradictions, produce a unity, which naturally will not come of itself, though it may—*Deo concedente*—with human effort' (ibid., para. 791).

I have often been struck by just that—the great and total 'human effort' that the patient puts into the therapeutic work at this difficult stage. He or she is often in a renewed state of depression, angry and sore, or again in an ambivalent mood towards me. The affect in dreams and phantasies is either painful, or split off. One patient, for example, who was recovering from a serious schizoid depression, dreamed of the parental pair in a car, under which there was a smouldering fire, perhaps a bomb, and the dreamer/son saved them just before the petrol tank blew up. Presence of mind—ego capacity—was required of him, as well as a warmth of feeling towards his parents. The dreams of a woman patient over many months grew around images of the limitless sea and then other kinds of water, with a gradual diminution of boundlessness, of isolation, of nameless terrors, and a steady growth of pictures in which some focus of safety was perceptible, places or situations where there were square enclosures or encircled areas, a potential coming-together, a possible *coniunctio*. Many months later, the images were again of a vast sea, greyness going on for ever. A renewed and strenuous effort had to be undertaken. Although the sea had no boundaries, there was fish pâté in a bowl on her kitchen table, ready to be made into sandwiches: bread from the earth, fish from the sea, a modern *coniunctio*.

The coniunctio and harmonization of internal imagos is unlikely to take place if the analyst does not find the right combination within herself of responsiveness and self-boundaries. If she can keep her sense of self, she will be able to become the internal representative of the union of the opposing pair. Unless she can respond from out of her own sense of healed self, the imagos do not come together well enough for the patient's healing to be soundly enough based.

The last chapter of *Mysterium Coniunctionis* is a mine of wealth. For example, 'The adept produces a system of fantasies that has a special meaning for him' (ibid., para. 694). 'The alchemists called their *nigredo* melancholia, "a black blacker than black" night, an affliction of the soul, confusion, etc.' (ibid., para. 791). 'It was ... of the utmost importance to him [the adept] to have a favourable familiar as a helper in his work.' That 'familiar' analyst knows in herself that *nigredo, mortificatio, separatio* and *divisio* precede *coniunctio*. The illustrations from the *Rosarium Philosophorum* and the use Jung made of them in *The Psychology of the Transference* (*CW* 16) are not always easy to connect in a living way with clinical material. Their initial impact can be one of major fascination, which is of little use in day-to-day work. When they, and Jung's other studies of the psychology of alchemy, are returned to—perhaps again and again with personal development having taken place in the meantime—then the possibility grows of applying them in understanding clinical interactions with patients whose experience of parental imagos has contributed substantially to splitting defences.

Mysterium Coniunctionis uses much material from alchemists living, broadly, at the same period as those men studied by the historian Frances Yates, whose works are now essential companions for students of Jung's work on alchemy. Most of those men were written about by both authors: they include Ramon Lull, Marsilio Ficino, Pico della Mirandola, Cornelius Agrippa, Paracelsus, Giordano Bruno, John Dee, Christian Rosencreutz and Robert Fludd. The search for harmony was the driving force behind many of the deep thinkers of the fifteenth, sixteenth and seventeenth centuries, men in turbulent public life as well as philosophers. The parallel between the archetypal yearnings for harmony and the researches of the alchemists gives added significance to the internal search for *coniunctio* of depressed patients. It happens to give me personally much interest and encouragement when I find the main lines of observations, thoughts and intuitions being followed in several arts and sciences. At the same time the differences between them must be taken into account, analogies must not be overworked, and there is also the danger of falling into the simplistic view that 'history repeats itself'.

The reconciling symbols have to be the alive ones for each of us. A particular patient may have no inclination whatsoever to make a living connection with the mythologies, or the periods of history or the particular arts which appeal to his analyst. Detailed descriptions of the clinical use of amplification would perhaps help those analysts who are chary of introducing their own cultural associations, who fear they might prevent the development of the patient's own imagery, or interfere with its potential flow. I do not think I have helped patients forward significantly when I have tried amplifying openly. It is rather, I find, that the implicit offering of a concentrated extract (so to speak) of my attempted inner harmonization, and of the work done so far on splitting and other defences, will be what the depressed patient who was once the child of a depressed mother will feed off and make his own. It is the psychology of conjunction which has to be understood and appreciated.

Summary

The hypothesis is offered that patients whose mothers were depressed during their infancy and childhood may be enabled to emerge from their own long-term depressions (or other consequences of early emotional difficulties) if in the therapy they are able to make use of their analyst's having achieved a reasonably viable sense of self, based on the internal *coniunctio* of parental imagos. Transference and countertransference manifestations of the workings of malign imagos and of the gradual emergence of benign and uniting symbols in phantasies and dreams are given in relation to the therapies of six patients.

It is suggested, implicitly, that current observations and studies of narcissistic deprivation, splitting defences, shadow material and hungry and envious attacks can be usefully furthered if they are related to Jung's exploration of the theme of *coniunctio* as having been the main psychological importance of alchemy.

REFERENCES

Fordham, M. (1974). Defences of the self. *Journal of Analytical Psychology* 19:2.

Gordon, R. (1980). Narcissism and the self: who am I that I love? *Journal of Analytical Psychology* 25:3.

Hubback, J. (1969). The symbolic attitude in psychotherapy. *Journal of Analytical Psychology* 14:1.

———— (1972). Envy and the shadow. *Journal of Analytical Psychology* 17:2.

Humbert, E. (1980). The self and narcissism. *Journal of Analytical Psychology* 25:3.

Jacoby, M. (1981). Reflections on Heinz Kohut's concept of narcissism. *Journal of Analytical Psychology* 26:1.

Kalsched, D. (1980). Narcissism and the search for interiority. *Quadrant,* 13:2.

Ledermann, R. (1982). Narcissistic disorder and its treatment. *Journal of Analytical Psychology* 27:4.

Schwartz-Salant, N. (1982). *Narcissism and Character Transformation.* Toronto: Inner City Books.

CHAPTER TWO

Success, retreat, panic: over-stimulation and depressive defence

Peer Hultberg

Hultberg's use of the concept of over-stimulation enables him to throw new light on depression, grandiosity and mania. The secret presence of grandiose phantasies attached to what would otherwise be realistic achievements in the concrete world makes these achievements feel like threats to psychic integration itself. From a personal–historical angle, the patient may have had pressurizing parents, or have been used as a cure for a parent's narcissistic wound. Then the tension aroused by achievement is unbearable because this is felt by the individual—in a sense accurately—to be against his or her own best interests.

Analysts and therapists will readily recognize Hultberg's depiction of underachieving patients with their fear of success. His usage of Jung's idea of 'regressive restoration of the persona', in which the individual denies ambition and aspiration, takes on

---

First published in *The Journal of Analytical Psychology* 30:1, in 1985. Published here by kind permission of the author and the Society of Analytical Psychology.

an added dimension when added to the list of neurotic counter-transference possibilities of which we are aware. In particular, the 'greyness' of meticulously conducted analyses certainly has to be reframed as a result of Hultberg's speculations.

Two sub-themes of the paper deserve mention: (1) the role of alcohol as a retreat from over-stimulation, and (2) the link Hultberg makes between Klein's work on gratitude and the coniunctio.

A.S.

T he concept of over-stimulation or hyperexcitement has until recently been used predominantly in connection with children. It has been discussed as an intense reaction of over-involvement resulting from too-strong stimuli from the outside, especially from over-close and over-taxing parents. However, in the past decade there has been a tendency to consider the concept also as an inner psychic phenomenon frequently observed in adults. This change of emphasis is mainly the result of work of American writers on so-called self-psychology, notably Heinz Kohut and his followers. Over-stimulation in this latter sense is, in the language of Kohut, defined as a 'mobilization of archaic exhibitionistic libido' (Kohut, 1971, p. 5) which threatens to flood the ego. This process may be triggered off by something in the outside world, or an inner stimulus or phantasy may be externalized. It is, however, in contrast to the classical concept of over-stimulation, essentially an endopsychic process. In the language of Jung one might say that over-stimulation in this sense is a process whereby conscious or unconscious psychic contents of an inflationary or grandiose nature are aroused and threaten to overwhelm the ego. The ego, however, is strong enough and has sufficient reality sense, as it were, to defend itself against both identification with the grandiose content and general non-psychotic states of inflation, and against irreversible submersion psychosis. The process, however, does call forth an excitement which is felt as highly uncomfortable and which gives rise to strong anxiety. The manner in which the ego defends itself against this anxiety is mainly by retreating. An ego which is especially prone to become hyperstimulated seems above all to protect itself by secluding itself from the wave or source of excitement. This is then generally experienced either as a state of resentful depressive hopelessness or as apathetic isolation and utter passivity, or both.

The process may be illustrated by the following story.

A young painter from a provincial town in Denmark held his first exhibition in Copenhagen. It was received well. Encouraged by this, he was soon afterwards able to arrange a second exhibition with a reception equally favourable, if not better. The young artist then went home to visit his parents in their idyllic little Danish town. As he was sitting in the train he suddenly felt as if he were about to burst, to fly into a thousand pieces. He was overwhelmed and entirely unable to control his phantasy that when the little local train eventually pulled up at the station a red carpet would have been laid out and a delegation headed by the mayor would be awaiting him with music and flowers. He got into a panic and started to pace frantically up and down the corridor of the train, imagining with dread the deafening sound of the brass band welcoming him. Overwhelmed by an inexplicable anxiety, he found his way to the small bar in the train. And when his parents met him at the station—needless to say without any municipal delegation or brass band—their son literally fell out of the train, totally drunk. Curiously enough, however, apart from the alcoholic poisoning his state of mind was tranquil and composed. He had mastered his excitement and the subsequent anxiety, and he no longer felt torn to pieces. Although his mood was somewhat sad and even resigned, at the same time he felt calm. However, for a very long time afterwards his creative powers seemed to fail him, and he was unable to paint properly for several years. He lived in something akin to a mild apathy and dejection and chose to finish a very conventional course of university studies rather than go on trying to make a career as an artist.

This small scene seems to speak for itself as an illustration of the problem of over-stimulation and retreat. Here was a man in his late twenties who all of a sudden sees the fulfilment of his most daring hopes. To become a painter and to be recognized as such was to him the supreme goal in his life. It had been so ever since he was a small, sensitive boy who, from the age of six, had to assert himself at school by means of his intellectual, and especially his artistic, talents. His parents never understood his situation. They did not see his plight and never considered his painting as anything of value. He quickly saw through his mother's superficial and sentimental praise of his efforts as a child and carefully kept everything he painted away from her lest she should use it for her own self-enhancement. The father was just not interested. And when he exhibited his pictures they were, in fact, both shocked and extremely embarrassed that their little boy could paint such big and such blatantly erotic canvases. On the other hand, they mildly flattered themselves on their son's success. The painter had thus never obtained any real recognition till the unexpected success with his first two exhibitions. But rather than finding strength and encouragement for further steady work he became overjoyed and subsequently hyper-stimulated. And this tendency to be almost torn to pieces at the fulfilment of his most burning wish had to be defended against in such a way that over-stimulation gave way to apathy and dejection for a long time to come. He fell into a state of emptiness; his initiative was blocked, and he felt paralysed. In short, he experienced a condition close to depression.

It is, however, important to underline that at no point was there any question of his falling into a manifest depressive psychosis. His ego seemed to function with a certain degree of reliability as it had always done, and he kept up his fairly good work record. In other words, he seemed quite early in life to have acquired a minimum of psychic cohesion, or ego strength, which prevented any complete submersion in the world of his phantasies. All the same, his ego did appear frail and seemed protected only behind rigid walls which then came under fierce attack through the realization of his burning ambition. It was, however, strong enough ultimately to withstand and to defend itself against the onrush of over-stimulation. The psychic tension could be regulated and the falling-apart prevented, albeit by rather immature or even archaic defensive manoeuvres.

The manner in which the walls are generally rebuilt after a flooding of over-stimulation—especially in the non-analytical setting—is also illustrated by this case. However, the following brief extra-analytical account may show even more clearly the essential features of this restorative process.

A woman violinist, on the strength of a very successful first performance, was awarded a scholarship to go abroad to study with one of the most famous of violinists. She returned home to give her second concert, which was a startling success. The audience recognized her as the national equivalent of the eminent violinist, and the enthusiasm was almost uncontrollable; people would hardly let her leave the platform. She reacted by getting into a panic after the concert. She hid in her dressing room, allowed no one to get near to her, cancelled immediately all further arrangements for concerts, and the following day decided to give up her career as a violinist entirely. It was impossible for anyone to persuade her to do otherwise. She broke away from her musical milieu and in due course obtained a post at a school as an ordinary music teacher, and she remained there for the rest of her working life.

For the young painter and for the violinist, the fulfilment of the greatest and most intense wishes of their lives led to a dangerous situation where the ego of each of them was about to be entirely flooded by grandiose phantasies. In both cases the ego defended itself by retreat and apparent emptiness. But when it came to a restoration it was, especially in the case of the violinist, unable to restore itself to its former dimensions. The young painter had to live for several years in a state much below the level of his artistic talents and possibilities and was, in fact, only helped out of this condition through analysis. The violinist lived like that for the rest of her life, contenting herself with a job that she found rather mundane; although her decision was naturally supported later by other defence mechanisms such as intellectualization, rationalization, and ideological and ethical arguments.

From a Jungian point of view, one notices here the resemblance, especially in the latter case, of this sequence of events to Jung's concept of 'the regressive restoration of the persona'. Jung coined this term in his 1916 lecture 'Über das Unbewusste und seine Inhalte' and elaborated it in the enlarged version of the lecture, 'The relations between the ego and the unconscious'. He uses it to describe one of the possible reactions to the breakthrough into consciousness of unconscious contents and illustrates it with examples taken from everyday life, since:

It would [. . .] be a mistake to think that cases of this kind make their appearance only in analytical treatment. The process can be observed just as well, and often better, in other situations of life, namely in all those careers where there has been some violent and destructive intervention of fate. [*CW* 7, para. 254]

The restoration of the persona in a regressive way means that the individual in question 'will have demeaned himself, pretending that he is as he was *before* the crucial experience, though utterly unable even to think of repeating such a risk. Formerly perhaps he wanted more than he could accomplish; now he does not even dare to attempt what he has it in him to do' (*CW* 7, para. 254). In other words, the person leads a life on a lower level than before.

The difference between Jung's description and the problem of over-stimulation as described here is that Jung uses the reaction to a catastrophe as an illustration of his concept: he takes as an example the case of a business man going bankrupt. In the context of over-stimulation, however, one is dealing with the reaction to an unexpected success, the fulfilment of a deeply nourished hope which threatens to upset the psychic equilibrium and create unmanageable inner tensions. The individual withdraws into isolation, either concretely as in the case of the music teacher or into an alcoholic aloofness as in the case of the young painter. But when they eventually emerge from their protective and calming isolation it is not with an ego which is better able to defend itself; it is with a patched-up psychic equilibrium. They emerge with an ego which is able to defend itself against the onrush of over-stimulation only because it has given up the ambitions and wishes the fulfilment of which caused the almost uncontrollable flooding. The healthy part of the psyche has not been strengthened; on the contrary, the psychic scope has been reduced and apathy adopted as a major defence mechanism. It might perhaps be said that here is a defensive mechanism which is the reverse of the regression in the service of the ego, and akin to Anna Freud's concept of ego-restriction.

Like the regressive restoration of the persona, the retreat after over-stimulation seems rarely to bring individuals into analysis. The retreat in itself is defence enough to keep them going. The avoidance of risks and of situations which may give rise to hyperexcitement generally assures a relatively smooth day-to-day functioning. And, as Jung indicated, the phenomenon is encountered perhaps less in analysis than among one's friends and acquaintances.

Over-stimulation in analysis

However, there is a group of patients for whom over-stimulation appears to lie at the core of their problems. These are people who in their youth and also as children have frequently given the impression of being very talented, at times even exceptionally so. However, they never really seem able to live up to the promise they initially inspired. Instead of developing and realizing their gifts they appear, often fairly early in life, to slip into a somewhat mild depressive state; and they tend to remain in it for ever, except perhaps for the odd short outburst of creativity in which they suddenly seem to rekindle the expectations they originally awoke. Generally, however, they live a reduced life, not in the sense that one feels that their intellectual powers or their creative talents have dried up, but merely that these never appear to have been led into channels where they may be fully and purposefully employed. The most typical feature, however, is that there is a specific task which they cannot accomplish, although they seem generously equipped to do so and also very well prepared for it. They may even come into therapy explicitly to be helped to perform this task, or it transpires very early in therapy that they are worried (or at times through rationalizations resigned to the fact) that they cannot finish their doctoral dissertation, that they have broken off their course of study a short time before the final exams (which naturally they had every reason to believe they would pass well), that they are simply unable to make the last preparations for their crucial recital, although the programme has been rehearsed for years. The rather absurd modern notion of concert abstinence seems to be a rationalization for such an inner state. Here a performing artist may rather retire than expose himself to the enthusiasm of an audience, as in the case of the violinist mentioned above. The following account may serve as an illustration of over-stimulation as a basic psychic problem.

Mrs Lake is an American. She is close to forty and has come into analysis with a 'man's disease'. She has a bad heart. She is

working overtime at her school without extra pay, is engaged in
trade union activities, and in addition gives courses in art history
almost every evening. The weekends are spent organizing
political work, and she has not had a holiday for more than two
years. However, she feels amply rewarded by the prestige she has
achieved as an ardent environmentalist and by the small political
organization devoted to these problems which, she feels, she
herself has created from scratch. Were it not for the heart,
everything would be well. In the initial interview she mentions a
curious fact: she, the prizewinner at school and at university, she
who won some highly coveted scholarships and whom everyone
expected to climb to the top of the university ladder, just cannot
finish 'her book'. After a sabbatical year to do research in Europe
she even had herself posted back to Germany to carry on the work
which was supposed to assure her a top position in her former
university department. 'Mark you', she adds in the initial
interview, 'when I have written my book and proved my point,
everyone working on Dürer will have to take it into account; and
all the encyclopaedias in Germany and subsequently in the whole
world will have to be revised.'

In the following session I try to test her claim, and as far as I
can see it is not just inflatory madness. She explains her ideas to
me painstakingly and accurately, showing me supporting reports
from museum directors and professors. It appears that she really
has a point which will throw an entirely new light on her topic
and she seems able to prove it.

The sore point, however, is that her book cannot be written.
She is now in her late thirties and it should have been finished
years ago. Everyone around her is encouraging, everyone
supports her; but the book stays where it has always been, in a
box of neatly filled-in index cards. It has long ago ceased to be
embarrassing to her. She has swallowed the hurt of disappointed
expectation, she just plods on. But still she cannot write, although
she has all the material she wants, and from an intellectual point
of view nothing prevents her.

This problem and not her heart quickly became the focus of the
sessions.

There was no difficulty in linking the problem up with Mrs
Lake's negatively experienced mother, but then everything
seemed to stop. Mrs Lake had been brought up by her divorced

mother who kept her, the only child, away from the father until his death. And it was not till she started analysis that Mrs Lake really began to see *how* brutally she had been exploited by her mother from childhood up till the present day. So we both tended to search for the root of her problem in her relationship to her mother.

Was the reason that she could not finish her book defiance against the mother? Was it revenge and an expression of rage in connection with the early trauma that she had never been accepted as she was but had always been exploited narcissistically in order to enhance the mother's self-esteem? Was she begrudging the mother the triumph of having a daughter who had published a book of her own? Or was it guilt over her success, because as the author of an important book she would finally have superseded the mother? Could it be just defence against competitiveness with the mother? Or had she through projective identification incorporated the inferiority and incompetence against which the mother defended herself so vehemently? Was she merely treating her book with the same demands of hyperperfection with which the mother had treated her as a child? Was the thesis her child, which she, unmarried and childless, would not permit to develop according to its own laws and of which she could not let go? Or was the block a deep prophylaxis against the shattering diappointment that the mother would after all *not* recognize her and accept her but remain as indifferent to her achievements as she had always been even after she had accomplished this, to her, tremendous feat? Did her block thus express deep doubts about her own worth and her own intelligence which could not be counter-proved by realistic self-esteem? Or was it just the *puella aeterna*'s fear of entering the world of the grown-up? Or a fear that growing up might mean irrevocably leaving the mother, and thus finally having to give up the neurotic entanglement with her, which had been almost the only form of human relationship she had known, or at any rate the most important? Or could it be a question of identity, a fear of abandoning the identity of the daughter as such, of the *doctoranda,* the eternal daughter of the Alma Mater? Or had the book been the only means whereby she could confirm herself to herself and maintain an inner continuity? Was she then clinging to it as a child clings to a transitional object? Or was she clinging to it because she had *not* been able to transform it into a transitional object, but kept experiencing it as a gift to the mother? Was the book one of the few stabilizing factors in her life; and would it then be possible for her to finish it if the analysis and I, in the transference, took over this stabilizing function? And, conversely, was the inability to get on with the work in the present context of the analysis, and in spite of my various interpretations, a transference phenomenon: she feared that just like her mother I might take the credit for her work if she were to finish it because of therapy with me; a fear that I, too, would exploit her for *my* narcissistic needs and treat her and her work as a feather in my analyst's cap. Or, worse still, a fear that I, like the mother, might choose just to ignore it and treat it as a matter of analytical course?

We looked into all these possibilities, and all seemed quite convincing. There was something about them all, but none of them seemed to hit the mark. Only one thing seemed certain: Mrs Lake was depressed in a restless, tooth-grinding way, not because she could not write her book, but in order *not* to write it.

It was not till the concept of over-stimulation was introduced that the reaction was more in the affirmative. It was even possible to speak about the classical 'aha-experience'. Things now seemed clearer. The book was the goal of her life. More she did not want from life; she had in advance decided against any further research. It was enough to her to think that when she had officially proved her point all the major encyclopaedias in the world would have to be rewritten and that her name from now on would appear in the indexes of all works on Dürer. She would expect nothing more from life. Perhaps this limitation of herself was a kind of anticipatory and prophylactic restoration of her persona in a regressive way. However, it did not succeed in curbing her over-stimulation and the subsequent anxieties at the thought of what might happen when she had finished her book. On the contrary, the confinement of her life's work to this single book seemed to have the adverse effect: it appeared to accentuate the absolute character of the fulfilment of that most burning wish and to exacerbate her fears of the consequences to her psyche when she had fulfilled her task. She was not afraid of being drained, or of the emptiness which might come over a person who has reached the goal he has set himself, nor of the feeling of sudden bewilderment which one might suppose comes over the donkey when it has suddenly devoured the carrot which for years has been dangling before its nose. What she was really afraid of was simply of bursting with joy, of being overcome with excitement to such an extent that she could not control it. And her feeling of emptiness as well as her severe work inhibition was her way of coping with this anxiety and defending herself against it. In these overstimulating phantasies the mother naturally also cropped up. One of the most hyperexciting phantasies was of an ultimate reconciliation with her mother. Through her success she would at last have replaced and even superseded and surpassed the father whom the mother had castrated so effectively. She would finally be able to compensate the mother for the severe troubles which the father in her eyes had caused her in the marriage, and thus in the end she would win the mother's love.

It now transpired that over-excitement and hyperstimulation were very important features in the life of Mrs Lake. She was, for example, totally unable to calm down if she had experienced some form of success in her professional life. She described how she would then talk incessantly to herself in her car or when walking in the street, where people would even turn round and look at her. At home she would argue with herself for hours, either sitting on the edge of her bed or pacing up and down in her study until five or six in the morning, when from sheer exhaustion and by means of a couple of glasses of Dubonnet she would at last collapse into bed for an hour or two. She was now herself able to connect this with her mother, who had never given her any admiration or recognition for her often exceptionally good achievements nor any sympathy in her worries. Mrs Lake then grew unable to feel any real joy in herself and in her accomplishments. Furthermore, she was provided with no measure by which to appraise realistically the value of her achievements. She thus had no inner joy in herself and in her activities and no inner criteria for judgement of herself. Indeed, many of her dreams pointed to this general depressive state of her soul; deep down, behind her often sparkling vitality and her 'green' environmentalist activities, there was a bleak psychic desert and a dream-ego deprived of any illusions. It was therefore understandable that she should react with terror to the thought of having to cope with the extreme happiness when she had reached her long-cherished goal; and that she should prefer her subdued, somewhat depressive and blocked state rather than risk exploding from a joy which she had no means of controlling. In this way she defended herself against the dread of over-stimulation, but at the price of a severe work inhibition.

Mrs Lake appeared fully able to accept the interpretation of over-stimulation as being at the core of her problem. And as a result of this she decided to abandon her ambitious project. The entries on Dürer in all the major encyclopaedias of this world are after all not going to be rewritten. Like most of her colleagues in the academic world, she chose to restrict herself to writing the occasional article. At the same time as she gave up the attempt to write her book she also approached her old college and was delighted to realize that she had not been forgotten. On the contrary, since she had always been an excellent and inspiring teacher she was offered her old position and returned to the United States in a composed frame of mind. And when friends and colleagues suggest that she might after all write a nice little popular book on Dürer, she can now cope with the stimulation and stem the flood of phantasies—and refuse.

Over-stimulation in the transference

In the analytical process as such, over-stimulation seems above all to manifest itself in connection with the transference and probably also the countertransference. In the transference it seems principally to evolve around an extreme sensitivity to the closeness of the analytical situation, especially at times when idealization or projective identification are at their strongest. The highest goal of the analysand at times is to be as intimate with the analyst as he possibly can, and the feeling that this wish could be fulfilled may again be too overwhelming. Subsequently, the analysand has to defend himself against this dangerous situation.

The manner in which the analysand experiences the perils of closeness is naturally highly varied and very subjective. The sharing of a joke can be as upsetting as the phantasies aroused when a confessing analyst feels he must disclose parts of his personal life as a reward for frankness, as a consolation, or as a surrender to more or less subtle emotional blackmail. A chance encounter outside can give rise to ideas of identical interests or identical life problems. Pleasure on the part of the analyst, as indeed his praise, can give rise to phantasies of being the chosen person, and so on. Behind all these phantasies lies the dread of being overwhelmed and of losing control as a result of reaching the unbearable state of intimacy and closeness. This may be expressed as a fear of being seduced by the analyst—seduction naturally understood in the broadest sense of the word, intellectual or ideological or theoretical seduction being often just as dangerous as sexual seduction. Here there is a dread that the analyst might abandon his self-control and initiate the wished-for closeness.

Kohut and his followers have pointed out an important fear in this context—the fear of being swept off one's feet by an interpretation which hits the centre of things (see, for example, Goldberg, 1978, pp. 9, 63, 83, 85). This fear has probably at least two main sources. It is naturally an expression of the fright at what might happen if an insight is suddenly achieved and hitherto unconscious contents are released and engulf the ego before it has had time to organize its defences. But it also seems to be a fear of being over-stimulated by the joy at having at last found a fellow human being who, seemingly by instinct or intuition or by extreme empathy, can feel the needs and the plight of the analysand even before he himself understands it. Many cases of prolonged silence in therapy may probably be put down to this anxiety, rather than being seen as an expression of unconscious aggression or defiance.

The following occurrence may illustrate this point.

A couple of years ago I was presented with a copy of the first edition of T. S. Eliot's *Four Quartets*. Since I was very happy both with the book and the thought behind it, I let it lie on a table in my consulting room, so that I might read a little in it between hours. An intelligent woman patient with a strong, rather dependent transference immediately noticed the book and remarked on it. As she was very interested in literature I fetched the book and read the passage about the wounded surgeon to her:

Our only health is the disease
If we obey the dying nurse
Whose constant care is not to please
But to remind of our, and Adam's curse,
And that, to be restored, our sickness must grow worse
[Eliot, 1969, p. 181]

We discussed briefly how Jungian, in fact, these thoughts are, and this led us, I believed, in a natural way into the hour.

As one too often does when breaking the rule of abstinence, I thought little of this and merely believed that we had discussed something of interest to her. I was therefore very much taken aback when she started her Monday session with a very earnest request: Would I please, please in future, *please* never more break the analytical neutrality and not introduce matters from my personal life; she was just unable to cope with it. At first I was perplexed and did not know what she was referring to; I believed it could only be an anecdote, not even concerning me personally, which I had produced to drive home an interpretation. Only then did she explain that it had to do with the poem. It seemed to her that I had talked about it in a very special way, as if I had felt the need to communicate something especially private and personal to her and to her alone, and exactly at this point in her analysis. She had registered my pleasure in the poem and interpreted this to mean that I had no one at all with whom I could share my joy and my interests. In that way I had made her my partner, I had seduced her, she felt, intimating a loneliness in my personal life, as well as deep problems, which were parallel to her own problems and her own loneliness. She had returned home after the hour overwhelmed by excitement and phantasies that after all she was the chosen one, that her feelings for me had echoed in me. She was at the time in a stage in her analysis where she did not retreat into an overt depressive mood as a result of the over-stimulation. However, she did feel that she was in danger of losing control over herself and experienced again a dreadful fear, almost like a fear of death, of losing herself to me, and thus entering into one of the fatally destructive relationships which she had previously known and in which she had entirely given up her own personality. For a couple of hours she was trembling all over her body, and it took her a full evening to calm down sufficiently so that she could write herself out of her excitement.

Furthermore, she spent the whole weekend studying Eliot in the belief that he had been the subject of my doctoral thesis.

The defence and retreat phenomena connected with over-stimulation in the transference are naturally very varied but aim predominantly at avoiding the threatening closeness. This may happen in a phobic way, by increasingly incapacitating anxieties, for example. Or, especially early on in analysis, it may lead to the analysis being broken off, often exactly when the analyst feels that things are going particularly well and a really good relationship is about to be established. The fear of praise may lead to snarls at the analyst, who has perhaps indirectly given vent to his pleasure at the good co-operation. Or the analysand may ostentatiously, and maybe even in a hurtful manner, forbid himself any interest in the life of the analyst as a defence against overwhelming phantasies. He may, as indicated before, appear drowsy, passive, be silent in a bewildering manner, rather than dare to expose himself to the friendly warmth and empathic understanding of the analyst. Or he may defend himself against being overwhelmed by his own idealization of the analyst by criticizing him, or seemingly rejecting the school of analysis to which he assumes the analyst belongs. Long tirades against Jung, often of a political nature, or the belittling of Freud's Viennese *petit bourgeois* background, seem to be instances of this, as are certain dreams, especially at the beginning of analysis, the contents of which poke fun at the analyst's theoretical frame-work or at the analyst as a person.

At this point perhaps one specific type of defence against hyperexcitement ought briefly to be mentioned: the use of the age-old depressant, alcohol. When the previously mentioned young artist was caught by the possibility of a fragmentation of his personality by his overwhelming, grandiose phantasies, he retreated at first into an alcoholic stupor. Mrs Lake likewise had, now and then, to lull herself to sleep with her glass of Dubonnet. This is almost a parody of the reality-orientated defence against over-stimulation, which is controlled retreat and organized withdrawal. But, when the source is internal, it is difficult to find a place to retire to and to do so in a regulated manner. It appears, however, that the healthy part of the psyche, in a highly inadequate way, uses alcohol to defend itself against disintegra-tion. When people with alcohol problems are faced with deeply

agitating phantasies and are about to be flooded by hyperexcitement, they seem able to quieten the intrusive grandiose
phantasies by drinking. Alcohol appears here to have a certain
ego-regenerating function. The individual is able to retire,
regress and isolate himself, and subsequently to restore his
personality through alcohol. Although drinking may naturally be
the revengeful reaction to a disappointment or an imagined
rebuff, it may also be caused by highly stirring phantasies
released in the transference, for example, through a misunderstanding of the analyst's friendly warmth. And the only way,
then, in which the ego seems able to defend itself against such
floodings of joy and excitement is by staging a flooding of its own.

Such a drinking pattern seems, for example, to be the basis of
the alcoholism of one patient who easily became severely
hyperstimulated. On one occasion he was overwhelmed by the
beauty of nature while wandering for days in an impressive
Alpine landscape. His happiness at such splendid scenery was so
great that he just could not contain it. The excitement grew so
painful that it became unendurable, and he had to have alcohol in
order to calm down: 'I just had to drink in order to become a
normal person again, otherwise I don't know what I should have
done for sheer joy', as he expressed it.

I am here reminded of Keats's 'Ode to a Nightingale', where
the poet 'being too happy in thine happiness' wishes for 'a draught
of vintage. . . . That I might drink, and leave the world unseen, /
And with thee fade away into the forest dim' (Keats, 1982, p. 207).
Hyperstimulation seems to have been a psychic reality for many
of the Romantics; and it was, in fact, observations concerning the
Polish Romantic poet Adam Mickiewicz which initially gave rise
to my interest in the phenomenon. In 'Ode to a Nightingale'
Keats also points to the ultimate regression in the face of
hyperexcitement:

> Now more than ever seems it rich to die,
> To cease upon the midnight with no pain,
> While thou art pouring forth thy soul abroad
> In such an ecstasy!
>
> [Keats, 1982, p. 208]

Perhaps the equivalent in the late twentieth century to such
sentiments is the experience of a recently married young woman

who on a glorious early summer morning drove her open car at very high speed in blazing sun down a motorway with her husband at her side. At a certain moment she suddenly became obsessed with the desire to drive her car straight into the pillars of one of the motorway bridges: life was so overwhelmingly beautiful that death seemed the only consequence of her rapture.

It seems important to mention the use of alcohol as a combatant of over-stimulation, since alcohol is so often mentioned in general discussions as the bringer of spirit. This might lead to a false understanding of some of the problems lying behind alcoholism or heavy drinking. In cases where over-stimulation plays a part one may even say that alcohol is used in its opposite, depressant way, to combat a surplus of spirit, as it were. And to see the alcohol problem as an expression of a thwarted spiritual search would be misleading, to say the least. On the contrary, alcohol here enables the ego to retreat in a defensive manner and thus withstand the threat of being swamped by spiritual contents. In other terms, it appears that just as one talks of anal defence against orality, one might here talk of an oral defence against an even deeper regression, a defence against the entire breaking up of the psyche. This mixture of defences seems clearly illustrated in the last case I will bring of the man who 'just had to drink to become a normal person again'.

T was a very meticulous and extremely hard-working and ambitious natural scientist—a true anal character, as one usually calls it. He had the habit of working late in the evenings at his laboratory. At a certain point he would start to drink. This, he felt, would enable him to work on a little longer. Soon, however, the quality of the work would be such that it was quite useless, and then he just drank on in a rather guiltless state, at times feeling that he was rewarding himself for being a genius. Hence he was able to muse about life for some hours, he could abandon himself to happy phantasies, or he was lost without anxiety in joy at having found a mistake or a fault in his calculations. Finally, in an alcoholic haze, he returned home from the laboratory. In the end his wife refused to accept this as 'the way scientists work'; she confronted him with the alternative of divorce or therapy, and this brought him into analysis. Here there seemed to be a defence against orality which, however, at a certain point broke through and clearly came to the fore when the scientist permitted himself a little drink, rationalized partly as a reward for his industry and partly as an excuse to get the energy to work on a little longer. At the same time, the drinking itself defended him against a feeling either of void or, more probably, of over-stimulation, when, for example, he finally found an insidious mistake; these feelings would invariably have overwhelmed him if he had finished his day's work without drinking. Without drink he would either feel exhausted and start doubting the meaning of all that he was doing, or he would get carried away by grandiose and anxiety-inducing phantasies. He had, for instance, terrifying phantasies of making an absolute fool of himself when receiving the Nobel Prize from the hands of the Swedish king. When he drank, however, he was able to control these phantasies, and they were not experienced as overwhelming. And rather than being terrified he would, in fact, enjoy them and could safely abandon himself to them, knowing that they would wear off as the amount of alcohol increased. Drinking in T's case is thus not only to be interpreted as a reward for industry (orality breaking through anal defences); it seems even more to be a defence against the hyperexcitement induced by phantasy products springing from what may be called anal industry. In this connection it also seems possible to argue that the well-known everyday phenomena of nightcaps and 'unwinding' after a day's work may be understood in this way. This may be a more fruitful interpretation than merely seeing them as oral compensations for the difficulties in life.

Countertransference

As regards the countertransference, a certain parallel seems observable to the situation of hyperexcitement in the transference, although the basic anxiety of attaining intimate closeness to the analysand may not be so pronounced. However, it can certainly not be ruled out entirely. There might, for example, be moments where the analysand is experienced as a parental figure whose approval and even admiration is sought through a strikingly correct interpretation or a convincingly good piece of advice. This may well happen if the analyst as a child has been called upon to advise his parents rather than being advised by them and to win their acceptance in this way, a situation which probably is not so uncommon for children who later become analysts.

In the countertransference two factors above all seem conducive to a flooding of the analyst's ego, admiration and success; and they may naturally be defended against in many highly different ways. The analyst may, for example, attempt to keep the analysis under tight control, guarding himself against getting too much from the patient, as it were. In this case he may play down the patient's achievements, either in the sense of not properly acknowledging material brought to the sessions, or not recognizing things achieved outside the analysis, either as a response to the analytical work or directly to gain praise from the analyst. This control may be rationalized as 'preventing acting out', or 'refusal to give narcissistic gratification'. All in all, such analyses may seem grey and dull or unduly severe, and the analyst will continually feel inadequate and complain that he never seems to achieve anything—feelings which naturally sooner or later will be picked up by the patient and damp all enthusiasm for the work.

It also appears that boredom in the analysis may at times spring from a similar source. It need not only be the analyst's response to resistances on the part of the patient. I remember a patient whom I found unbearably boring; I dreaded the three weekly hours with him and could hardly restrain myself from confronting him with this. Only when I realized that it was, in fact, mainly my own problem and that I was defending myself against archaic idealization on his part, could I cope with my boredom. This was so much more excruciating, and hence highly defensive on my part, as the patient's idealization was of the type which is intensely intrusive, and thus it was felt by me as being very aggressive. I had simultaneously to defend myself against something both intrusive and idealizing, and for some weeks that was too much for me.

I wonder whether the fear of closeness on the part of the analyst, which may arise as a reaction to a patient's over-stimulating admiration, might also find expression in a certain apprehension regarding inquiries into the patient's personal life, or directly in avoidance of phantasizing about him. This would naturally mean that the analyst was depriving himself of one of the best tools for interpretation. In any event, it does appear that fear of over-stimulation can hamper interpretation to a great extent. The analyst may fear the impact of the correct interpretation in the same way as the patient, either because of the consequences which it might have on the patient, or because he is afraid of the over-stimulating effect on himself of his skill in hitting the mark. This is a dread that his own virtuosity may finally bolt away with him and flood him, an anxiety which it seems is also felt by many artists.

The fear of admiration or of idealization, that is, the fear of being praised, with the resulting avoidance of closeness, is likely to lead to rather uninspired analyses where not much happens. This is often rationalized as steady work on the part of a reliable analyst. Over-stimulation, however, may also take the form of fear of being flooded in the case of evident success. This could lead to an unconscious avoidance of success altogether. One of the many ways of preventing success is to terminate analysis prematurely, or even break it off, an act which might again be rationalized, for instance, by advocating principles of not binding the patient too strongly to the analyst, of not believing in over-long analyses, of wishing the patient to take the responsibility for his own life.

The following example, not of an analyst but of a physiotherapist in her early thirties, may illustrate the problem of over-stimulation in the helping professions, that is, the fears aroused in the helper by his own powers. Mrs Nielsen was highly gifted in her field. However, like all people whose skill approaches virtuosity, she was also an exceedingly hard worker who had gone to great lengths to improve her skills and training. As a result of this she was able at times to achieve cures which were almost miraculous: people condemned to the wheelchair were able after some months of treatment to get up on their own and take their first steps; a spastic baby whom everyone had given up and who had given himself up and turned all but autistic gained control of his motor apparatus, started smiling at his mother, expressed frustration and understandable rage, and became very curious about the world about him. At a certain point Mrs Nielsen grew frightened of her own powers. The events taking place in her practice were nearly too much for her to contain or to cope with. They seemed uncanny to her, and she felt that she possessed almost supernatural powers or, conversely, was possessed by such powers. She was partly fearful lest she should 'grow into the skies and become a megalomaniac', as she expressed it, and partly afraid that something fundamental was wrong with her since she could achieve these stunning results. In her worries about her successes she was at a point where she wished to put an end to it all and just become an ordinary run-of-the-mill physiotherapist. She did not know where the whole thing would lead to otherwise, she said.

After a thorough discussion of her cures she and I agreed that there was, in fact, nothing supernatural about them. She had not consciously or unconsciously entered into a pact with the Devil, whatever shape he might take in the psyche of a late twentieth-century woman. Her seemingly miraculous successes sprang from a combination of conscientious hard work and an uncommonly good training combined with an excellent diagnostic intuition based on her trust in her subliminal or unconscious perceptions. She felt her situation had also become worse during her analysis because she had achieved an even better contact with her unconscious. Moreover, her enthusiasm for her work combined with her confidence in her unconscious, especially in her unconscious observations, gave her pronounced suggestive powers which contributed further to her fears. She could carry people with her and awaken their own trust in themselves and in the possibility of what they had hitherto believed was impossible. And this naturally was a necessary condition for a cure. Because of this insight into her inner and outer reality it was possible to halt her tendency towards retreat in the face of hyperexcitement at her astonishing cures. She built up a realistic self-esteem which prevented her from flight in terror from her own successes or from thwarting them. She no longer saw herself as being like a faith healer in the grip of mysterious powers which would grow or wane without her control. She realized that she was simply a highly-skilled professional woman who had a fine career ahead of her.

It seems then that the main defence mechanism against over-stimulation on the part of the analyst is the well-known device of ego-restriction, be it in the form of a restriction of his human response, his empathy, his attention and vigilance, his interpretative skills, or his general performance. However, one feature might be particularly considered in this context, and that is the rejection, if not the direct rebuff, of the patient's feelings. This may take place as a reaction to idealization where the analyst in the countertransference, for example, may reject parents who have idealized him as a child instead of letting him idealize them, thus depriving him of guidelines and leaving it to him to fend for himself and perhaps for the parents too. But, naturally, a rebuff of the necessary idealization from the analysand may also be a question of idealization felt as too much, that is, as the fulfilment of the most cherished wish. In this connection one specific aspect of the rejection and rebuff should be pointed out—the rejection of gratitude.

Gratitude

Melanie Klein was certainly right in emphasizing the importance of both envy and gratitude for the human being. However, in general, too little attention has been paid to gratitude for the human being. This may certainly be felt at times as exceedingly uncomfortable. In the case of Mrs Nielsen, the physiotherapist, the worst moments for her came when patients, especially ordinary simple people, expressed their profuse thankfulness to her for her remarkable cures. Often these patients were extremely moved, and she had the greatest difficulty in not belittling their feelings as well as her own achievements. The embarrassment was aggravated because, like Mrs Nielsen herself, the patients had generally no particular religious beliefs. Hence they could neither thank their God for their cure, nor could Mrs Nielsen thank hers for her gifts. Her ego had thus to carry the full weight of the gratitude which in former times might have been bestowed on God or on a saint as well as on the healer. And it seemed very understandable that she should cringe away and retreat from this task with its inherent possibility of gross inflation.

In the analytical setting, over-stimulating may manifest itself not only because the analyst senses that he has been successful in his work with the patient, but also because he fears being swept away himself if he allows the feeling of gratitude as such to emerge in the analytical situation. Maybe he himself has never really experienced this feeling, either in his personal life or in his analysis; hence he is forced to perceive it as dangerous and threatening to his psychic equilibrium. Perhaps it should be emphasized that rejection is being discussed in connection with over-stimulation and the subsequent dangers of flooding of the ego and not in connection with cases where the analyst thwarts his own success out of envy of the patient for the feelings which the patient experiences as a result of his analysis with him. There are probably quite a number of analysts who envy their patients their good analysts, in the same way that certain parents may envy their children their good parents.

The analyst's rebuff of the patient for fear of his own over-stimulation induced by gratitude may thus have very serious consequences for the outcome of an analysis. It may again be rationalized; for example, by advocating conformity to rigid rules of not accepting tokens of gratitude, of not giving narcissistic gratification. However, it may be argued that gratitude is one of the most important feelings to emerge in analysis.

One of the goals, if not even the principal goal, of analysis might be said to be an experience of the feeling of gratitude. It is one of the feelings associated with the experience of a relationship to something greater than the ego. It may not necessarily be the aim of an analysis for the patient to experience this feeling solely in relation to the actual parents. There will always be cases in which this cannot be achieved, however profound the analysis. The parents may have to remain rejected. But the important thing is that gratitude is experienced at all.

Speaking in Jungian terms, one might say that the feeling of gratitude is very close to being the feeling equivalent to the experience of the psychic totality, of the supraordinate personality, the conjunction, or whatever name one uses. This transcending factor may initially be projected onto the analyst. But even thus the feeling of gratitude seems to be a step not only towards the realization of good inner and outer objects but also towards self-awareness.

However, the feeling of gratitude also implies a corresponding degree of ego-awareness. And thus it seems that a relation between the ego and the self may be built up which is not a merger of the ego into the self with the corresponding danger of grandiosity or inflation. Gratitude appears to ensure that the two psychic instances are kept apart but at the same time remain intimately related.

Over-stimulation and the related depressive defence may be observed in connection with a very wide range of psychic phenomena. It is encountered within analysis but perhaps even more often outside. The defence, in other words, seems to be particularly effective, especially perhaps in cultures where qualities like modesty, self-effacement, non-competitiveness are considered primary moral values. The defence against hyperexcitement ranges from shyness and a general tendency to hide one's light under a bushel, to an attitude of humility on principle, to fears of healthy competition and fear at one's own achievement, to severe doubts about the value of oneself and of one's accomplishments, and it may end in serious work inhibition, sterile regression, and empty depressivity. The defensive manoeuvres may be supported by a whole arsenal of secondary rationalizations and of references to ethical, social, and religious ideals; and even psychological self-labelling may be employed, like references to one's introversion or one's sadistic super-ego.

Jung has called attention to the important phenomenon of the regressive restoration of the persona. This concept is extremely valuable when one considers the subsequent reactions to the defence or retreat against hyperexcitement. Jung has shown how the walls are rebuilt after a flooding of consciousness by unconscious contents, and how the individual lives a life on a lower level than before, being 'smaller, more limited, more rationalistic than he was before' (*CW* 7, para. 257). One may, however, be entitled to ask whether it is possible to observe a manic defence against the depressive defence against over-stimulation and against the regressive restoration of the persona. The question may sound sophistical yet it appears that a characteristic feature of the regressive restoration of the persona and of the depressive retreat after, or prophylactically before, over-stimulation is often an almost compulsive manic activity. And this hectic activity may then secondarily be used as a rationalization for avoiding situations which might cause hyperexcitement. In the cases mentioned above, for example, Mrs

Lake entered therapy with heart difficulties as a result of her exorbitant political engagement, and the young painter also developed heart problems during his later university career. In these instances, where it is directed against the depressive state connected with over-stimulation, the manic defence appears to be particularly fierce and even virulent. There seems little doubt that this may be explained only by assuming that it is reinforced by an intense narcissistic rage of a highly self-destructive nature. Neither the regressive restoration of the persona nor the retreat phenomena connected with over-stimulation thus imply a state of lethargy. On the contrary, appearances may be strikingly deceptive. Behind the smiling façade of the astonishingly energetic but self-effacing individual who merrily labours himself to death, claiming no reward, there may be a frail and deeply anxious ego which fears the unmitigated onslaught at any moment of its own grandiose phantasies, if it has not already experienced this.

Summary

Over-stimulation is discussed as an endopsychic process, whereby psychic contents of an inflationary or grandiose nature threaten to overwhelm the ego thus causing anxiety. The ego under consideration is, however, able to defend itself more or less successfully against this anxiety and does not succumb irreversibly to it. The defensive mechanisms employed by the ego have the character of a retreat which is experienced as a state of empty depressivity. This depressive defense is linked with Jung's 1916 concept of the regressive restoration of the persona. The phenomenon is treated theoretically with reference to Jung and to the modern American writers on self-psychology, notably Kohut. It is illustrated by extra-analytical occurrences, where the depressive defences seem to function. Subsequently it is considered as a focal point in analysis, and it is then discussed in the context of the transference and the countertransference. The connection with the use of alcohol is specifically underlined. In conclusion, the concept of a manic defence against the depressive defence is briefly sketched without being further elaborated.

REFERENCES

Eliot, T. S. (1969). *The Complete Poems and Plays.* London: Faber & Faber.

Goldberg, A. (ed.) (1978). *The Psychology of the Self.* New York: International Universities Press.

Keats, J. (1982). *Poetical Works.* Oxford: Oxford University Press.

Kohut, H. (1971). *The Analysis of the Self.* New York: International Universities Press.

CHAPTER THREE

A psychological study
of *anorexia nervosa*:
an account of the relationship
between psychic factors
and bodily functioning

Eva Seligman

In this chapter on anorexia, Seligman shows that she is aware of the background in family and marital dynamics and how she works this into her analytical approach. The part played by the father and by siblings is therefore fully acknowledged alongside a more internal perspective.

In many respects, the paper serves as an introduction to the treatment of psychosomatic disorders generally. For in many or all of these, we can see what Seligman calls 'metamorphosis in reverse'—a move from 'the multi-faceted ostensibly somatic syndrome to its basic, primary emotional constituents in infancy.'

Though Seligman's use of a teleological approach is implicit rather than explicit, the reader will see how, for her, any understanding of the aetiology of anorexic symptoms is bound up with a consideration of the unconscious purposiveness of the

First published in *The Journal of Analytical Psychology* 21:2, in 1976. Published here by kind permission of the author and the Society of Analytical Psychology.

illness: what is the anorexic aiming at, desiring, trying to achieve?

A.S.

Psychosomatic illness constitutes a cry of despair and of hope, and may represent an unsuccessful attempt at a search for wholeness. It points to a division within the individual, and any therapeutic confrontation needs therefore to attempt to encompass all aspects of the patient. When a psychosomatic disorder such as a severe eating disturbance manifests itself, and could threaten the continuance of life, the pressure on the analyst to focus primarily on the symptom may become difficult to resist.

A scanning of current psychiatric literature on *anorexia nervosa* is a herculean task. *Psychiatric Briefs,* 8:I, 1975, alone contains eleven extracts from the most recent publications on this topic. In the present cultural environment, and at a point in time when sylphlike slimness is at a premium, eating disorders foist themselves as a socially acceptable manifestation on to the disturbed psyche of the individual. Furthermore, the very real danger to health, and, indeed, to survival, together with the acute distress that these patients cause their relatives and medical practitioners, is matched by their resourceful guile and cunning in sabotaging traditional medical and psychiatric measures. Their scheming to resist a 'cure' is equal to that of alcoholics.

Though 'behavioural' and 'conditioning' techniques are widely favoured because, ostensibly, they produce a considerable percentage of 'successful cures', I am inclined to suspend judgement on their long-term efficacy and retain the view that it may be futile to aim only at a cure of the physical condition, which masks a fragmented, stunted personality. As Jung and others have shown us, a heart ailment, for instance, need not arise from the heart only; it can also arise from the psyche of the sufferer, and then its resolution may evolve from symbolic growth, that is, a gradual *inner* transformation. Meier concludes that healing can take place only through the constellation of a symbol, or the archetype of totality (Meier, 1963).

My own interest in eating disorders was triggered off when I found myself working simultaneously with four patients whose ostensible central preoccupation was with food. Their lives were taken over by incessant compulsive eating rituals of alternate starving and gorging, often followed by vomiting. They went through either acute phases of elation, or feelings of guilt and worthlessness, and I need hardly add that all four were alarmingly underweight or overweight at times. I will now quote you a standard psychiatric textbook description of *anorexia nervosa.*

Anorexia nervosa occurs typically in girls in their later teens and in young unmarried women; it is doubtful if the same syndrome is found in men. A typical triad of symptoms is *anorexia, amenorrhea* and loss of weight. Vomiting is common, representing repressed disgust; it is rapid and easy, occurring without nausea. The illness has an emotional basis.

These girls tend to come from families with a history of nutritional disturbances, obesity and *anorexia*. There is a refusal to take an adequate diet, or phases of compulsive overeating countered by vomiting and excessive purgation. A remarkable feature is tireless activity in spite of emaciation.

The patient may declare that she is perfectly all right. She may exhibit the *belle indifference* of the hysteric. Depression may be prominent, with feelings of guilt and isolation and suicidal thoughts. Obsessional, anxious and hypochondriacal traits are encountered. There are food fads and alimentary preoccupations. There may be a severely disturbed mother/ daughter relationship, the patient being at one and the same time unduly dependent and rebelling against maternal domination. The prognosis is poor; only 10–20 percent recover. [Henderson & Gillespie, 1969]

What heightened my interest was the fact that only one of my four patients appeared to fit the above description closely, though even here not only the mother but the father too entered significantly into the constellation of her illness. This, my first case, concerns Alice, a young unmarried woman in her early twenties. I had known her parents on and off for approximately five years in connection with marital problems.

The mother was as thin as a beanstalk, had many physical illnesses, and was remote and detached. She gave the impression that she felt in some strange way triumphant about her husband's marital and sexual deviations. On the other hand, she had an unusually close relationship with Alice. For instance, they used to bathe together and to scrub each other's backs. The intimate marriage seemed to be between mother and daughter and not between the parents. Not surprisingly, it was Alice's father who contacted me on this occasion, whereas before he had come only reluctantly and under duress from his wife. He told me that Alice had recently returned from her first stay away from home, depressed, ill and with severe eating difficulties; she had lost four stone in weight and her periods had stopped.

Hilde Bruch, in her book *Eating Disorders and the Person Within,* stresses the importance of involving the family in the treatment process (1974). She further points out that whatever the *anorexia* patient does is not for herself but for her parents' sake, though it can never be sufficient to please them. It frequently happens that the patient's mother is dissatisfied with her marriage and endows the child with the task of compensating for her own disappointment. Thus she suffocates her daughter's pull towards independence. Both parents conceal their deep disillusionment with each other. Secretly, they carry on a sacrificial competition. Each desires the sympathy and support of the child, whose energies go towards satisfying the competitive claims of the parents so that too little is left over for investment in her own development. A quote from a recent article emphasizes these points:

> It appears that ultimate progress for the patient is importantly related to the initial levels of psychoneurotic status of the parents. The overall findings in the study support the view that *anorexia nervosa* is often importantly and dynamically related to parental and family psychoneurotic morbidity and stress the importance of investigating the illness in terms of the family pathology and the probable related importance of involving parents in the treatment programme. [Crisp, Harding & McGuinness, 1974]

To return to Alice: when her father suggested that he and his wife should come and discuss their daughter's illness with me, I thought this device of excluding Alice might prejudice any prospect of my working with her and her parents in the future, and so I proposed that all three come together. From previous contact with them, I had a hunch that a conjoint technique might be the most appropriate. I knew this approach had been used successfully by many other therapists in the past, as this abstract suggests:

> The marital relationship was inadequate, allowing J. to be inappropriately involved in the parents' affairs. The family's pattern of functioning was characterized by over-protectiveness, lack of privacy for individual members, denial of the existence of any problems other than J.'s illness, and a failure to resolve marital conflicts which remained concealed by the parents' preoccupation with J. Her symptoms were therefore reinforced within the family circle. [Liebman, Minuchin & Baker, 1974]

Alice looked like a Giacometti sculpture: emaciated, withdrawn and distraught. Her father was noticeably depressed and agitated, as if in some way he felt to blame and implicated. Her mother once again seemed least affected, almost as if exulting in the catastrophic manner in which Alice had returned to the fold. Most of the talking was done haltingly by Alice and her father. The dominant theme was Alice's acute guilt and agitation about having left her mother in pursuit of a life of her own. Father seemed only too well aware of his neglect of his wife, and how he had handed over responsibility for her to Alice.

I explained that guilt tends to produce illness with the unconscious purpose of restoring the *status quo*. In the process, inevitably someone is made to suffer. I pointed out to them how the family problems were being passed around between them like a parcel. As usual, the weakest link in the chain, Alice, had become lumbered with the parcel, not daring to unwrap it or to pass it on. She had become the casualty, while her father, in spite of his depression and feelings of blame, was still able to keep up appearances and to function in the world.

Towards the end of the interview the mother mentioned casually that, at their request, their family doctor had referred Alice to a Psychiatric Outpatients' Department. Why, then, I asked myself, had they come to see me at all? In retrospect, I think it was to find absolution, and not a resolution. I could not, because of the arrangements they had committed themselves to, continue with them, and this I told them. The unconscious conspiracy to treat the symptom and to neglect the person within had won the day and sabotaged a potentially favourable prognosis engendered by this first family session.

Within a week, and before she had been seen at the Outpatients' Department, Alice's mother sent me a letter from which I quote: 'Alice is looking better; some of the strain is leaving her face and she is eating more normally. Her weight is increasing. I feel she is being repaired.' Some nine months later, however, I heard from mother again. Alice had had a course of electro-convulsion therapy and was on anti-depressants and tranquillizers. Mother and father were also being treated with drugs. Alice had regained some weight but was still depressed and not menstruating, nor able to function in any facet of her life. She was continually asking, 'When will I be allowed to talk to someone?'

This brief and frustrating encounter with Alice has had a happier sequence; she recently telephoned me out of her own motivation, asking for therapy. Just two years after our first meeting I have seen her once and plan to take her on regularly.

I was struck by her frail beauty. She looked like a fairy-tale princess, waiting for her prince to awaken her, and as if made of fragile precious china.

Alice told me that she had become dissatisfied with her treatment, was still on drugs and receiving five minutes' follow-up therapy fortnightly at the Outpatient Department. She felt annoyed when told that her parents were narrow-minded Christians, and that she should take herself off and have sex. Her weight, however, has stabilized at 114 lbs under the threat of hospitalization if it falls below 112 lbs.

Her parents have meanwhile moved to another city and have set her up in an apartment in the house of an elderly couple who stand in for them. Alice is lonely, having no friends of her own age, is doing a rather low-grade job well below her capacity, and is still depressed and feels too fat.

I should here like to quote an abstract from another article on this topic, entitled 'Mind over matter':

> The more accessible material suggested that all dimensions of psychic life were experienced in terms of the quantity of their flesh and the oral activities directly related thereto. All described a deliberate decision not to eat based on the dual concept that they were too fat and that eating was bad. Their

attitude towards feeding others was much more accepting. ...
The patients were encouraged to lose the fear of pleasure from
which many of them clearly suffered. [Galdston, 1974]

Alice has bouts of stealing food from the couple that she lives
with, and has carbohydrate binges, stuffing herself with 'forbidden' food. On the other hand she has difficulties about eating in
company, is afraid she may be pressed to eat starch—yet steals it!
She is also afraid of being cheated of her due, of being denied that
to which she feels entitled, and is touchy about being offered a
smaller helping or else forgotten altogether. These contradictions
pinpoint my view that food is a stand-in for love and caring. Alice
also finds herself acutely critical of what other people eat, a
manifestation of her resentment of her parents.

She feels 'unattractive and babyish', obsessed with and
anxious about feeling left out and of not being given enough. Her
mother, who is a poor housekeeper and cook, encourages Alice to
spend her weekends with her parents, preparing their meals for
them. Yet Alice feels her parents are 'not really there' and, most
of all, not there for *her,* being still very entangled with her
mother, whom she sees as lonely and not appreciated, although
father has told her 'mother is stronger than you think'. In spite of
struggling to distance herself from her parents, their mutual
entanglement is still very strong; Alice sees herself as the only
one who really understands how her mother feels.

Alice avoids involvement with other people, ostensibly because
she would then have to eat with them. If, nevertheless, she
becomes attracted to a man or makes 'a conquest', she persuades
herself that she has become 'bored' with him. Her acquaintances
are married couples, and she befriends the husband on an
intellectual level which she feels 'safe'. At 25, she continues to
feel that no one takes her seriously, or cares enough to show true
concern either for herself or for her mother. Whenever she allows
herself to think about all of this, she gets profoundly upset on
behalf of the mother in her, and of her baby self.

I recently came across an article in the *American Journal of
Psychiatry* on the effectiveness of 'Family therapy in the
treatment of *anorexia nervosa*' (Barcal, 1971). The author's
experiences accentuate my own. Thus, he describes how the
anorexia families he has worked with manifest concern and
interest for one another while denying personal wishes and

interests. Family members had to guess in order to determine the other's wishes; a direct expression of need was taboo, thus creating flux states of involvement together with abandonment. Their bodies were strange and alien to them. He further stresses that the families were living under an umbrella of falsehood; a person who is unable to differentiate between hunger and other needs becomes anorexic as a perverse way of solving conflicts. He points out the necessity for 'peace at all costs', engendering guilt and an abdication of responsibility, isolation and a power struggle for control. The aim of his therapy was to enable the patient to take over the responsibility for herself, and to neutralize the eating symptoms. If successful, an inadvertent and alarming reaction tended to occur in the other family members, as was the case with Alice, whose parents were not only an important component of her illness, but subsequently became so disturbed that they too received drug therapy at the Psychiatric Outpatient Department where Alice was being treated.

In a paper entitled 'Hungry patients: reflections on ego structure' (Plaut, 1959), the author outlines the basic problems of patients who were predominantly occupied with food and eating, and I will summarize the gist of his article as follows: somatic symptoms have a psychic basis. Hungry patients have not yet acquired the capacity to relate to whole persons or images, but only to parts. There is an absence of ego boundaries, i.e. a stage of magical identity in which there is no distinction between I and you. The aim is to unify the ego sufficiently to distinguish between itself and the other, between an inner and an outer world. Experiences of wholeness remain exclusively linked with the object which stands proxy for the patient's own ego. Bodily experiences in infancy have not been satisfying.

Personally I should go even further, and describe my own patients as more than hungry; they are *craving* not for food but for love. The state of magical identity referred to above appears to have become one of the primary identity, i.e. *anorexia* patients try to achieve an imaginary state of bliss and contentment associated with the original fusion between subject and object, between baby and mother. This illusory primary object is the ever-nourishing breast—they are obsessed with it. The exclusive, inexhaustible supplier of nourishment comes closest to how they would like to perceive themselves. This identification temporarily enhances their tenuous self-esteem and promises the approval of others. It gives them a sense of power and achievement. To maintain it, however, they must ensure that they are in absolute control as the sole manipulator of all nourishment dispensed, withheld or rejected. Thereby their mother is divested of her positive, feeding, loving qualities; she is, as it were, dethroned, if not mutilated. This engenders acute guilt in the patients, and fears of mother's hatred and revenge. Thus the idealized breast has been transformed into the terrible one, and the powerful, manipulating patient sees herself as the perpetrator of the deed. This complex cycle leads to an intolerable psychological trap in which the patient revolves from a temporary state of bliss and effectiveness to becoming a depleted and greedy monster. In fact, both the subject and the object have turned into monstrous breast-witches, and the identification is so complete that it cannot be disentangled.

At this point, we have moved closer to some understanding of why these particular patients appear to become fixated at the primary oral level rather than develop other forms of neuroses. In all my four *anorexia* cases, the patient's *actual* mother is seen as precisely fitting the fantasy monster/breast just described. There is an uncanny correspondence between the internal fantasy and the external reality, the one reinforcing the other. Their mutual stranglehold takes on archetypal proportions, not mediated by redeeming personal experiences.

One way out for patients in these situations is to retreat into a state resembling an intra-uterine, conflict-free shelter, a depressed withdrawal. There are two alternatives—to starve until they almost disappear, or to seek relief in an eating binge in which they once again get on to the bandwagon, creating for themselves an illusory ever-full breast. But then their excessive greed evokes revulsion, anxiety and shame, and the vomiting mechanism usually becomes active at this point. The whole syndrome is cyclical and repeated endlessly. Indeed, I have observed that those of my anorexic patients who have children of their own perpetuate this pattern in the next generation, both over-indulging and excessively controlling them, while plagued by fantasies of ridding themselves of them for good and all.

I am quite convinced that inadequate and unsympathetic mothering experiences set the stage for the subsequent pathology of *anorexia*. Wilke (1971) also stresses the predominance of the mother-complex and any immaturity of personality in heart neurotics. In the same way *anorexia* patients have never been able really to depend on anyone, and even in infancy lacked the experience of a need being adequately met. Thus they fail to differentiate other signals of discomfort from pangs of hunger, and food provides a temporary relief, whatever the source of deprivation or anxiety. Severe love bereavement leads to mistrust of the legitimacy of all other feelings and ultimately has an annihilating effect. There is therefore a desire to become larger and larger, or else to disappear and, perhaps, to have a new beginning, a rebirth.

Other psychosomatic disorders and psychosexual problems frequently accompany *anorexia*. In any encounter with the opposite sex, for instance, an overpowering craving for affection clashes with fear and revulsion. During an erotic act, their fragile sense of personal ego consciousness disappears, sweeping with it the last vestige of an identity of their own. The encroachment of the partner's ego is intolerable, yet longed for.

Two of my four patients suffered from migraine and attacks of dizziness, which I understood as a shrinking from a longed-for, yet feared, sensation of autonomy. The connection between asthma and migraine makes good sense in this context. These symptoms exemplify opposites—the fear of the suffocating mother and the complementary dread of separateness from her. One of my migraine patients has an asthmatic child. Kierkegaard's words spring to mind: 'Freedom looks down into its own possibilities, and then grasps desperately for limitations in an attempt to survive.'

The basic task for the analyst with *anorexia* patients, as I see it, is to focus on their *real* needs, and not to focus on the illness. Any attempt to persuade the patient to eat or not to eat should be avoided; the underlying disturbances, however, have to be brought into the open whenever possible. Any dwelling on vomiting or other somatic symptoms only leads to a neglect of vital but hidden aspects. As suggested earlier, the analyst will try to find a way to stand proxy for the missing ego in lieu of the person with whom the patient is identified. As the ego boundaries grow stronger and more flexible, interpretations become increasingly possible and certainly necessary. The emphasis needs to be on the implicit regression to earlier levels and on a reconstruction of them. In the main, however, therapy with these patients consists in listening to them, an experience they have missed out on. The therapist who presumes to know the answer plays into his patient's belief that somebody else has the magical solution, in the same way that mother purported to have.

My next case is an example of the atypical within the familiar. Barbara displayed the usual somatic manifestation of *anorexia*; in fact, after two previous analyses she had become, and was determined to remain, a chronic case. She was already in her fifties but looked even older and haggard; she was married and had had children. In addition to her eating problems, she demonstrated another characteristic feature of *anorexia,* namely the pathological envy of whoever is perceived as the best-loved within the family setting—most often it is the sibling of the other sex. In her case, these acute feelings of envy culminated in murderous attacks on the one she perceived as her parents' favourite son, or else in futile attempts to become like him, and even to surpass him.

A negative prognosis was determined from the start, when she insisted she could only come once a week. It was clear to both of us that her resistance to change was paramount; all my interpretations on this point were stonewalled by her. Nevertheless, because of the empathy between us I became a perfect foil for her *anorexia nervosa* mechanisms. Whenever something incisive had taken place in a session, she vomited it out in the form of a meaningful but almost illegible scrawl which she posted to me, telling me in substance that she had been fed too much, so that it had turned bad inside her, and she would starve herself by not coming next time. In this self-defeating manner she wasted my time and her money, while remaining craving and desperate. The only time that she felt any good was when she could produce a dream; however innocuous the dream might be, it provided her with a sliver of confirmation that she possessed some inner life that was her own.

In an early session she drew my attention to an arrangement of wild flowers in my room. She disapproved of my liking for 'rubbish', as she called it. She also seemingly disapproved of my liking of her. The next day she wrote as follows: 'I was offended when you told me in connection with these weeds that everything, however apparently valueless, can be accepted and treated as something that has meaning. I want so much from you, yet I get nothing. Good things in excess turn bad.' Not surprisingly, she was a compulsive, self-induced vomiter.

A few sessions later she wrote: 'Loving feelings are dangerous and obliterate boundaries. They make one take other people inside one's self and get mixed up with them, and one has to get rid of them, suddenly, violently. I have to spoil things to protect them from the murderous feelings inside me. Then I become an empty shell without life. I don't know where I begin and end. I am drained and impaired.' Her one relief was strenuous and endless wailing to the point of exhaustion.

Her mother was seen by her as dominant and insecure, narcissistic, a 'Virgin Queen', and childish. Mother had food fads and starved herself on a nature cure diet. Father was seen as only interested in mother, and never stood up for Barbara. Mother constantly criticized Barbara, calling her greedy, fat, ugly, awkward, stupid, and frequently pointed out to her that her mouth was permanently open, and that she was ashamed of her. Barbara had had thirteen governesses in twelve years! She further described her mother as a 'jealous prima-donna' who never accepted any 'nice' feelings from her. She remembered an occasion when she borrowed her mother's bicycle without permission and slightly damaged it. Her mother rejected her plea to be allowed to repair it, and instead pulled Barbara all the way home by her hair.

Barbara's eating habits followed the characteristic pattern: she ate too much of the 'good' things and vomited, or she starved herself, or she ate the 'wrong' food. 'Greed takes over', she said, 'and I feel ugly.' She also had the typical distorted body image which I hope shows in the little primitive self-portrait she drew (Figure 2). It shows a scarecrow-like person with a tiny pinched-in waist, two minute appendages instead of legs, no hands, but greatly magnified buttocks. Behind this figure it is just possible to detect another, a portrait outline of a timid-looking young girl. I felt this depicted her undeveloped young self.

Barbara did not know how to use her hands, and was prone to say that it was as if she had none. She explained 'words are better'; she read greedily but could never retain any of it. When I

FIGURE 2

interpreted to her that she dared not use her hands because of her murderous impulses engendered by her envy, she remembered confirmatory data. She had tried her utmost to be a tomboy—a tougher and better boy than her brother. On one occasion in her teens when her brother taunted her with being 'jelly-muscled', she throttled him until he was blue in the face, and then bashed him so hard that she broke his nose.

Barbara left me abruptly when a distressing event occurred in her life, and when she could have done with maximal support. She bequeathed an unpaid bill as the surviving bond between us.

Munch's 'The Scream' haunted me while I was gestating this paper. I feel it projects cogently the agony of the *anorexia nervosa* patient confronted by the monster within and without, and catches the expression I have often seen in the faces of these patients.

Both Eileen and Douglas, my third and fourth cases, have now moved in the direction of integration. They have had long analyses with frequent sessions, though interestingly their *anorexia* symptomatology only became prominent in certain phases of their therapy. Eileen, like Barbara, was atypical in that she was married with children, and she was menstruating regularly, though with much accompanying disturbance. Her relentless pursuit of thinness is a recent development, and follows many years of frequent and acute attacks of migraine, severe phobic states and hypochondriacal preoccupations, as well as compulsive over-eating with obesity and numerous psychosexual difficulties. She was obese when she first came to see me, and subsequently did a complete turn-about. I shall be confining my comments to her starvation phase from which she is in the process of emerging.

She was the daughter of a suffering mother who was said to have conceived Eileen in her sleep, and who sobbed her heart out when she gave birth to a girl; to be female was a catastrophe! It meant a life of misery. Eileen had to be her mother's perpetual 'sunshine', so had never really been a child; she never played, was always called 'sunshine', and never heard her own name. If she *was* like a small child, mother would become ill and suffer. She was smothered by her mother. Everything that happened was said to be Eileen's fault. She felt compelled to be what her mother needed of her and felt incessantly watched, assessed and judged. To be unhappy would have implied an insult to her mother's supposed superiority. Thus Eileen acquired the façade of adequate functioning and learned to mistrust the legitimacy of all her own feelings, suffering severe love deprivation, for which she attempted to compensate by a promiscuous phase in adolescence which revolted her and made her ashamed. Unable to live a life of her own, she lived by proxy through other people.

I quote a relevant extract from a recent publication:

> From the psychodynamic point of view, the reduction in food consumption is an expression of an unconscious revolt of the anorexic patient against her own body. The condition is associated with an abnormal affective relation between mother and daughter; the former is excessively anxious and concerned about the well-being of the latter, who feels that her growing body frustrates her unconscious desire to remain a child [Rolandi, Azzolini & Barabino, 1973]

As already described, a sense of hollowness within can be temporarily ameliorated by filling up with food; the eating stands in for satisfaction of needs in other areas, and provides a momentary sense of spurious power. With Eileen, elation, however, did not last, and she would soon say that she wanted to disappear, or at least to have a boy's figure like her brother so as to be admired. She would then make herself vomit by putting her finger down her throat. Her eating habits became so highly ritualized and followed such a precise sequence that they acted as an anaesthetic. She was weighing herself several times a day, and each fresh loss of weight gave her a sense of triumph; it was a 'bonus' which made her feel superior because it proved her powers of self-control, but it was never good enough, and she set herself a yet lower target than before.

Her distorted body image which, like Barbara's, was of bizarre proportions was, however, gradually becoming more realistic, and her anorexic symptoms were beginning to phase themselves out. To achieve this she had to go back and begin again as a baby with a different mother figure—that is, myself.

> The aim of the first phase of therapy is to continue the role of the mother with the exclusion of the negative aspects. A 'transference' can be achieved only by attempts to break through the voluntary self-isolation of the patient. [Schenk & Deegener, 1974]

In fact, when Eileen made insistent demands on me to be treated as a baby, I felt the vital turning point towards health had begun. Even so she still felt too large, all bulk without appeal, useless, with ugly hands, neither in nor out of the womb. 'I am a stone walking about, a stone feels nothing.' She would avert her eyes, looking without seeing, and imagining like a baby playing hide and seek that *she* would not be seen either.

Nevertheless, her face that she has hated has become less fixed and staring, her mouth less pouting and sulking, and she has learned to smile as well as to become very sad, because she has relinquished her exclusive living through others. She has become alive and rebellious:

> Why should I do what is expected? As long as I have a beginning I can persevere. It's my turn now; it has never been my turn. I have been crippled, and feel the pain of a crippled child. When I am I, you can be you! I am detaching myself *inside* myself. I want my own face which I don't know yet. I am

growing up, and am experiencing and beginning to like my body. I want to be *me* now.

Gradually, she started crying from her guts; for years she had shed invisible tears. She explained: 'When I howl there is so much inside me. I feel myself getting smaller and smaller, three years old, and then only four weeks old, and then I begin to exist as me.' She often now eats normally, no longer having to starve or to gorge herself constantly, and to make herself sick, and no longer feels constantly watched, assessed and judged. She is finding herself and how to be alone without a sense of intolerable rejection.

Douglas, my last case, is also atypical in being a man, and in his sixties. He has come perilously close to death on several occasions—accidents in which he seems to have had to test out his own resources for survival to the ultimate point. He is still alarmingly emaciated, and he used to sprawl on the chair as if he had no body structure at all. He had been totally controlled by his mother, the more so after his father had died when Douglas was only three. Recently it has become noticeable that Douglas sits up tall and becomes more of a person when an interpretation goes home and reaches his core. Latterly he has had two crucial dreams. In one he shouted, 'I have had enough of interfering women!' He then 'forgot' to come for his subsequent session, in spite of his over-meticulous time-keeping; his dependence/ rebellion conflict in relation to me as his mother had become too much for him. Shortly afterwards he had a dream in which his mother's hands were round his neck, and she had a stranglehold on him from behind. He bit her and shouted, 'Let go of me!'

Attacks of uncontrollable vomiting have recently only occurred when he goes out for a meal and eats in public; then he again feels dependent and controlled, or guilty and anxious because of his greed and extravagance, or else overcome by his frustration and rage because the food or the service have not come up to scratch. Attacks of migraine and dizziness, frequent at one time, have become spasmodic. They have always been linked with his having it too good, some achievement or success for himself which was not of immediate benefit to his current mother figure, or with an increasing sense of new-won freedom which frightened him. He is now almost ready to terminate his analysis but scared to death of an ending which, in his case, actually coincides with the afternoon of his life.

I will now summarize my main points. I had originally called my paper 'Metamorphosis in reverse', because the transition which will hopefully take place is not from the simple to the complex, as in nature, but from the multi-faceted ostensibly somatic syndrome to its basic, primary emotional constituents in infancy.

With anorexic patients a distorted attitude towards, and an abnormal preoccupation with, food is central to their lives and constitutes a regression and fixation to an early oral level of development. The nutritional function is used in an attempt to solve or camouflage complex emotional and interpersonal problems.

The triggering-off point for the subsequent syndrome appears to be the mother's inappropriate response to her infant's needs from birth into adulthood, and one must hypothesize that unsatisfying feeding experiences occur together with continuing distortions of communications on other levels. These factors lead to a stunting or deformation of the ego structure, a distorted body concept and arrested psychological growth. Because of these defects, the patient's eating disorder constitutes a futile attempt to be in control of his own life. The symptoms constitute a pathological attempt at acquiring some identity and trying to fulfil the insatiable craving for seemingly unobtainable love.

I have drawn attention to the uncanny degree of correspondence between the subject and the object, i.e. between the patient's fantasy image of herself as a powerful menacing breast/monster and her experience and perception of her actual mother. A mutual stranglehold situation results in which both the child and the mother reject each other, while being indispensable to one another, thus engendering murderous feelings in both. The fathers in all my cases did not intervene or rescue the child. Sibling rivalry is more than usually acute, the sibling of the opposite sex always being perceived as the favourite child, and the patient unsuccessfully endeavouring to demolish the rival, to surpass him, or to turn into him by changing shape.

Psychosexual disturbances, other psychosomatic symptoms and a preoccupation with death as well as the longing for a new start are encountered. The anorexia patient attempts to become omnipotent and indestructible by over-eating, or else tries to do away with herself by starvation and shrinkage, in the hope of resurrection as the best loved. If therapy fails, she will eventually die, but hopefully she will survive and evolve towards experiencing herself as a person to be cherished.

REFERENCES

Barcal, A. (1971). Family therapy in the treatment of anorexia nervosa. *American Journal of Psychiatry* 128:3.

Bruch, H. (1974). *Eating Disorders and the Person Within*. London: Routledge & Kegan Paul.

Crisp, A. H., Harding, B., & McGuiness, B. (1974). Anorexia nervosa—psychoneurotic characteristics of parents: relationship to prognosis. A quantitative study. *Journal of Psychosomatic Research* 18:3.

Galdston, R. (1974). Mind over matter: observations on 50 patients hospitalised with anorexia nervosa. *Journal of the American Academy of Child Psychiatry* 13:2.

Henderson, D. K., & Gillespie, R. D. (1969). *Textbook of Psychiatry* (10th rev. ed.). Oxford: Oxford University Press.

Liebman, R., Minuchin, S., & Baker, L. (1974). The role of the family in the treatment of anorexia nervosa. *Journal of the American Academy of Child Psychiatry* 13:2.

Meier, C. A. (1963). Psycho-somatic medicine from the Jungian point of view. *Journal of Analytical Psychology* 8:2.

Plaut, A. (1959). Hungry patients. *Journal of Analytical Psychology* 4:2.

Rolandi, E., Azzolini, A., & Barabino, A. (1973). Present possibilities of neuroendocrinal study in anorexia nervosa. Report of a clinical case. *Archives E. Maragliano, Pat. Clin.* 29:1.

Schenck, K., & Deegener, G. (1974). Therapy of anorexia nervosa. *Medizinische Welt*, 25:24.

Wilke, H-J. (1971). Problems in heart neurosis. *Journal of Analytical Psychology* 16:2.

CHAPTER FOUR

Object constancy or constant object?

Fred Plaut

In this iconoclastic chapter, Plaut challenges the mental health values of both psychoanalysis and analytical psychology—object constancy and individuation, respectively. He feels that there has been an idealization of both of these concepts which excludes other paths to psychological fulfilment, less sanctioned by psychotherapeutic criteria.

Actually, Plaut points out, in analytical psychology a place has been made for a valuing of the less than whole, less than perfect, less than fully object-relating. Provided there is a cultural context (often of a religious nature), then the shared dimension brings in a qualitative change so that graffiti-like imagery has to be understood as having an unconsciously sacral intent.

Plaut challenges the illusion that we ever 'master' our objects. To some extent, then, he disputes the very idea of psychopathol-

---

First published in *The Journal of Analytical Psychology* 20:2, in 1975. Published here by kind permission of the author and the Society of Analytical Psychology.

*ogy. On the other hand, I do not think he wishes to be heard as
arguing for the mental health value of* all *schizoid phenomena.*

A.S.

Psychoanalytic theories of child development employ the
useful concept of object constancy, which forms a milestone
in the relations between the developing ego and its images,
technically referred to as objects. When for one reason or another
this milestone, which is also a formidable hurdle, has not been
passed, the crucial question arises whether the person can
nevertheless make progress towards a viable mode of living,
including stable relations with others. Some of the differences
between psychoanalytic theory and analytical psychology may be
semantic rather than fundamental: when it comes to the
application and aims of therapy, the similarities may well
outweigh the differences and incompatibilities of theory. Therefore a mutually acceptable model of child development may well
emerge.

There is however one aspect in which analytical psychology
may claim a uniquely different orientation and point to an
alternative mode of development. I shall refer to this as the
constant object, in contrast to object constancy.

For the newly-born a need-satisfying union is established
between mouth and nipple (or teat of feeding bottle). To this must
be added a number of other sensory modalities, such as warmth,
skin contact, smell, surrounding arms and gazing eyes, all of
which create a secure situation required for satisfactory nourishment and growth. An object-less phase of fusion has been
postulated to begin with, but some measure of differentiation
soon occurs. For example, the infant will notice that not every
feed and contact is equally satisfying, and he begins to
distinguish between good and bad experiences, which become
internalized (introjected) and charged with corresponding affect.

It is assumed that in the earliest stages the emerging ego is
unable to link good and bad experiences, to maintain a continuity
between opposite affects and also to associate these with one and
the same organ, the nipple, which is his first part object. Later on,

when the manifold sensory impressions have coalesced, it is possible for the infant not only to focus on the nipple but to become aware of its connection with a whole body, a person and a specific person: his mother. But, for the time being, good and bad are experienced as totally disparate qualities without continuity, functioning on an all-or-nothing principle, even if the oscillations from one extreme to the other can occur quite rapidly. It is not difficult to understand that such a division into opposite qualities and affects comes naturally to an immature ego and that it requires effort and pain to link the two. When for some reason the growing infant or child cannot make this connection, we say that an ego defence, splitting, has been called into operation. It looks then—and this can happen right throughout life—as if opposite experiences could not possibly stem from the same source. If the source is thus perceived as divided, the 'I' which responds affectively is divided too. No division of objects, without division of ego. Or, as Hartmann wrote, 'Satisfactory object relations can only be assessed if we also consider what it means in terms of ego development (1964, p. 163).

The next developmental step comes about with the help of our increasing capacity—given favourable environmental conditions—to create continuity out of memories, which leads to a dawning awareness of the inseparability (and relative unpredictability) of good and bad feelings within ourselves and in relation to objects. Thus a precariously balanced state of *constancy* is established in the relation between ourselves and our objects. The acceptance of this state of affairs presents a harsh reality because it requires the surrender of a comforting illusion whereby every experience could be made into a good one and all pain and frustration counteracted and avoided by means of splitting. The time of the first giving up of this illusion in return for object constancy coincides with the Kleinian 'depressive position', during which ambivalence and despair change into the ability to feel sad. The reward, if one may so call it, for the sacrificed illusion of an only good (idealized) object is a reduction of anxiety. For while the bad object was repressed it also became persecutory in the unconscious, and, conversely, the ego retaliated with punishing sadistic fantasies and subsequently expected similar treatment from the split-off, bad object. Once object constancy has been achieved, the good and bad aspects of one and the same object are no longer denied. A degree of fusion of characteristics has come about and with it 'object constancy'.

It cannot be over-emphasized that this developmental attainment is slow and remains permanently threatened by the impact of extremely good or bad experiences at any age: regression to splitting remains a lasting human propensity both in individuals and in human groups. Jung recognized this when writing about the dissociability of the psyche (*CW* 8, paras. 365–366) and the child's struggle for an ego (*CW* 8, paras. 771–773). Within the present frame of reference object constancy is seen as the prerequisite of all human relations which are based on 'reality' rather than on idealizations and projections. It results from the ability to reconcile opposite qualities both within ourselves and in others.

The burden of this constant struggle is rewarded when the outcome is 'the establishment of lasting emotional relationships' (Jacobson, 1965, p. 63). But there exists an additional aid in the form of an intermediate area in which the boundaries may be blurred and where play, experiments and illusions have their rightful place; it is the area which Winnicott referred to as transitional-phenomena and -objects to which we have recourse throughout life (1958, pp. 224–242). Art and religion are, from the psychological point of view, the grown-up counterpart of the child at play, a situation in which he is partly inside and partly outside himself. (Here one may see an obvious parallel with Jung's technique of active imagination.)

Let us suppose that despite varying terminologies and vested interests in theories, the above represents a widely acceptable although incomplete outline of intra-psychic development leading to desirable and satisfying relationships. The question remains whether object constancy could also be attained in a different way, and could indeed have a different meaning. Could a part object, in the absence of a steady enough environment but given suitable cultural conditions, find symbolical expression and thus act as a focal point of reference and meeting place for people of a similar cast of mind? And, if so, could this part-object-become-cult-object lead to lasting relations between people, not primarily because of the balance of good and bad feelings established in the course of each individual's development, nor because of a stabilizing social structure, like the family, but because of shared celebrations of a cult based, for example, on the mythical elaboration of phenomena in nature or events in history?

The answer to such questions could have far-reaching consequences on psychotherapy, but it cannot be given in a sweeping way. In order to reach a point of view, let us consider some illustrations of part objects in Jung's work. Differently put, the question is whether the development of object constancy is the only valid stepping-stone to personal relations and individual development or whether there are indications that alternatives have existed in other cultures which are (under various guises) still with us today.

Among the illustrations in Jung's *Symbole der Wandlung,* 4th and final edition (1950), which have been omitted from its English translation as *Symbols of Transformation* (*CW* 5), there are two in particular which I reproduce here as being relevant to my theme.

Figure 3 appears in the text of the general chapter heading, 'The hymn of creation'. Jung's footnote, which gives a reference to the phallus worship here depicted, is affixed to a sentence in which he states that religious experience in antiquity was frequently conceived as a bodily union with the deity (1950, p. 113).

Figure 4 appears in the introduction to the second part of the volume. Here Jung speaks of the creative deity and refers the reader back to figure 4. (As both pictures have been omitted from *CW*, the cross-reference cannot, of course, appear either.) He adds that the phallus was thought of as independent, 'an idea that is found not only in antiquity, but in the drawings of children and artists of our own day'. This independence with which we are sufficiently familiar through *graffiti* could simply be regarded as

FIGURE 3

FIGURE 4

expressions of infantile sexuality, were it not for the wings, which are a striking feature of both illustrations.

Just as light is a standard symbolic device for depicting awareness, so wings, when attached to a human or animal shape (other than birds), are widely used to indicate the divine or daemonic nature of a creature (Interestingly enough, our first illustration is meant to convey worship, while the second is an amulet or charm worn to avert evil.) Of course, light, especially in the form of a shaft of light, lightning or a halo *and* wings, often appears in combination, as we know from numerous mythological or religious paintings that symbolize impregnation by a divinity.

The difference is that the wings in our illustrations are attached not to a whole human figure, but to a part. Nevertheless the reader familiar with Jung's interest in transformation of the libido from lower instinctual to higher spiritual levels will also remember the picture series that Jung used to illustrate his *Psychology of the Transference* (CW 16). Figure 5 of that series shows the king and queen having intercourse beneath the water. In figure 5a entitled 'Fermentatio', the alchemical analogy of a psychological process, the queen is preventing intercourse, and both she and the king are now bewinged, indicating that a 'higher' development is on its way. The series ends, as will be remembered, in the winged hermaphrodite, the new composite and complete being. (Cf. *CW* 5, plate 38a, for an illustration of a numinous but terrifying breast.)

I have previously drawn attention to the extraordinary intensity with which part objects are experienced, and therefore suggested that they are comparable to luminosities (Plaut, 1974). Although we know that their brilliance and fascinating quality stems from reflected light (projections which are re-introjected), the part object is nevertheless perfect to the beholder. Such perfection does not vary; it is constant for the devotee. It differs markedly from the completeness which, according to Jung, is an attribute of the self archetype imposing surrender of ego power and suffering. The encounter with the self therefore makes the same demands on the individual as the surrender of omnipotence when object constancy is realized. But whether he responds to the luminosity of an apparently perfect object or to the demand for tolerating the reality of complete rather than ideal relationships, the individual's ego has to find an appropriate attitude towards the 'master' whom he is going to serve. In either case he is forced to abandon the illusion of *mastery* over his objects.

In the paper referred to I pointed out that although the breast–penis is the first part object, if no object constancy (in the sense described above) develops, other objects may take the place of earlier ones. Thus the miser is more or less possessed by his money, the alcoholic by the bottle, the addict by the drug, the artist by the medium in which he works and the religionist by the deity he worships.

In the winged phallic images reproduced here we are, no doubt, dealing with idolatry. Omnipotence has been surrendered but is, in the form of endless creative power, attributed to the part object. This is magic and from the theological point of view heresy. But as psychologists we have to admit that in practice the boundary between it and superstition on the one hand and the worship of religious objects on the other is hard to define.

Wings and light are not the only symbolic devices by which the unvarying (constant) power for good inherent in an object can be portrayed. Several others spring to mind. Within the field of visual representation we find various other images of part objects but in abstract form, such as the Lingam and Yoni statues of India which are garlanded and worshipped. There is also the ritualization of sex in the stylized and elaborate forms and techniques of Tantra art. The power of the object is constant; sexual organs are in constant tumescence, god and goddess in constant copulation. The power is always for the good (but *not* good in the sense of pleasurable; see Kali as slayer of man), but for good in terms of renewal of the life cycle, an affirmative, creative power.

The idea that the sexual act as such can be sacral is by no means dead in our civilization, as the following quotation from an important writer, Heinrich Böll, a Catholic, shows:

> It is impossible for me to despise what is erroneously called physical love; it is the substance of a sacrament ... there is no such thing as purely physical or purely spiritual love, both contain an element of the other, even if only a small one. [Böll, 1962, p. 12, translated by the present author]

If for physical love we were to read union of sexual parts, regardless of the personalities involved, we could not avoid the comparison with a part object relationship. Such pre-object constancy (promiscuous) encounters which do not lead to the development of personal relationships are nevertheless credited by Böll with spiritual potentialities. Jung refers to the frank eroticism of the coitus pictures and almost apologizes to the reader, whom he reminds that the pictures were drawn for mediaeval eyes and that the analogy of this illustration is 'a little too obvious for our modern taste, so that it almost fails of its object' (*CW* 16, para. 460). Since he wrote these words nearly thirty years ago, pornography has spread, and 'modern taste' is used to even stronger meat. But one wonders whether the capacity for understanding sexual symbolism, without which, as Jung says, the sphere of the instinct becomes overloaded, has grown at all. (The omission of figures 3 and 4 from the *Collected Works* edition may indicate that the editors or publishers had little confidence in the readers' comprehension of symbolism.)

Be this as it may, the perfection with which part objects (incomplete by definition) can be endowed seems characteristic of specific life styles. Thus we find people who with single-mindedness devote their lives to a deity, a muse, or an ideology. We may therefore come to the conclusion that they have elected to serve a constantly good object. But the persons concerned may prefer to describe the situation as having resulted from a call, a vocation. At this juncture one could ask whether what I called the constant object is identical with the Kleinian 'good internal object' which 'forms the core of the ego and the infant's internal world' (see Segal, 1964, p. 57). This question cannot be answered by theorizing, but two practical points arise from the comparison: if the ego-core with its 'good internal object' were resilient enough, there would be no reason why object constancy with all its subsequent socializing benefits could not be attained. Secondly, because 'good' means a great deal better than 'perfect' or 'idealized', are we able to supply such goodness and bring about a fundamental change which did not happen at a critical phase of development, by means of analytical endeavours? The answer to such questions is of practical interest but must remain open. For while it is all too easy for us to attach pathological labels to people whose life is ruled by a constant object and who have not achieved object constancy, clinical observations make me wonder whether we do not idealize object constancy.

Whether we look at some individual's relations or the state of our civilization there must surely be some doubt as to our enduring capacity to combine 'good' and 'bad' feelings towards one and the same object. The suffering involved is so frequently expressed in disease and even violence that one may question whether 'good' relations and the stability of our family-based society can lay claim to being the standard model of mental health. So what is pathological?

Jung writes in 'The stages of life': 'The meaning and purpose of a problem seem to lie not in its solution but in our working at it incessantly' (CW 8, para. 771). What really matters is whether analysts can keep an open mind towards patients whose capacity to develop along the path of object constancy is severely limited. Given some talent such patients may have for expressing their devotion to a constantly good object, they may nevertheless lead satisfying lives. For them the alternative, which I called the constant object, may be therapeutic, as I outlined in my earlier paper under the subheading, 'Devotion versus addiction' (Plaut, 1974).

Does this mean that individuation is out for such persons? In order to arrive at an answer we have to consider briefly by what psychodynamic changes we move towards individuation. If the answer is that without object constancy there can be no ego constancy, and that without a sufficiently coherent ego the completeness required in personal relationships cannot come about, the conclusion is obviously negative. If, on the other hand, we hold that acts of devotion to an apparently perfect object—in whatever form it may appear—are in themselves arduous and demand the surrender of personal ambitions for the sake of a common or ultimate good, then even a divided (pre-constant) ego may be held together by an apparently perfect (albeit) part object. A life led under such auspices could potentially be rich and fulfilling.

It is likely that this alternative path of development where there is very little ego cohesion is charged with the dangers of inflation, paranoia and depression. Yet it is of practical importance to make allowance for this alternative path rather than to insist that without object constancy there can be no integration of the personality.

Analysts will probably agree that combinations, compromises and diurnal fluctuations between object constancy and constant objects are more commonly found in practice than the word 'or' in the title suggests. However, a theoretical standpoint is best stated in extremes. Clinical examples have been omitted here, and considerable detail would be required to give flesh and blood to the present outline. Words like 'perfection', 'completion' and 'wholeness' are large counters, and the small change of clinical examples is required to illustrate their meaning.

On the other hand the question which this paper poses constitutes only one aspect of the still more fundamental problem facing depth-psychology: to what extent and by what means can we supply or make substitution for what was lacking or went awry in the history of an individual's life? Being somewhat less tied to a psychogenetic theory of neuroses and personality disorders than psychoanalysis, analytical psychology is in a favourable position to show how the wider problem could be broken down into smaller, more answerable questions.

To sum up: Object constancy implies the ego's ability to combine opposite qualities and affects in one object. Conceptually this does not seem difficult. In practice, however, the demands thus made on the unfolding and even on the developed ego are so exacting that it is regarded as impossible to fulfil the desiderata of object constancy at all times and in all circumstances. Perhaps we should take our limitations more to heart, in Eliot's phrase: 'Human kind cannot stand very much reality.' Therefore, a relatively constant object, even if it is derived from, and bears the hall-marks of, a part- as well as cult-object, is a valuable and necessary standby. This can serve as a focal, concentrating point for a personality that would otherwise be in danger of disintegration. Provided only that the ego does not become totally absorbed by it, the constant object offers the person a viable alternative, a chance to integrate around an alternative core.

A third factor which is not an inherent aspect of personal and social relationships stands as a central point of reference outside it: the constant object cannot be classified as either 'good' or 'bad' in the Kleinian sense. It is fascinating and awe-inspiring—in short, numinous. As such, it may be identical with Jung's self. If so, my contribution does no more than highlight a specific way in which the psyche may find a viable alternative form of development which combines physical and spiritual qualities.

REFERENCES

Böll, H. (1962) *Brief an einen jungen Katholiken*. Köln, Berlin: Kiepenheur & Witsch.

Hartmann, H. (1964). *Essays in Ego Psychology*. London: Hogarth.

Jacobson, E. (1965). *The Self and the Object World*. London: Hogarth.

Jung, C. G. (1950). *Symbole der Wandlung*. Zürich: Rascher.

Plaut, A. (1974). 'Part-object relations and Jung's 'luminosities'. *Journal of Analytical Psychology* 19:2.

Segal, H. (1964). *Introduction to the Works of Melanie Klein*. London: Heinemann. [Reprinted 1988, London: Karnac Books.]

Winnicott, D. W. (1958). *Through Paediatrics to Psychoanalysis*. London: Tavistock.

CHAPTER FIVE

Narcissistic disorder and its treatment

Rushi Ledermann

This chapter is one of a series by Ledermann on the aetiology, phenomenology and treatment of pathological narcissism. It exemplifies the way in which sensitive application of psycho-pathological understanding serves, rather than injures, an approach to the patient as an individual. For, as Ledermann points out, the manifestation of apparent ego strength could easily convince the clinician that she or he was confronted with neurosis rather than with a serious personality disorder. If that were to happen, then the well-thought-out understanding of the analytic needs of such patients, as described by Ledermann, would not take place.

Ledermann combines insights from psychoanalysis with the developmental theories of Michael Fordham. From Jung, she takes the notion of the inevitable presence in the unconscious of

First published in *The Journal of Analytical Psychology* 27:4 in 1982. Published here (with revisions) by kind permission of the author and the Society of Analytical Psychology.

something opposite to what is presented on the surface. It is this conviction that enables her to hold on to hope in a fraught situation, such hope being available for the patient to draw on when he or she is ready.

Ledermann's technique is notable for the use in tandem of interpretation and a flexible response to the patient, which departs from a strict adherence to the 'rules'.

A.S.

Introduction

Before discussing the treatment of narcissistic disorder, I shall outline my view of its nature, since I believe that this syndrome differs from other personality disorders. Some points I made in my previous papers on the subject will recur. Psychoanalysts and analytical psychologists are well known to disagree, in some respects, about the nature of narcissistic disorder. Both consider it to be a disorder of the self, but they work with different concepts of the self. According to the *Shorter Oxford English Dictionary* (1944), narcissism is 'a morbid self-love or self-admiration'. In fact, narcissistic disorder is the inability truly to love and value oneself and hence the inability to love another person. As I said in my previous papers, narcissistic patients suffer from severe defects in their object relations, which make them appear self-absorbed. They are fixated on an early defence structure that springs into being in infancy—when, for whatever reasons, there is a catastrophically bad fit between the baby and the mother, frequently compounded by the lack of an adequate father and by other inimical experiences in childhood.

Babies, thus deprived, grow into persons who lack trust in other people. They replace mature dependence by spurious pseudo-independence and delusions of omnipotence. They experience their lives as futile and empty, and their feelings as being frozen or split off. In severe cases these patients feel themselves outside the human ken and suffer from a terror of non-existing. This terror and emptiness are frequently covered over by a superficially smooth social adaptation, sometimes by feelings of aloofness and superiority, at times even by grandiose ideas about themselves.

In my previous papers I have discussed how Fordham's theory of deintegration and of the earliest defences of the self in infancy has helped me to understand the origin of narcissistic disorder. I speculated that with such early defences the process of deintegration is defective from the start. This leads to a badly formed ego, in my view, which is an essential feature of narcissistic disorder. I was interested to see that Kohut also speaks of self-nuclei not yet stably cohesive in what he terms borderline patients (quoted in Schwaber, 1979, p. 468). It is remarkable how close he comes to Fordham's theory of ego formation, but it is beyond the scope of this paper to elaborate this point.

A baby who, in phantasy, does away with the mother, has the experience of, one might say, being himself baby and mother, lonely and omnipotent. He does not expect any good to come from the outside world and cannot put his trust into anything good that even an unsatisfactory mother provides. Moreover, as he has abolished his noxious mother in infancy, he sometimes feels as if he had killed her. If his mother is incapable of being a mother to him and appears to be impervious to his demands, or, if an inborn defect in the baby makes it impossible for him to use her motherliness, then the delusion that he is murderous gets reinforced. Such a baby, of course, lacks the foundations of object relations which are based on his relationship to his mother. It is not surprising that such patients have enormous resistance against relating to the analyst. I have further postulated that a baby with stunted oral deintegration also suffers from pathological deintegration at the anal stage of development. Moreover, deintegration at the anal stage is not object-related because he has 'abolished' the object. The healthy mother of a healthy infant, as it were, detoxicates her baby's angry faeces that, in phantasy, he expels into the part-object, the breast. The narcissistically damaged baby has intense destructive impulses. But as he cannot (in phantasy) discharge them into the mother, he expels them into what he experiences as nothingness or outer space. There they are uncontained, undetoxicated, and they become enormously threatening. This, it would appear, is why narcissistic patients feel so bad and so persecuted and at the same time deny their personal hate. This unrelated aspect of the anal phase reinforces the experience of the stunted oral phase: that of arid power.

Clinical manifestations

A description now follows of the main clinical manifestations of narcissistic disorder; I shall divide it and discuss it in six sections. Needless to say, these divisions are interconnected and overlapping, hence somewhat artificial. Some of the material appeared in my previous papers in a different context. The six sections are:

1. the barrier against the analyst; power in place of eros;
2. the negative non-humanized archetypal experience of the analyst;
3. an insistence on turning the clock back;
4. massive splitting defences against disintegration;
5. difficulty in symbolizing;
6. pathological defences of a deformed ego.

Some or even all of the first five features may be manifest also in other personality or borderline disorders. It is the sixth feature—the way in which a narcissistic patient forms and defends a pathological, at times quite strong, ego—that gives narcissistic disorder its specific character.

1. The barrier

Narcissistic patients tend to experience relationships in terms of power only. Mrs B, a patient whose psychopathology was also discussed in my previous papers, was haunted for years by a gruesome vivid dream; it illustrates the terrible sado-masochistic situation in infancy which she relived in the transference.

> There was a very weak man who was attached to, and totally dependent on, a big cruel sadistic man. The big man wanted to destroy the weak man. He gouged his own eyes out and extracted his teeth, so as to induce the weak man to do the same. Despite these destructive actions the big man became increasingly strong and the weak man increasingly weak until he waned away.

This dream also indicated that Mrs B imagined her psychotic mother 'feeding' on her when she was a totally helpless baby. This gravely weakened the baby but made the mother stronger and at the same time increasingly self-destructive, like the man in the dream, until she had to be taken into a mental hospital in a strait-jacket. I felt in the countertransference that her libidinal attachment to me and her murderous impulses against me had not separated out. In severe cases patients see the analytic situation as an issue of killing or being killed, because they have the phantasy that they have abolished their mother and that their mother has demolished their existence as a person. Hence they put up a barrier against the analyst, all the more, as 'feeds' (sessions) with him are experienced like those of the noxious infancy mother. The more severe the disorder is, the more difficult it is for the therapist to penetrate this barrier. It is as if these patients came to sessions with a big poster in front of them saying KEEP OUT. Yet it is remarkable that none of them ever stopped coming.

In the early years of therapy those patients could not relate to me either with love or hate. Mrs B pulled her cardigan over her head in almost every session and kept her eyes averted from me for months. At times she was gasping for breath and terrified that she would suffocate if she breathed the air in my consulting room. She seemed either to experience the air as an extension of the noxious analyst/mother, or to flee in phantasy into an impersonal airless womb. As I mentioned in a previous paper (Ledermann, 1979), she said to me for months, like a gramophone needle stuck in a groove: 'You are a stupid useless monster and if you don't help me I shall kill you and then myself.' This was said with icy detachment and despair.

Less severely ill narcissistic patients talk about the abyss or the unbridgeable gap between them and me. Another patient expressed the narcissistic barrier and the fear of his murderous impulses by a severe stammer. He also had breathing problems, as if he, too, retreated into the inside of an archetypal mother. These breathing difficulties contributed significantly to his stammer. Even a much less severely disturbed narcissistic patient cut herself off from me. When I referred to the couch as an extension of the analyst's body, she said: 'The couch has nothing to do with you; it is *my* couch and the rug is *my* rug.' She could not 'feed' in my presence with her eyes, with her ears or with her tactile senses. After two years of analysis she still claimed that she had no idea what my hall or my consulting room looked like, nor what I wore. Whenever I made an intervention, she gave the impression that she had not heard it. When I commented on this, she said: 'I put it in my pocket and use it at home when I am by myself.' It is interesting that, as a child, she stole food from the larder although there was plenty to eat at mealtimes. She also resisted the tactile experience of the couch and experienced herself as suspended a quarter of an inch above it. She frequently seemed to escape from me into the inside of an impersonal mother. In her outside life she could not understand why, when shopping, she frequently had to hurry home suddenly for no apparent reason. We understood this as her flight back into an archetypal womb.

Some patients dare not use the couch at all and want to be barricaded in the armchair, which becomes their fortress. Others experience the couch as their impenetrable castle, with me on the other side of the moat. Both, whether called fortress or castle, seem to represent the archetypal mother into whose inside they retreat. When such patients feel the slightest danger of becoming more intimate with me, they panic and in phantasy send me flying to the other end of my consulting room. This barrier is also expressed by images in patients' dreams: the patient is locked in a castle, or in a room with all the shutters down. All these patients complain about feeling 'dead'. In my previous paper there was a reproduction of the gruesome picture of a 'dead thing' drawn by Mrs B (Ledermann, 1979). It had no mouth, ears, hands or feet to connect with the analyst. The patient with the severe stammer frequently pointed to his abdomen and said that he had a dead baby inside him, hence found it difficult to relate to me. He was told by his mother that, as a baby, he used to nestle in the hollow of her shoulder instead of feeding at her breast. Another patient had felt as an infant that she could not expel her anger into her mother. This made her imagine that her faeces were deadly dangerous. She re-lived this experience in the transference. For quite some time, an hour or so before setting out for the session, she had violent abdominal pains and had to defecate several times before she could risk the journey to me. In this session, whenever an angry feeling threatened to come up, she fled to my lavatory to deposit her 'anger' by defecating. She felt that she could not put her anger into the 'analytic breast'. She also held back her tears of anger and grief for years, and could only cry at home when nobody was present. Mrs B was also unable to cry in the analysis for several years.

Another manifestation of the barrier is that narcissistic patients frequently experience the analyst as non-existent, like the abolished mother of their infancy. It would appear that a baby that denies the existence of his mother's body feels as if he, himself, also had no body. This is repeated in the transference. The patient feels disembodied, and I become a 'mother-hole', 'a shadowy outline without a body', as one patient put it, or 'animated clothes walking around', as another patient said. Furthermore, I wondered whether a baby that has been unable to latch on to the mother lacks the experience of being moored and of having gravity, because two of my patients had the terrifying experience of floating in space forever, unable to land. The borderline patient experienced separation from me as if I had 'snipped the string, and she was a balloon floating away into nothingness'. Similarly, the patient with the stammer said, 'I have a balloon in my abdomen. I try to keep it moored to the couch as otherwise I would float away and disappear forever.' Although these are, of course, phantasies, they are pre-symbolic and have an almost delusional quality for some patients.

2. Non-humanized archetypal experiences

The second feature of narcissistic disorder is the failure of the mother to humanize her baby's archetypal experience of her. As is known, the baby has inborn potential for archetypal Great Mother images. In health, the images both of the good mother and his archaic love for her and of the devouring witch-mother and his murderous feelings towards her become humanized, mediated and modified by the actual mother who is loved and wanted by her baby and, on the whole, satisfies his needs. When the mother is not able to do this for her baby, he finds himself in the hopeless situation of feeling emotionally threatened and flooded by archetypal images, in particular that of the devouring witch-mother. One patient, when a young nun, was terrified of going into the Reverend Mother's room because she imagined that her cupboards were full of half-eaten nuns. Similarly, the patient who had to defecate before she came to the session told me that, whenever she experienced me as gentle and motherly, an experience she longed for, she simultaneously felt as if she were being pushed into shark-infested water. The terror of being gobbled up can, of course, be seen as a reversal of the baby's unconscious phantasy of scooping out the mother. In narcissistic patients it also seems to relate to the memory of early childhood when the patient felt as if both parents devoured him in that they did not allow him to exist in his own right. 'I was not allowed me-ness', one patient said.

In the transference I frequently become the witch-mother who lures the patient into her dark evil realm. Sometimes these terrors are displaced on to a copy of a Cézanne landscape that hangs above the analytic couch. It becomes populated by evil monsters and black sinister witch-like creatures or huge black bottoms that represent faecal breasts. Thus the present analytic situation, like the original environment in infancy, is experienced by patients as non-human and persecutory; pain and terror of their non-modulated destructive impulses reign supreme. Needless to say, they do not experience the analytic situation *only* as bad and dangerous; otherwise they would not come with great regularity and persistence. But the good experience is denied for a long time.

3. *Putting the clock back*

This brings me to my third point, the patient's unconscious wish magically to turn the clock back and be a baby, with the analyst as his ideal infancy mother. Because narcissistic patients' experience of the analyst as the devouring witch-mother goes hand-in-hand with a desperate yearning for the archetypal all-good mother, they hate the analyst for not fulfilling this longing. Together with the longing goes a strong impulse to set up the original *bad* situation of infancy so as to blame and punish the analyst for it. The narcissistic patient has felt bad—in serious cases, bad beyond redemption—throughout his life. He has the almost delusional belief that he could only feel good if he could demonstrate to himself and to the analyst that it is the analyst who is bad. This would prove to the patient that it was the mother who was bad and not he, the baby. This is how the patient's argument seems to go: if I set up the infancy situation, then I, the good patient/baby, suffer under the bad analyst/mother who leaves me for twenty-three hours every day and for weekends and holidays. Hence it is evident that the analyst/mother is hard, uncaring and unreliable, and I am able to believe, for the first time in my life, that I am good. Moreover, I can punish my mother by making her feel thoroughly bad and useless, as I have always wanted to do (a 'useless stupid monster').

The argument continues: when I have succeeded in making the analyst/mother feel bad, then I can make her feel guilty and remorseful about what she had done to me. This will make her wish to repair the damage by doing everything I want her to do. It makes patients believe that they can only get better if they put the clock back or 'rewrite history so as to give it a happy ending', as one patient put it. Such patients often set up this sado-masochistic situation also in their outside life. Two of the patients mentioned were married women. In the early stages of their analysis they experienced themselves as the victims of their husbands, whom, like the analyst, they considered to be bad and cruel. Both patients believed that they must leave their husbands, as they could not stand their marriages any longer.

4. Splitting defences

The fourth characteristic of narcissistic disorder is the collection of massive splitting defences that such patients develop, so as to ward off disintegration. These defences now operate in the transference. This is well illustrated by the following childhood incident which a patient reported. As a little girl one day she threw her favourite china doll high up into the air in the presence of her family. The doll of course was shattered to pieces, and the patient was inconsolable. Everyone, including the patient, was bewildered by this inexplicable action. In the analysis we came to understand that the doll represented her brittle self and that she had desperately wanted proof that her family could save her from disintegration by catching the doll. By telling me this story she expressed her fear as to whether I should be able to save her from shattering. Many narcissistic patients feel hollow and empty, and they frequently compare themselves with wooden Russian doll toys. The experience of hollowness, in my view, is due to the fact that they have split off and denied their basic feelings and drives.

In infancy they seem to have only minimally related to objects with love, hate, greed, rage, jealousy, envy and the need to depend. Hence their elemental impulses are unintegrated, and their inner world feels devoid of healthy objects. They fear that they might 'collapse like a house of cards', as one patient put it.

The absence of internal objects also contributes to the feeling that they have no body, as mentioned earlier. They feel two-dimensional. Alternatively, such patients feel that they have bizarre, freakish objects inside them: their grossly defective relationship to the breast was of a bizarre nature. Hence they sometimes experience themselves as a 'gargoylish monster' or as a 'diluvian monster full of warts trampling about mindlessly', as one patient described herself.

Alongside the denial of the patient's own feelings goes the denial of the analyst's good feelings. This further contributes to the experience that the analyst, when not felt to be downright bad, is experienced as cold and indifferent; the session is a business transaction for the purpose of making money. The analyst's good intentions are denied or, if acknowledged, deemed to be utterly useless.

5. Difficulty in symbolizing

The fifth facet of narcissistic disorder is the patient's very limited ability to symbolize. As I said, narcissistic patients could not internalize their primary object and their impulses towards it in infancy. Owing to this disability they appear, for a long time, to be unable to internalize the symbolic maternal care of the analyst. Even when a patient gradually lets go of his defences and develops some trust and good feelings for me, for a long time he lacks the capacity to 'keep me alive' when he leaves the session. Moreover, the patient has to deny the analyst's existence when away from him because he is too terrified of his impulse to destroy him when he is not reassured by the analyst's living presence. Also, for a long time the patient is convinced that he needs a mother and not an analyst. Thus he is outraged that the analyst is not always present when he wants him. In severe cases, the patient finds the hours away from the analyst painful, dehumanizing and terrifying. 'When you leave me you force me back into a living death', Mrs B used to say for years. I think this accounts for the narcissistic patient's adhesion to the analyst. I use the term adhesion to denote clinging in place of depending.

6. *Pathological defences of a deformed ego*

Finally I come to my sixth point: pathological ego defences. Patients suffering from non-narcissistic personality disorders frequently have a weak ego. The ego of narcissistic patients has a certain strength in the way it manipulates and controls the outside world; but it feels located in the head and is a highly pathological ego (see Ledermann, 1981). With this deformed ego such persons often make a superficially good adaptation to the outside world, but, of course, they cannot enter into real relationships with people. A pathological ego tends to produce pathological defences in childhood and adolescence, superimposed on the pre-ego defence of the primal self in infancy. These defences can manifest themselves in a stammer (or at least contribute to the formation of this symptom) or in a work block (defence against feeding). They can lead to grandiose ideas about themselves—two of my patients initially considered themselves to be geniuses. Or the defences can take the form of exaggerated social compliance. Some narcissistic patients express this particular pathological ego defence by exaggerated striving in social and work situations as a defence against a strong desire to drop out altogether. Two such patients defended their deformed egos in childhood by creating an unfeeling, computerized robot personality which I have discussed in another paper (ibid.). With this robot, one of these patients achieved good adaptation to the outside world. Another patient, when she left home in adolescence, changed from being a sulky, messy, awkward, badly performing child into a witty, entertaining, highly efficient young girl. She even changed her name at that time, so as to leave the hated child behind for good. In the analysis she recognized that it was essential for her to make contact with the discarded miserable child, as this was a vital part of her real self. As mentioned before, these typical narcissistic defences, protecting a specifically deformed ego, differentiate narcissistic disorder from other serious personality disorders.

Ovid's myth of Narcissus

Various authors who have written about narcissistic disorder
have used this term because of the many parallels with the myth
of Narcissus as related by Ovid in his third book of *Metamorphosis*. Jung stressed the fact that myths can be helpful guides
in analytical treatment as they express deep universal and eternal truths about men; also, the parallel between the myth of
Narcissus and clinical manifestations that I observed in narcissistic disorder emphasizes that this disorder has an archetypal
dimension. Gordon also drew attention to this myth in one of her
papers on narcissism (1980). I am indebted to the psychoanalyst,
Padel, who has pointed out some inaccuracies in my presentation
and interpretation of the myth in a previous version of this paper
(1988, pp. 164–165).

I now present a new version of these parallels. (I am
paraphrasing F. J. Miller's translation of the Latin text.)
'Narcissus had reached his sixteenth year. ... Many youths and
many maidens sought his love; but in this slender form was pride
so cold that no youth, no maiden touched his heart.' This relates to
the spurious pseudo-independence and the delusions of omnipotence in narcissistic patients which I mentioned. Narcissus calls
to the nymph Echo: 'come ... here let us meet', and Echo 'comes
forth from the woods that she may throw her arms around the
neck she longs to clasp. But he flees at her approach and fleeing,
says: "Hands off! Embrace me not! May I die before I give you
power o'er me!"' Thus spurned, she withdraws into the woods and
'lives from that time on in lonely caves.' As I have pointed out, the
essence of the plight of the narcissistic patient is that he has
enormous fear of and resistance against letting himself depend on
anybody, which includes the analyst. I have shown in my clinical
material that narcissistic patients, from infancy onwards, have
displaced depending and relating—that is, eros—by a striving for
power and control (unrelated anality). This is so because
depending means a partial abdication of power; the needed person
has power over the needy one, and in infancy this proved to be
disastrous. Hence, like Narcissus, the narcissistic patient feels
that he would rather die than give the analyst power by
depending on him.

Later on, the myth tells us that, so as to punish Narcissus for
mocking nymphs and men, one of the scorned youths cries out 'So

may he himself love, and not gain the thing he loves!' We know that as Narcissus lies down by the pool, 'he is smitten by the sight of the beautiful form he sees [his own reflection in the pool]. He loves a hope without substance; he believes a substance is there which is only a shadow.' Although the myth calls it 'love', this kind of love clearly relates to the narcissistic patient's morbid self-absorption and self-aggrandisement, which look deceptively like self-love. One could say that, like Narcissus, he 'loves a hope without substance; he believes a substance is there which is only a shadow.' Equally, the narcissistic patient feels disembodied, because, like Narcissus, he tries to mirror himself instead of being mirrored by the mother/analyst in the way I described. This special mirroring is an essential prerequisite for residing in one's body.

In the myth Narcissus pines away. Narcissistic patients speak of their terror of non-existing, of being in a 'living death'. One patient described herself as belonging to the 'undead dead'; psychologically such patients pine away unless they get help. It is interesting that Narcissus' parents already foreshadow an important aspect of the narcissistic problem: power in place of eros and relatedness. His father, 'the river-god Cephisus, embraced the Nymph Liriope and ravished her while she was imprisoned in his stream.' The issue of this rape was the child Narcissus. The seer Tiresias, when asked whether this child would reach well-ripened age, replied 'If he ne'er know himself.' The narcissistic patient thinks that he knows himself and that he does not need the mother–analyst to help him to discover his real self. Only if he can be enabled to give up this delusion can he, with the help of therapy, hope for real and meaningful living.

Treatment

I hope that I have described my view of the nature of narcissistic disorder sufficiently to demonstrate in what way treatment of this disorder differs from that of ordinary neurosis. In my experience the treatment of narcissistic disorder does not differ *basically* from the treatment of any serious personality disorder. But as narcissistic patients have a distorted ego and frequently have such strong, albeit pathological, ego defences, there is a great danger that the nature of the disorder is not recognized and that the patient is treated as if he suffered from a neurosis.

To simplify the exposition I shall describe therapy as falling into two phases; as the two phases overlap, however, we are concerned more with an emphasis than with a strict division.

The first phase, which in severe cases may last for several years, has similarities with the treatment of any serious personality disorder. As narcissistic patients have minimal trust, the basic aim in this phase is to create an empathic warm analytic environment in which trust can grow. Moreover, the purpose of this containing environment is to enable the patient to continue the deintegrative processes that were so badly impeded in his infancy. As Fordham says: 'The patient's self must become active' (1980, p. 315). Since the narcissistically unsatisfied baby scarcely gets into the relation with his mother that would be essential for healthy deintegration, libidinal and destructive impulses appear to remain fused. They exist as potentials inside the baby's primary self. This is reminiscent of Freud's concept of primary narcissism, of which Fordham reminds us in his paper 'Primary self, primary narcissism and related concepts' (1971). According to Freud, it is a state in which libidinal and aggressive energies are not yet defused. In Jungian terms, these instincts exist as archetypal potentials in the primary self but have not become active in the baby's relationship with the mother. Hence such patients have large areas of the primal self not yet deintegrated. Their deintegrative processes are severely stunted. To help the patient to defuse his libidinal and aggressive impulses by bringing him into relation with the analyst in the transference seems to be the first task in treatment. This will gradually lead to a state when the patient can relinquish unrelated power and by relating to the analyst can form healthy internal objects. To achieve this he must be helped to recognize his extremely destructive power which he dreads and denies yet which is instrumental in making him feel desolate, unanchored and unlovable. This recognition also eventually releases his loving feelings for the analyst. Furthermore, the analytic environment must provide the integrative function that the patient so badly lacks; the glue, as it were, to join together the deintegrates—or, as Gordon says, 'the links between the various internal objects' (1980). This will gradually change his deformed ego into a healthier one. It will also slowly transform his pathological ego defences, his 'survival kit', as one patient called it, such as the robot, the false façade, or the grandiose ideas, into healthy ego defences. It will enable the patient eventually to experience in the transference the impulses of which he has been terrified all his life and that he has encapsulated, split off, frozen and denied.

The analyst must remain in a state of syntonic countertransference, using Fordham's term, and at the unconscious level, whenever possible, feel alongside the patient. This could be seen as mirroring the patient. However, it differs from Kohut's concept of the mirroring transference (1971) defined as the 'therapeutic reactivation of the grandiose self'. I do not fully agree with Kohut's view, but to elaborate this point goes beyond the scope of this paper. Mirroring, in Winnicott's sense, means 'a long-term giving the patient back what he brings' (1971, p. 117). Although this is essential for the narcissistic patient, it is not sufficient. The analyst needs to detoxicate the patient's predominantly bad feelings, cut them down to size and give them back to him in a form that he can handle; furthermore, as Meltzer puts it, the analyst must 'modulate the patient's mental pain' (1981, p. 181).

The syntonic countertransference may encourage in the patient a feeling of merging with the analyst, which, again, somewhat relates to what Kohut says when he speaks of the narcissistic patient merging with the self-object. His view, like Neumann's, is that the neonate is without a self, and that the baby's self develops through interaction with various self-objects (Kohut & Wolf, 1978). Here I agree with Fordham's view that the baby does not experience his mother as self-object for any length of time but gets into relation with her (1971; 1980). Likewise, a patient needs to be helped not to experience the analyst as a self-object; on the contrary, he urgently needs to develop object relations to the analyst.

It is true that some patients experience me as if I were part of them: initially they are in a state of adhesion instead of dependence. However, I have come to see this adhesion as a pathological defence, namely their imagined safeguard against destroying me with their elemental infantile 'pre-ruth' love and hate. 'If the therapist is not a separate person, I can neither gobble him up nor kill him', so their argument goes. Obviously one needs to work through this defence and not collude with it. The resulting prolonged syntonic countertransference may raise hopes in the patient that the analyst will become his infancy mother. Hence for a long time many patients consider me as thoroughly bad (1) because I am not always there when they want me to be, (2) because I have no physical or sexual relationship with them. What they really mean, of course, is a concrete relationship with the infancy mother's body, not adult sex. These apparent failures of the analyst contribute to the phenomenon of the barrier that I have described and to the patient's feeling of hopelessness. Another difference from ordinary analytic practice is this: whereas a neurotic patient may feel strengthened by being confronted with his denied or repressed aspects, the narcissistic patient should, to begin with, only gently be made aware of his split-off, denied impulses. His resistance and his defences should be interpreted only gradually. For quite some time the patient needs to feel resistance and pain as an alternative to feeling nothing. Schwaber, in her paper 'On the self within the matrix of analytic theory' (1979) quotes the psychoanalyst Gedo who also makes the points: (1) that the patient prefers his pain to the experience of nothingness, and (2) that in resisting help the patient feels more real. He puts it succinctly: *Nego, ergo sum*—I resist, therefore I am (Gedo, 1975). This seems to be the adult equivalent of the baby's resisting the mother for the sake of survival, hence confirming Fordham's theory of the defences of the self (1976, p. 91). For a very long time in such cases the analyst must tolerate the patient's negative therapeutic reaction, like being called a useless stupid monster. Schafer in his paper 'The idea of resistance' also notes: 'unless we identify also the affirmations implied by apparently negative behaviour we are committed to using the idea of resistance pejoratively' (1973).

When one begins to interpret, one should do so only reconstructively. The patient must for some time be held in his delusional transference and be allowed to see his bad bits in the analyst. The importance of refraining from premature interpretations of the patient's denied impulses and of his bad bits was brought home to me many years ago: a narcissistic patient had persistently warded off my interpretations by saying, 'You are like a bloody Spitfire, te, te, te, te, shooting your interpretations at me. I am longing, one day, to vomit all your breast muck on to the tiles of your fireplace'. He had been stuck for some time, and when I stopped interpreting he began to progress. Also, I learnt from Mrs B that when I interpreted these denied impulses too soon, she returned into a state of icy isolation.

Instead of confronting the patient it is essential to give him repeatedly, and over a long time, insight into the genetic roots of his present experiences. Again Schwaber, in the paper mentioned (1979), came to the same conclusion. She says, 'One must always analyse from past into present'. Such genetic interpretations are essential as they help the patient to feel understood and gradually lead him to understand himself, as he is bewildered by his inability to use the analyst.

Another important principle in the first phase of treatment consists in not confronting the patient with reasonableness or reality, as he does not live in the real external world. Similar findings have been reported by Kohut (1978, p. 423) and by Schwaber (1979). For example, when I go on holiday a patient must be allowed to be in a delusional transference. Mrs B said for a long time on such occasions: 'You are sticking a knife into me; you go on holiday because you think I am rubbish and because you enjoy torturing me'. Even in a situation where a patient has to miss sessions for reasons of his own he will, like a young child, blame the analyst for not being there. This must be sympathetically understood and not analysed away, so to speak, by stressing the reality of the situation. Moreover, as I have explained, blaming the analyst is also intended to make him feel bad so that the patient can feel good. The therapist must be able to receive the patient's bad feelings lovingly. For a long time bad feelings are predominant. The patient loathes to acknowledge any good in himself and in the therapist. When he has a good experience he takes fright and withdraws: he thinks that, like in his infancy, good milk always turns sour. Indeed, with a part of himself he makes the analytic experience turn sour so as to reconstitute the familiar situation.

It is important that the analyst always greets the patient with warmth and openness, irrespective of what had occurred in the preceding session. This loving acceptance, I think, corresponds to Kohut's idea that the narcissistic patient needs to see the gleam in the analyst's eye; the gleam that he, as a baby, did not see in his mother's eye. I only partly agree with this: a patient does not benefit from praise or reassurance, but from affirmation, recognition and acceptance of his good and bad aspects. I should add, moreover, that the narcissistic patient initially also needs to see the *beam* in the analyst's eye, namely, the projection of the patient's own unacceptable impulses. This creates painful countertransference feelings that have to be endured. The wish to ward them off by interpretations must be resisted. However, to understand what the patient is doing makes the countertransference more bearable.

The analyst knows Jung's theory of opposites: the patient must also have some love, hope and trust hidden away somewhere, and this needs to be communicated to him. It makes the patient's often prolonged hopelessness more tolerable both for analyst and for patient. Moreover, the analyst must enable the patient to feel that his bad feelings also have value if he learns to handle them. Indeed, it is to be considered a therapeutic achievement when the patient finally reaches his personal hate for the analyst. On the other hand, whenever the analyst perceives a glimmer of trust or of a loving feeling in the patient, he needs to point this out to him. It gives the patient the hope that, after all, he is not all bad. A third important aspect in the first phase of treatment is that, as justice needs to be seen to be done, so does the analyst's loving care need to be seen to be done. By this I mean that the analyst must, in severe cases, be willing to make considerable sacrifices: for example, curtail holidays and be prepared to offer weekend sessions. He must be available on the telephone, in extreme cases even at night, although narcissistic patients seem to abolish the analyst to such an extent that it is usually impossible for them to telephone when in distress. Furthermore, I found that in the early stages narcissistic patients are unable to make demands as they dread the enormity of their greed. Whereas ordinary patients gain by being enabled to handle frustration, narcissistic patients must not be expected to cope with more than minimal frustration in the first phase of treatment.

I think that, occasionally, there are times when the patient needs to be given a token: a symbolic equivalent of a feed, to use Hanna Segal's term; e.g. a drink, as Frieda Fordham (1964) pointed out, or a cushion to take home. I do not consider this therapeutic in itself, but it can be seen as a 'rescue operation' when the patient feels flooded by a fear of going mad and is in utter despair. At the same time the analyst must give an explanation of this action to the adult part of the patient. Some patients are creatively finding what they need, not unlike a baby that finds a transitional object. When Mrs B had reached the stage when she could ask for something, she brought a packet of sweets to the session. She asked me henceforth to give her one of them at the end of each session to take home so that she could remind herself in the evening that I go on existing for her. Although *she* had had this idea and *she* brought the sweets, I was to give them to her. This is also the beginning of symbolizing, the 'as if' or 'let's pretend' stage of the child. For a long time such a patient will attack the analyst with his insistence that he can only get better if the clock is turned back. This causes great strain on the analyst's capacity to handle his countertransference hate and at times his exasperation.

I fully agree with Kernberg who says (in his book, *Borderline Conditions and Pathological Narcissism*, 1975) that seriously damaged narcissistic patients require a therapist 'with a true capacity for object relations and a great deal of security in himself. He needs to be non-self-centred and self-accepting and must be in control of his hostility. Unresolved narcissistic problems in the analyst are an unfavourable prognostic element for the treatment of such patients' (Kernberg, 1975). This may be a somewhat idealized picture of a therapist, but it is important to strive towards it. With such patients the therapist must be a real person and, occasionally, step out of his analytic shoes. By this I do not mean that the analyst should ever show his anger or make personal confessions. This would burden and not relieve the patient, as he desperately needs a calm, unruffled therapist who does not get alarmed or anxious on account of the patient. What I mean by the analyst being a real person is shown in the following example: Mrs B had a psychotic mother who had never cooked a proper meal for her as a child. At times Mrs B found it impossible to cook for her family; she had an overpowering yearning to be the child for whom the mother should make the meals. After she had come to see why she had this problem, we used two sessions to make menus for a week, and she wrote all the dishes down. Since then she has felt that at home the analyst/mother is inside her to help her with the cooking, and she has not reported any more difficulties with it. On another occasion she brought her guitar and overcame her extreme nervousness by playing it. Since that occasion she has derived pleasure and solace from this activity.

As a narcissistic patient's relationships to people are so defective, I think that such patients sometimes need help to find pathways for emotional communications. One of my patients persistently complained that she could feel neither anger nor hate for me, yet we both knew that these feelings were 'some place inside her', as she put it. She could not find them. At this point, after about four years of treatment, she made a creative suggestion which again had an element of a transitional phenomenon. She said that she could never express her despairing anger as she imagined that I, like her mother, would not hear it. She needed to make a big noise, like a hammer on an anvil. It occurred to me that I had an old anvil and a hammer in my garage. At this stage I had enough trust in her to know that she would not smash up my room, although she had occasionally expressed the wish to do so. She brought a tin for baking buns to the next session and set about flattening the breast-like shapes of *her* tin with *my* hammer on *my* anvil. She made a deafening noise. This continued through several sessions, until finally the cast-iron anvil broke in two under her violent blows. It helped her to have found this pathway for her anger and to test out whether I would accept it. Also, her hammering released a scream in her for the first time; something she had been longing to do. But she said despairingly: 'This is impersonal anger; I cannot yet feel anger at *you*. I fear if this should happen it would have the destructive power of an atom bomb, and neither of us would survive'. It was another year before she could reach her hate and anger at me.

In severe cases the anger, when finally reached, is at times expressed in pre-verbal noises like roaring, hissing, screaming, howling and growling. I think that after a time the patient benefits if the analyst puts into words for him what these noises communicate. The analyst needs to indicate that he is affected but not damaged by these communications. Also, narcissistic patients need help to find a way to express their grief and enormous pain. I mentioned a patient who could not cry in my presence. She felt that her tears were frozen, as in infancy and childhood she had not been able to deposit her pain and anger with her mother. These frozen tears could be understood as anaesthetized grief and anger. The analyst's warm acceptance of the patient, however despondent he may be, will thaw his frozen tears. He will be increasingly able to 'dump his grief and rage with the analyst', as one patient put it.

I mentioned that the analyst's voice should never be raised. Whenever there is an edge to my voice, my patients distance themselves and become once more cold and withdrawn. It is important that the therapist gives audible responses to everything the patient says. The analyst's silence causes terror in the patient.

Now I come to the second phase of treatment that gradually evolves out of the first phase, a process that with serious cases may take several years. With patients who have only areas of narcissistic disorder the first and second phases seem almost to coincide. The second phase is much more like analysing patients who have a fairly viable ego. Often a patient will at this stage still be intent on turning the clock back in order to become a baby. But now I interpret this defence, and we persistently work through it. The patient's trust in the goodwill and competence of the analyst will have grown, and his paranoid feelings will have lessened. His capacity to feed and to symbolize is increasing. Analytic work can now proceed with the usual transference interpretations. The patient can now be helped to own and to integrate his formerly split-off impulses and to modify their infantile absoluteness.

Patients gradually become able to bring love and hate together and no longer insist 'that you cannot have a black and a white slide in your projector simultaneously', as one patient used to say. Frozen tears are now thawing, and, for example, Mrs B cried for a whole year throughout every session. The patient who had imagined herself suspended above the couch unable to feed could now sink into the couch and take in the room and the analyst. It was moving when this woman, who formerly could not 'hear' my interpretations, said: 'I now find interpretations very helpful. They give me the stamp of existing.' Patients are now able to benefit from symbolic feeds and gradually understand that they need an analyst and not a mother. They are much less intent on using the unrelated power of their infancy, pseudo-omnipotence and pseudo-independence, to manipulate the analyst. By realizing that he has an impact on the analyst, the patient discovers that he has genuine potency. This makes it possible for him to allow the analyst also to be potent and effective. The patient can gradually let go of his pathological ego defences, such as the robot and the false façade, and have a more realistic appreciation of himself as a human being, more good than bad. We can now work through the depressive position and through oedipal feelings.

All the patients mentioned in this paper have become increasingly creative in their work and in their relationships. Mrs B visited her overseas home last summer to forgive her psychotic mother whom, for a very long time, she had wanted to kill. She also made peace with her father, who had left the family when she was little. But she has still some way to go in daring to contact fully her colossal destructive anger. Considerable improvement was brought about in the patient who stammered and was blocked in his work. He is now sought-after as an author and lecturer. The two patients who, at the beginning of analysis, had been about to dissolve their marriages now have a viable relationship with their husbands. Indeed, the husband of one patient, who had been impotent, is now intermittently potent on account of the change in her. However, another patient, not mentioned in this paper, who had a deformed ego and characteristic narcissistic defences, suffered a collapse of his ego as a result of having to move from his familiar surroundings, his home town, his family and friends. As it was not possible for him to have therapy more than once or twice a week, he could not be helped by analytical treatment.

I shall end by illustrating a patient's development in the course of the first three years of her analysis, describing the progression of child images as they revealed themselves in her dreams. The archetypal child can be seen as representing a person's potential future. In the early stage of the analysis the patient dreamed that she was nursing a friend who was dying of cancer of the womb. This friend, although married, had in reality had an abortion because she had felt too deprived herself to be the mother of a child. The friend was an aspect of the patient. Instead of a live child there was a cancer in her psychic womb, and she was in danger of psychic death. Then an actual child appeared in a dream, but it was disguised so as not to look like a child. She still tried to deny the existence of her inner child as she denied her infantile impulses. Then her dreams contained undisguised images of babies and young children. At first it was a deformed baby, blue and nearly frozen to death in the far corner of a room. It could not cry. The patient thumped and kicked the baby in order to bring it to life. Then she picked it up and cuddled it and warmed it back into life.

In another dream the baby had a blemish, and its parents wanted to discard it. It was soaking wet, having been left unprotected in the rain. This time again the patient wrapped it in a blanket and hugged it. But she was worried that the baby was unable to kick. It will be obvious that this dream represented her inner child rejected by the mother as *she* had felt in her childhood. The rain might have represented the inimical environment and/or her at that time unexpressed tears. The baby could not kick as her aggression was still inhibited. Also, the patient was still the do-it-yourself mother. I was not yet permitted to help her inner child. Unrelated power was still replacing eros, relatedness. This is illustrated by another dream: a little child on a sledge was magically going up a snow-covered hill backwards. There was nobody pulling the sledge. It landed inside a hut that was guarded by a black dog. The patient ran up the hill, tackled the dog and freed the child. Again we have the magic omnipotence of the child that does not need anybody to pull it up the hill. The patient felt that going backwards was a retrograde movement, and the snow depicted that she still experienced the analytic environment as cold. The black dog, her fierce aspect, tried to stop her from making contact with her child qualities. But she overcame the dog and reached her inner child.

Then she dreamed of a child that fell over the balustrade of a high balcony into a river. The patient panicked and called ambulance men who saved the child from drowning. The patient's being too high up and separated from the child represents her arrogant aloofness, a characteristic narcissistic defence. The river can be understood as the lethal archetypal womb into which the child falls. However, it is now no longer her omnipotent self that saves the child, but ambulance men—an archetypal representation of the analyst.

As my patient made more contact with her infantile impulses and began to latch on to me she dreamed of a frenzied destructive little child; but when his mother picked him up he calmed down and was content in her arms. It is again no longer the patient herself but this time 'the mother' who holds the child—a tentative recognition of the analyst. Then she dreamed of a rubber-like puppet child that lived locked up by her father in a castle with all its windows covered by dark shutters. A woman clowned so as to amuse the child. The patient urged the father to open the shutters and let the sun and air in. 'It is beautiful outside', the dreamer said, 'and it will do the child good.' Clearly the castle with all the shutters down is her narcissistic barrier; the father, her controlling non-relating aspect that locks her inner child away; the clowning woman one of her narcissistic defences which I mentioned. You will remember that she used to amuse people by clowning and being witty. But here is the recognition that letting sun and air in will be good for the child. The environment inside and outside the analysis is no longer experienced as hostile.

The patient's development, like all psychological development, went in a spiral movement. She dreamed again of a three-year-old-child—the age of the analysis at that time—that was only half alive. It was unaware of its surroundings, leaned over the edge of a canoe and fell flat on its face into the water. The dreamer saw this happening from a window, again high up on the second floor of a building. She ran down and screamed, 'A child is drowning!' A woman helped her to save the child. The patient was still too high up and divorced from her inner child that was not fully alive nor aware of reality. It is saved by a woman, but again she dare not yet identify the woman with the analyst.

I see one of her recent dreams as giving the quintessence of her development. In this dream she walked on the South Downs and saw a horde of invaders coming towards her. She thought that they were hostile and dangerous and fled into a cave. Then she realized that the invading army was friendly and on her side. In the cave she saw a tiny child with a woman. She thought the woman looked like me. The child shot down some stairs as if propelled by an invisible force. 'There was no holding it back', she said; the stairs were an exit into the sunny world outside. This seems to me to depict a kind of birth of her inner child. She had once more fled into the womb of the archetypal mother, the cave, because she had experienced the analytic invasions into her psyche as hostile. But her trust in me had become established; the dream tells her that the invading forces are her allies. The child, in the presence of the analyst, can enter into a world that is now experienced as warm and sunny. The patient is well on the way to recovery. A person suffering from narcissistic disorder has usually a fairly strong but deformed ego that arose from stunted deintegration in infancy. This has resulted in replacing eros, i.e. relatedness, with ruthless power. This pathological ego is experienced as being located in the head. The patient develops specific defences to guard against going to pieces.

In the treatment I consider it essential to create an analytic environment in which further deintegration can take place. The analyst must enable the patient to release in relation to him the impulses that have been split off and denied. He must refrain from interpreting those destructive impulses *per se* since it is, as yet, too difficult for the patient to take responsibility for his evil aspects. All he can tolerate at this stage is a reconstructive interpretation about his destructiveness in the light of his severely defective infancy situation which he is re-living in the transference.

In the second phase of treatment the usual analytic interpretative work can proceed.

REFERENCES

Fordham, F. (1964). The care of regressed patients and the child archetype. *Journal of Analytical Psychology* 9:1.

Fordham, M. (1971). 'Primary self, primary narcissism and related concepts'. *Journal of Analytical Psychology* 16:2.

———— (1976). *The Self and Autism*. Library of Analytical Psychology, Vol. 3. London: Karnac Books.

———— (1980). The emergence of child analysis. *Journal of Analytical Psychology* 25:4.

Gedo, J. (1975). On a central organizing concept for psychoanalytic psychology. *Journal of the American Psychoanalytical Association,* Spring.

Gordon, R. (1980). Narcissism and the self: who am I that I love? *Journal of Analytical Psychology* 25:3.

Kernberg, O. (1975). *Borderline Conditions and Pathological Narcissism*. New York: Jason Aronson.

Kohut, H. (1971). *The Analysis of the Self*. New York: International Universities Press.

Kohut, H., & Wolf, E. (1978). The disorders of the self and their treatment: an outline. *International Journal of Psychoanalysis* 59:4.

Ledermann, R. (1979). The infantile roots of narcissistic personality disorder. *Journal of Analytical Psychology* 24:2.

———— (1981). The robot personality in narcissistic disorder. *Journal of Analytical Psychology* 26:4.

Meltzer, D. (1981). The Kleinian expansion of Freud's metapsychology. *International Journal of Psychoanalysis* 62:2.

Ovid [Publius Ovidius Naso] (ca. A.D. 2). *Metamorphoses*. Loeb Classical Library: 42/43, 1916.

Padel, J. (1988). Theoretical concepts: narcissism. A commentary on the series. *British Journal of Psychotherapy* 4:2.

Schafer, R. (1973). The idea of resistance. *International Journal of Psychoanalysis* 54:3.

Schwaber, E. (1979). On the self within the matrix of analytic theory—some clinical reflections and reconsiderations. *International Journal of Psychoanalysis* 60:4.

Winnicott, D. W. (1971). *Playing and Reality*. London: Tavistock Publications.

CHAPTER SIX

Reflections on introversion and/or schizoid personality

Thomas Kirsch

Kirsch's chapter is noteworthy for several reasons. First, he is attempting to clarify differences and similarities between the terminology of analytical psychology and psychoanalysis. He notes that what may be conventionally pathologized as 'schizoid' overlaps with what Jung termed 'introversion' (see below). But he has also formulated ways in which the two states are different. Second, what he has to say about the matching of types in analysis speaks to the issue posed by Edwards (and mentioned in my Introduction): the whole question of a fit between patient and analyst. Here, as elsewhere in the chapter, Kirsch is quite open about his changing views. Third, Kirsch shows how the personality of the analyst influences his interpretive stance—and does so with a wealth of clinical detail.

For some readers, typology may be an unfamiliar subject. It is a system developed by Jung to demonstrate and ascertain

First published in *The Journal of Analytical Psychology* 24:2, in 1979. Published here by kind permission of the author and the Society of Analytical Psychology.

different modes of psychological functioning in terms of 'psycho-logical types'. Some individuals are more excited or energized by the internal world and others by the external world: these are introverts and extraverts, respectively. But, in addition to these basic attitudes to the world, there are also certain properties or functions of mental life. Jung identified these as thinking—by which he meant knowing what a thing is, naming it and linking it to other things; feeling—which for Jung means something other than affect or emotion: a consideration of the value of something or having a viewpoint or perspective on something; sensation—which represents all facts available to the senses, telling us that something is, but not what it is; and, finally, intuition, which Jung uses to mean a sense of where something is going, of what the possibilities are. A person will have a primary or superior function: this will be the most developed and refined of the four. The other three functions fall into a typical pattern. One will be only slightly less developed than the superior function, and this is called the auxiliary function. One will be the least developed of all. Because this is the most unconscious, least accessible and most problematic function, it is referred to as the inferior function.

Using the two attitudes and the superior and auxiliary functions, it is possible to produce a list of 16 basic types. Several psychological tests exist, based on Jung's hypotheses. These are used by some analytical psychologists clinically and also have educational and industrial application. There is a difference of emphasis in analytical psychology between those who welcome the scientific tenor of typology and those who use it as a rule-of-thumb approach, the value of which lies in providing an overall assessment of a person's functioning.

Jung worked on his typology as a means of understanding the differences between himself and Freud (to put it concisely, he felt he was introverted and Freud extraverted). It seems to be the case that interpersonal dysfunction can be understood in terms of typological difference.

A.S.

This chapter is in large part an outgrowth of a previous paper (Kirsch, 1980) on an extravert's approach to dream interpretation. In that study I examined my work with people who did not know I was a Jungian analyst. I found that I tended to relate their dreams to outside reality rather than to the subjective contents of the unconscious. I attempted to discuss some differences in dream interpretation depending upon the psychological type of the analyst. By contrast, Jungian studies tended to emphasize the introverted subjective aspects of dream interpretation. Early in my professional life I had tended to agree with that approach, yet through my own analysis I came to realize that my own natural extraversion needed another way of approaching dreams.

A further interesting facet emerged from this previous study in that I found that, in my practice, there existed a large sub-group of introverted women. As a group these women were generally successful in their chosen careers but felt extremely isolated in their interpersonal emotional life. It was the latter that usually led them to seek analysis, since their emotional isolation brought on various forms of depression. That I seemed to work well with women of this group I attributed to two basic factors: (1) psychological type differences, and (2) orientation towards the mother complex.

As an extraverted intuitive-feeling type I could do most of the work in bridging the relationship and, therefore, help the analysand feel more at ease. I was able to 'sense' intuitively certain feelings which these analysands would have and present the possibilities to them. This tended to open up various affects and emotions that they were unaware of. I had to be careful about these 'hunches' because, at times, I would be wrong and then be at complete odds with the patient. Furthermore, analysands have an ambivalence to exposing these feelings, so defences would arise. It would feel to them as if they were being invaded by something quite alien to their own natures. I have become aware that one must be extremely careful with one's intuitive feeling hunches because they can cause as much harm as good. Clinical examples of this phenomenon will be given later.

All these introverted women had a deep negative mother complex which was a primary factor in their emotional isolation.

They were usually profoundly self-critical and full of negative judgements towards themselves, and they generally viewed the world in a pessimistic fashion. The future was bleak, and it was felt that nothing could change to make life more meaningful. My own orientation towards the mother complex was positive, and I saw life as full of possibilities and growth. At first I was extremely naive in my overall optimism. Often, therefore, a polarity was constellated between the patient and me which had to be thrashed out in each individual situation. As my life went on and my analytic experience grew, I realized that it was not correct to label all the behaviour patterns of these women as introverted. There was something other than introversion at work, and it was more than a matter of helping shy women to ovecome their shyness, introversion or whatever. In other words, there was clearly a pathological complex at work, and I found these people could best be described as schizoid. A conflict arose for me at this point between the psychiatrically oriented nomenclature of the schizoid personality disorder and Jung's description of psychological types based on normal psychology. For instance, much of what is described as schizoid by psychiatry analytical psychologists would consider to be normal introversion. In Freedman and Kaplan's *Comprehensive Testbook of Psychiatry* (1967), the authors describe the schizoid in terms of 'a tendency to avoid close or prolonged relationships with other people. A corollary of this is the tendency to think autistically ... the cornerstone of the adaptive defensive system in this instance is withdrawal. ... In his isolation, he may invest his energies in non-human objects and with sufficient talent and persistence ... [to] provide an adaptably useful structure for his life.' Some of these attributes may just as well describe the introvert.

So wherein lies the difference between the two terms? Is it important to make the distinction? But I think that there *is* a great difference between normal introversion and schizoid personality disorder. The difference lies in the fact that the introvert is able to make a meaningful interpersonal connection when he chooses, whereas the schizoid person is unable to do so.

Clinically, one may ask, what difference does it make? Analytical psychologists in general are not greatly interested in diagnostic categories, and if the analysis works, such categories do not matter. But I have found that it is important for me to have some formulation in order to assess better where the patient is. Some of these patients have done extremely well in analysis, but others have been among my most outstanding failures. Knowing, therefore, what can be seen as introversion and what can be seen as schizoid has been most helpful in the analytical work. Furthermore, within the category of schizoid it has been most helpful for me to assess the degree of isolation. Often these patients present a thick barrier through which it is extremely difficult to penetrate. It is the degree of isolation which, ultimately, determines whether analysis is possible or not. A colleague (Melvin Kettner) has described this sort of person as a 'workable schizoid'. I have seen a large number of such women, and I think they are drawn to a Jungian analysis because they see in Jung a legitimization of their psychology. Jung accepts the reality of the inner experience and does not reduce it to a pathological entity.

I should now like to present some clinical examples of such schizoid persons.

One case in which the analysis did not work well was a young, single woman in her mid-twenties. She had become interested in Jungian analysis through taking a course. She had been seeing a married man with whom she felt quite involved, although he did not appear to reciprocate her interest. In the initial phase of analysis we discussed this relationship extensively, and she expressed much affect, crying frequently and seemingly feeling vulnerable. She came to see herself as playing the little girl rôle vis-à-vis the man and eventually was able to disengage emotionally from him. Over a period of twelve months her outer life became stabilized. Her job went satisfactorily; she was involved in courses and had a few friends and the analysis seemed to go well. She presented dreams which mainly centred on her childhood home.

Her history revealed that she was born of a Jewish father and a Catholic mother, both of whose families had emigrated from Europe. She had always been competitive with her mother and favoured by her father. Her background through high school did not seem unusual, but at college her life became somewhat chaotic. She changed colleges each year until graduation, after which she went to Europe for several months. In Europe she became unable to cope on an emotional level, and her mother had to bring her back home. After several months of recuperation she obtained a job and gradually found herself involved in one short-term relationship after another.

None of these had been particularly significant until the one which brought her into analysis. I felt that the therapeutic relationship was good. She expressed warm, positive feelings towards me, and I liked her. The analysis was working. Then she became genuinely involved with a man ten years younger than herself—she was 29, and he was 19. She felt it was crazy, but they were both in love. Life was going better for her until he began to pull away from her because he wanted more independence. She began to withdraw more into her shell, and all my extraverted feeling could not bring her out. She reported fewer dreams and then began to leave the sessions early. She claimed that she had nothing to say, and after a few attempts on my part to get her to talk more, I began to let her go early. This pattern continued for a year until after I returned from a summer vacation. She came to the first session after my return extremely heavily made up, which was unusual for her. She announced that she was going to stop therapy, that it had reached the point of diminishing returns. I urged her to continue and see if we could work through the block, but her decision was final. At the last session she was on the verge of tears throughout the session, but she would not give in to them.

I have reflected on this case because it concerned a type of patient with whom I have usually done quite well. Furthermore, the initial phases of the analysis had progressed favourably. After two years of therapy with this patient I had dreamt that I was married to her. I had taken this as a positive sign that I was deeply connected to her, but I did not understand the further meaning. Now I think it has to do with the schizoid aspect of my own anima seen in projection on this patient and which I sought to bring into more intimate relationship with my ego. With the actual patient there had only been a partial resolution of that schizoid nature. She did make many changes in her psyche over the four years of therapy; but she was not able to break out of a certain schizoid isolation which remained untouched. She became more comfortable in her professional life, but she was not able to form a meaningful relationship, either to a man or a woman.

Perhaps it is too early to say, but I do not think that she will return for further therapy.

Another example follows in which the problem of distinguishing schizoid personality from introversion became important. The patient, a woman in her mid-thirties, married, but with no children, came to me after she had been in therapy with another man for three years. Her previous therapist had a bio-energetics orientation, and a conflict had developed between them about his approach. She decided to leave him in favour of someone with a Jungian orientation, since she thought Jung's approach would validate her more readily. She particularly liked his theory of psychological types, and she saw herself as an introverted thinking person.

Her early history showed that she had grown up in a small town with an intact set of parents and two older brothers. The family was extremely poor during her youth, but the parents always put on a good persona for the community. She never felt close to her mother, and the father had had serious brain surgery during her adolescence.

The initial three months went quite easily, until I made some comments about masculine and feminine aspects in one of her dreams. Before the next session I received a long letter, a warning of sorts, not to label things in masculine or feminine terms. I tried to explain how Jungians use these terms and that they represent attitudes and are not specific to one sex or the other since we all have both. We were able to come to some sort of agreement in that I would be careful how I used the words masculine and feminine, as they were so loaded in the general culture.

The next major issue was my interpretation of a dream. She had dreamt that she was going to a doctor's office in a clinic; she was going to tell him a dream. She did not tell the dream to the doctor, however, but went to the next office where her husband was. I saw this dream as presenting a major problem. In reality she was telling dreams to her husband before she brought them into the analytic hour. I experienced the energy as going away from the analysis rather than coming into it. I suggested that she tell the dreams to me first, and then talk them over with her husband if she wished. She reacted extremely negatively to my suggestion.

We began a battle that lasted for the remainder of the therapy. She felt that since it was her analysis she could do whatever she wanted, whereas I tried to explain my orientation in terms of the alchemical container, where it is important to keep the material contained and not have a leak, which dilutes or drains the content. In actuality, she found that it made a big difference whether she told me or her husband the dream first. If she told him the dream first, most of the energy would be dissipated by the time she came for the analytical session. A related issue was that she would only talk about dreams that were weeks or months old. She would not relate recent dreams that she had not yet herself assimilated. She required a certain distance from me, and I felt that I was working too close for her comfort.

Another major issue concerned the use of tranquillizing medication. She required tranquillizers to calm her diffuse anxiety. She was taking more than the recommended dose, and I felt that she was becoming psychologically and physically addicted to them. My medical conscience would not allow me to prescribe such large doses for her. Again it was the issue of who was in control of the therapy. I ended up by writing the prescriptions, cautioning her, at the same time, of overuse.

A further issue was money, but not in the usual way that it came up as a problem. She and her husband were not in the best of circumstances financially during much of the time of the analysis. As a result I did not raise her fee when I made a general overall rate increase for my practice. When I made a second rate increase, I hesitatingly asked her for the first increase. She became furious with me for not telling her about the first increase. Why did I take it out of her control and decide unilaterally not to raise her fee the first time? She ended up by paying me retroactively so that her fee was like that of everyone else.

These vignettes highlight the issue around control in which we were engaged. It appeared that she had a solid wall around her, her schizoid character, which I, with my extraverted feeling, was unable to penetrate. I felt genuinely supportive towards her and that I wanted to help her. In other words, my anima functioned generally positively in relationship to her. She did not want to let me in because that would have been too threatening. As I saw it, she could not allow me to enter her world with her, and I was always outside. Behind the defensive armour there seemed to be extremely positive feelings towards me. She always came punctually, gave much time and thought to the analysis, and she did not wish to end with me. However, after three years I found I had worked to the limit of my tolerance of being excluded from the process, and felt that we were locked in an endless and destructive power struggle which was not helping either of us. I suggested termination, with referral to another Jungian therapist, a woman. This was done, and I understand she is now doing much better.

If I look back and wonder what went wrong, I think it has to do with the two factors I had thought would be helpful with this type of patient. It seems that both my extraverted intuitive feeling responses and positive mother complex threatened her. She felt attacked by my reaching out or wanting to give to her. Instead of helping her to come out from her shell, it made her retreat more behind her defensive armour.

A third and less complicated example concerns a woman, married, in her middle thirties, with a successful career as a book editor. In addition to being quite isolated interpersonally, she had phobic symptomatology, such as not being able to be in crowds, stores and so on. In the early phases of treatment she had several dreams in which she tried to meet me, but something would be wrong, such as the time or the place of meeting. I felt that this had to do with a resistance to the analysis. In thus failing to make a connection with me in the dreams, she was unable to make a connection to herself as symbolized by me.

Initially, her ability to express affect of any kind was quite limited. Dreams and crying were her major modes of expressing anything deeper than personal issues. For instance, during this phase of the analysis she would enter each session and cry for the first ten minutes without being able to say why. It seemed as if a dam were breaking, which had been holding her emotions in check by only the greatest of efforts. The dreams centred mainly upon family matters, particularly relating to childhood. In many dreams she was in her childhood home with her five sisters and mother and would be unable to talk because there was too much noise in the room. She sensed that she was caught in the 'participation mystique' of the family and could not express her individual needs. She felt completely implicated in the subliminal demands, attitudes and expectations of the family, and hence she could not find an individual mode of expression. The family values were typically mid-western and caught her up in an extraverted life. We were able to trace the sense of isolation that developed in spite of her being surrounded by the rest of the family. Many dreams included an interaction with her mother, wherein the analysand felt duty-bound by the wishes and expectations of the mother. These dreams were most helpful in the reductive aspects of the negative mother complex.

The analysis progressed more or less smoothly for several years, until a crisis situation developed. In the marriage the pattern had been for her to take all the initiative. She planned all social events, even made her husband's appointments with his doctor and generally took charge, though in not too overbearing a manner. The crucial time came when her husband had to decide about a change of job. His local office was closing, and he expected to be transferred. In a subliminal way she was being asked to make a decision for him: should he move with the company or look for another job locally? She became quite anxious and phobic, with a return of many of her initial symptoms. After several months of indecision we threw an *I Ching* on my suggestion. The result was 'Waiting' with no changing lines. It seemed that she needed to wait and let events happen as they would. She should not try to influence her husband in any way. Difficult as it was for her, she did wait and let him make the decision. On the last day of his old job he found work in another division that was not being re-located, and they remained.

Shortly afterwards she had a dream which indicated that she was ready to finish therapy. She dreamed that I was visiting her home, and she was showing me her kitchen. Afterwards we walked through the hallway into the living-room, and then I walked out. After all those early dreams in which we did not connect, she had finally brought the symbolic me into her house. I suggested that it was time to terminate therapy, and, after her initial surprise, she concurred.

My extraverted intuitive-feeling approach proved most helpful with this schizoid woman, who was also an introverted sensation type. She had gradually been able to drop many of the extraverted expectations placed upon her and accept her own more natural introverted way. My intuition had raised numerous possibilities where her own associations were quite sparse. She had been able to pick on those possible interpretations that seemed to be right for her and was then able to continue with her own associations: a meaningful dialogue ensued. She had also needed my feeling function and positive mother complex to help her feel comfortable. Of the three examples this one had by far the most favourable outcome.

Analytical psychology generally does not place much emphasis on clinical diagnosis. We speak rather in terms of psychological type, or the activation of a particular complex. When I began analytic work I tended to over-use the terms 'introvert' and 'extravert' as a way of describing certain of my analysands. It has become important for me to be more specific, especially in relationship to the over-use and over-evaluation of the term introversion. In each of the three cases described there exists a schizoid element above and beyond normal introversion. An important consideration is whether this schizoid element can be changed or not. In each of the three cases presented that element has been analysed with varying degrees of success. I have pondered what effect my own psychological type and positive mother complex has had on the process. At first, I thought that my being able to reach out would have a helpful effect. It has turned out that the results have been mixed. Some schizoid introverted women can respond to my extraverted feeling, nurturing approach, whereas for others it is pure poison. The deciding question is whether I am able to reach behind the barrier and tap into the emotional isolation. If I can, then such women become the 'workable' schizoid. Thus, contrary to my original notion, my psychological type is not always as helpful as I originally thought. These clinical reflections have been extremely important to me since the variations on this theme of introversion-schizoid account for approximately one-quarter of my practice.

REFERENCES

Freedman, A., & Kaplan, H. (1967). *Comprehensive Textbook of Psychiatry*. Baltimore: Williams & Wilkins.

Kirsch, T. (1977). Dreams and psychological types. In I. Baker (ed.), *Methods of Treatment in Analytical Psychology*. Fellbach: Bonz.

CHAPTER SEVEN

Reflections on Heinz Kohut's concept of narcissism

Mario Jacoby

Jacoby's aim is not to stress that many contemporary ideas in psychoanalysis concerning narcissism and self-psychology have been anticipated by Jungians. Rather, he is exploring similarities and differences between two major strands of theorizing. As he says, he is, if anything, looking at analytical psychology through the eyes of Kohutian self-psychology.

A further interest of the author's is to consider the implications for technique. It can be seen that Jacoby, a training analyst in Zürich, is quite clear that attention to transference–countertransference processes is a central feature of analysis. When first reading the paper, I was struck by the sensitive and self-aware way in which Jacoby dealt with his patient's idealization—not in a manner that dismissed it as 'defence', but somehow managing to allow for growth inherent in such a transference (along the lines of Kohut's model).

First published in *The Journal of Analytical Psychology* 26:1, in 1981. Published here by kind permission of the author and the Society of Analytical Psychology.

Finally, what Jacoby says about the 'Jungian self' repays study.

A.S.

There is much diversity in current psychoanalytic litera-ture, but for many years now my attention has been particularly drawn to Heinz Kohut's works on narcissism (1966, 1971, 1972, 1977). Kohut has struck me in many ways as a kindred spirit, his views being akin to my own on psychology and his therapeutic approach similar to mine, which, in itself, is closely related to C. G. Jung's analytical psychology. While reading Kohut's often microscopically subtle, descriptions and interpretations, traits of various analysands, including the analysand I am for myself, would immediately come to mind. I was also struck again and again by how close Kohut seemed to analytical psychology, even in the way he sees the basic problem of psychological theorizing. Because he firmly believes that 'all worthwhile theorizing is tentative, probing, provisional—con-tains an element of playfulness' (Kohut, 1977, p. 206), Kohut is tolerant about possible inconsistencies in psychological theory. As he writes, 'I am using the word playfulness advisedly to contrast the basic attitude of creative science with that of dogmatic religion' (ibid., p. 207). Here we have a striking parallel with Jung, who, in his memoirs, complains about Freud's dogmatism with the following words, 'As I saw it, scientific truth was a hypothesis which might be adequate for the moment but was not to be preserved as an article of faith for all time' (Jung, 1963, p. 148).

Furthermore, Kohut postulates, for example, that so-called 'narcissistic libido' goes through a progress of formation and transformation and can, in the course of a lifetime, stimulate the maturation processes of a personality. The results of this maturation he calls empathy, creativity, humour and wisdom. This view is quite contrary to that of classical psychoanalytic theory, according to which in healthy development narcissistic libido always transforms into object libido. In contrast, Kohut believes that so-called narcissistic libido has its own capacity for transformation and maturation. Such an observation immediately makes us wonder if Kohut is not using this rather prejudiced term to refer to the phenomenon that would be called, in Jungian terminology, introversion, or, even more specifically, the urge towards individuation. Moreover, in his most recent book, *The Restoration of the Self* (1977) Kohut dares to introduce a theory that reaches far beyond the bounds of traditional psychoanalysis: a new theory of the self as centre of the psychological universe. This is a big step within psychoanalysis, an essential innovation of great consequence. The analytical psychologist is then faced with the obvious question of whether Kohut's *self*, centre of the psychological universe, corresponds to the psychic experience that Jung describes and ascribes to the self. In order to answer this question we have to investigate first of all exactly what Kohut means by the term *self*.

Generally speaking, we have to remember that as time went on psychoanalysis could not avoid introducing the concept of the self. Heinz Hartmann was the first to use the term *self* in psychoanalysis, in 1950, and to suggest a conceptual differentiation from the term *ego*. In contrast to the ego which is only one instance within the psychic apparatus, *the self* refers to 'me as a whole person'. It means 'I myself', the way I experience myself and the ideas I consciously or unconsciously entertain about myself. And thus, the specific term 'self-representation' is used, which means the way my being is, as it were, represented in my own mind—in contrast, for example, to the way objects are represented. This inner image of myself may be realistic enough and form the basis of tolerant and constructive self-evaluation. But it can also be distorted, exaggerated, superior, inferior, unreliable or labile. In the latter case my self-perception or at least my sense of self-esteem is in some way disturbed.

For many psychoanalytic authors this concept of the self is a *content* of the ego. In analytical psychology my image of myself—to the extent that it reaches awareness—would also be attributed to the ego. But the unreflected parts of this image belong to my personal unconscious and are related to my life history. Thus, it seems that analytical psychology could also attribute this notion of the self to the psychology of the ego. However, experience has shown that the way a person sees himself can have intense emotional effects and tends to colour his entire outlook and the basic feeling tone of his personality. This is a condition that is beyond the control of ego consciousness and cannot be easily modified by deeper insights. We must therefore assume that the feeling tone underlying self-perception and self-evaluation has deep archetypal roots. Thus it might be related to the self in the specific Jungian sense.

But Kohut does not seem to be completely satisfied with the psychoanalytic concept of the self either. As I mentioned above, he is taking a step which he tries at great length to justify: side by side with the self concept in the 'narrower sense' accepted by psychoanalysis—as a content of the ego or of the whole psychic apparatus—he places an enlarged concept of the self, as the centre of the psychological universe.

The consequences are varied and decisive. The drives and their vicissitudes, considered by psychoanalysis till now as primary, become merely a part of the self in formation and serve in its development. The self is an independent configuration, greater than the sum of its drives. What classical psychoanalysis calls drive fixations and their respective defence mechanisms would, in Kohut's view, be products of decomposition due to momentary or chronic instances of disintegration of the self. Thus, the disorder in the coherence of the self would be primary and the drive conflict secondary. This is a tremendous innovation within psychoanalysis.

It is natural for Kohut as a psychoanalyst to go on to investigate the genesis of the self and its disorders. Always basic for the formation of the self is the 'empathic' presence of so-called self-objects. By this Kohut means, for example, a mother who is experienced by the infant in fusion with her as a part of his self. As he writes,

> The crucial question concerns, of course, the point in time when, within the matrix of mutual empathy between the infant and his self-object, the baby's innate potentialities and the self-object's expectations with regard to the baby converge. Is it permissible to consider this juncture the point of origin of the infant's primal, rudimentary self? [1977, p. 99]

This hypothesis seems quite similar to Neumann's concept of the primal relationship: an instance when the self, or rather the functional sphere of the self, is incarnated in the mother (1973, p. 18). The mother is thou and self at the same time.

The earliest primal relationship with its mother is unique because here and practically only here the opposition between automorphous self development and thou relationship which otherwise fills all human existence with tension does not normally exist [Neumann, 1973, pp. 14–15]

According to Kohut, a coherent self evolves in the following way. First of all the infant's magical feelings of omnipotence and his spontaneous 'exhibitionistic' activity must be greeted with joy and empathic mirroring by a maternal self-object. 'The gleam in the mother's eye' has become a sort of formula which Kohut repeatedly uses to decribe this necessary condition. With the inevitable step by step frustration of its boundless needs, the child slowly learns to recognize its limitations, and thus its phantasies of omnipotence and need for admiration can gradually mature to become realistic ambitions and an adequate sense of self-esteem. When there is optimal frustration, the mother who (in accordance with her function as self-object) mirrors in an empathic way is progressively internalized and gradually becomes what Kohut calls a 'psychic structure'. In other words, optimal maternal empathy lays the foundations for a healthy feeling of self-esteem that allows one to take and protect a 'place in the sun' corresponding to one's personality; one is then neither obsessed with ambition nor inhibited, ashamed nor plagued with guilt about being 'seen', about being exposed. The need to be well 'regarded', to be someone of 'regard' in the world and to enjoy 'distinction' makes me think of how this need is originally related to 'the gleam in the mother's eye'.

We are all in continual need for recognition, of having our existence and our own worth acknowledged by others. As Eric Berne humorously formulated it, we need a certain measure of 'strokes' or 'stroking' (1964). Kohut is right in comparing emotional resonance with the oxygen we need for survival (1977, p. 253). When, however, someone is all too dependent on continual approval and admiration, when he becomes addicted to unceasing narcissistic supplies, then we can no longer speak of *healthy narcissism*. This rather indicates that his sense of self-esteem is unstable or disturbed and that a tendency to narcissistic vulnerability predominates; in such a condition the sense of the coherence of the self can from time to time be threatened.

The developmental lines of self formation that vitally need the empathic mirroring of a maternal self-object are what we normally consider as narcissistic. They are connected with the vital question of 'self-approval'.

But Kohut believes that something else also occurs during the formation of the self. Not only does the developing self want to be admired by the self-object; in its turn, it also admires the maternal or paternal self-object and experiences it as omnipotent and perfect. But as the self-object is hardly differentiated from the self's own world, its perfection also entails the self's own perfection. There is fusion with the idealized, seemingly omnipotent and perfect self-object. Progressive disappointment about the real parents' omnipotence, omniscience and perfection can, as we have said above, lead to their 'transmuting internalization' (Kohut, 1977). This is an important process that makes possible the formation of psychic structures forming the matrix of future ideals.

Whether an infant can survive physically and emotionally, can feel valued and 'whole', thus depends essentially on a good enough empathic attitude on the part of the self-object. The necessary process of gradual liberation from this dependency finally reaches its end when the system of parental values has been internalized in the structure of the super-ego—Kohut calls this 'the idealization of the super-ego' (1971)—that is, when the Oedipus complex has been overcome.

In other words, self esteem can also develop and be sustained when, out of fusion with the idealized self-object, ideals have been born that stimulate worthwhile commitment. There are, for example, always people engaged in minor or major tasks that transcend their immediate, personal needs, people who are completely devoted to greater or higher aims. Their conscious intention is by no means to raise their own sense of personal worth; rather, their devotion to greater matters—be they scientific, artistic, religious or social—seems to give their lives a certain transpersonal meaning. The fact that these matters might have their infantile roots in the idealization of a self-object is probably responsible for a well-known phenomenon: often these higher aims appear in personified form, embodied, for instance, in an admired and idealized person or in all kinds of charismatic leaders. Certainly commitment to matters transcending one's personal needs does not sound like what we normally call narcissism—on the contrary. And yet, the main purpose of such endeavours is maintaining narcissistic equilibrium. I feel, however, that the prejudiced term 'narcissism' is a bit out of place here. In his most recent book, Kohut replaces the expression 'narcissistic equilibrium' with a preferable term, 'the coherence of the self'. Thus we would say, the coherence of the self can also be attained by fusion with an idealized self-object; and, it can be maintained via the formation of ideals.

Jung is no doubt referring to similar phenomena when he speaks of the search for transpersonal meaning and of neurosis as the 'suffering of a soul which has not discovered its meaning' (*CW* 11, para. 497).

According to Kohut the archaic grandiose self and the archaic phantasies of omnipotence are gradually transformed. In a favourable development the result is the emergence of realistic ambitions and mature ideals. The self that emerges at the end of this development has to be considered as bipolar. There is, on the one hand, a pole of ambitious initiative that strives for admiration and, on the other, a pole consisting of meaningful goals and ideals. The tension span between the poles is regulated by the talents and skills a person possesses. This means that ideally both poles of the self operate together when vigorous, spontaneous energy is directed toward goals that the person feels are meaningful and worthwhile. It is, therefore, understandable that narcissistic personality disorders are often marked by a loss of energy, a sense of inner emptiness and general lack of interest.

Is then what Kohut considers 'the self, as centre of the psychological universe' the same as what analytical psychology understands under the concept of the self? At first sight it hardly seems so. Kohut's idea of the self seems more personalistic, close to what Jung means by ego, compared with what he means by self. And yet I must point out here that Kohut also speaks of what he calls 'cosmic narcissism' (1966), which transcends the boundaries of the individual: here wisdom would consist in reflecting on the finiteness of all being and on the transitoriness of individual existence. Furthermore, in Kohut's view, there is no original or primal self present at the time of birth (cf. Fordham, 1976, p. 12). According to Kohut the self has slowly to develop its coherence from a state which Freud called 'primary narcissism'. Here

Jungian psychology would rather say that the self is the *imperceptible,* central ordering factor responsible for psychic development, transformation and, at the same time, psychic balance. This might be the essential difference, if Kohut did not go on to say, among other things, that man's ultimate goal might be 'the realization, through his actions, of the blueprint for his life that had been laid down in his nuclear self' (1977, p. 133). And so we see that Kohut believes that the nucleus of the self has to do with a blueprint for life. And we are thus once again quite close to the Jungian idea of the individuation process. The parallel becomes even more apparent with Kohut's statement that 'the self, whatever the history of its formation, has become a centre of initiative: a unit that tries to follow its own course' (1977, p. 245). Furthermore, we have to remember here that Jung at different times considered the self as both the psychic totality *including* the ego and the archetypes *and* as also being the central archetype of order, distinct from the ego and perhaps from all the other archetypes. According to Fordham, those are two incompatible theories of the self that do not form an essential paradox, but merely create unnecessary confusion. He therefore suggests that a distinction be made: the term self would only be used to refer to psychic totality; otherwise the term central archetype of order would be preferred (Fordham, 1973).

I must admit that I am not quite sure whether those two theories of the self belong together as a paradox or not. Logically they are mutually exclusive, but we know that this has little meaning when we are dealing with the reality of the psyche. The distinction suggested by Fordham has the advantage of clarifying matters, but it has the disadvantage of separating out things that we may experience as belonging together. Yet Fordham argues that he is referring only to the place of the self in the *theoretical model* of the psyche and not to the *contents* of the self, which can, in accordance with experience, be stated paradoxically (1973, p. 34). For Jung, an essential aspect of the nature of the self lies in the fact that it cannot be clearly defined. And here again we find that Kohut has come to the same conclusion when he writes at the end of his book, *The Restoration of the Self,*

My investigation contains hundreds of pages dealing with the psychology of the self—yet it never assigns an inflexible meaning to the term self, it never explains how the essence of the self should be defined. But I admit this fact without contrition or shame. The self is ... not knowable in its essence. [1977, pp. 310–311]

For Kohut too, then, the self is many-faceted, and thus it more or less escapes definition. But in comparison with Jung, what is lacking is the wealth of symbolism and any *direct* reference to the religious experience which might be inherent in the self as God-image. For all his insights, Kohut remains here within the psychoanalytic tradition. Jung arrives at his insights mainly through his experience with, and amplification of, the wealth of images from the unconscious. Kohut's method is based on introspection and empathy with his patients' experience. It is, therefore, especially in the feeling realm of analytic practice that I find Kohut's observations, with the special attention they pay to transference–countertransference phenomena, most valuable.

But also here there are parallels with Jung's views. Kohut, for example, believes that the termination of analysis can be considered successful even if 'not all structural defects have been mobilized, worked through, and filled in through transmuting internalization' (1977, p. 48). Compensatory, creative solutions are also possible; as he says,

I have observed a number of patients who began to devote themselves during the terminal phase to some deeply absorbing creative endeavor. The evaluation of the analysand's total behaviour pattern—especially an attitude of quiet certitude— led me to the conclusion that the creativity of such patients ... is not a manifestation of a defensive manoeuvre meant to prevent the completion of the analytic process, but rather an indication that these analysands have at least preliminarily determined the mode by which the self will from now on attempt to ensure its cohesion, to maintain its balance, and to achieve its fulfilment. [1977, p. 38]

Fine and good, the analytical psychologist may say. Finally, a great psychoanalyst has come to realize what Jung discovered over fifty years ago. He may also get a bit angry and find it unfair that Jung is not even mentioned here. Is Kohut an opportunist who does not mention Jung for fear of stirring up his psychoanalytic colleagues' prejudices against his ideas? In not mentioning Jung is Kohut dressing in borrowed finery? I feel we should be careful in making such accusations. At any rate, we have to recognize the author's courage, the courage it takes to step beyond the relatively tabooed boundaries of psychoanalytic theory. And I feel we can believe the author when he says that there would have been 'only one way out of the morass, of conflicting, poorly based, and often vague theoretical speculation' (1977, p. xx). The only way to progress was 'the way back to the direct observation of clinical phenomena and the construction of new formulations that would accommodate [his] findings' (ibid., pp. xx–xxi). Kohut wanted to present these findings without having first to compare them with other theories of psychology. In a similar vein, Jung says that in the lack of orientation he faced after his separation from Freud, he decided first of all, before formulating any hypotheses, to wait and see what the patients had to say for themselves (1963, p. 165). I am impressed by the closeness of the parallel.

I personally find Kohut's works so interesting precisely because he does not simply repeat Jungian ideas: but, rather, with a completely different approach, he comes up with similar results. This is much more valuable for the analytical psychologist; it is encouraging and stimulating at the same time.

In any case, Kohut's theoretical views lead to innovations in psychoanalytic techniques that partially coincide with, or at least can be correlated with, those of analytical psychology. From Kohut's findings it becomes clear that empathic understanding of the patient's concerns is the most important therapeutic agent.

Such a view seems to stand in contradiction to Freud's famous dictum that analysts should 'model themselves during psychoanalytic treatment on the surgeon, who puts aside all his feelings, even his human sympathy' (1912, p. 115). In order to relieve the psychoanalyst of any and all guilt feelings he may have when not following this dictum, Kohut quotes passages in Freud's later correspondence where he informally expresses views that are clearly at variance with the injunction cited above (1977, p. 255). Kohut rightly feels that neutrality on the part of the analyst is not to be equated with minimal response. In his opinion, a lot of a patient's resistances may be due to a 'certain stiffness, artificiality and strait-laced reserve' in the analyst whose attitude does not provide the essential 'empathic resonance' (ibid., p. 255). The extent to which this empathic resonance is of greater concern to

Kohut than adhering to any strict and sancitifed rules can be seen in the following quotation:

> If, for example, a patient's insistent questions are the transference manifestations of infantile sexual curiosity, this mobilized childhood reaction will not be short-circuited, but, on the contrary, will delineate itself with greater clarity if the analyst, by *first replying* to the questions and only later pointing out that his replies did not satisfy the patient, does not create artificial rejections of the analysand's need for empathic responsiveness. [1977, pp. 252–253]

As I have already said, I find comparisons with Kohut that merely stress the superiorities of Jungian psychology of little interest. Instead of pointing out how unoriginal all of this is and how much has already been said by Jung—at least fifty years beforehand—I feel that Jungian psychology is basically open enough to be able to integrate some of the results of Kohut's findings. I have found this to be a profitable way of refining one's own therapeutic procedure. (This is obviously true not only of Kohut but also of various other approaches according to the specific needs of each individual case.)

In practice I particularly see the usefulness of the two transference–countertransference models related to the bi-polar self. As is well known, Kohut differentiates between mirror transference and idealizing transference. In the first case the analysand expects the analyst to provide empathic resonance to his very being, a yearning for 'the gleam in the mother's eye'. The idealizing transference, on the other hand, stems from the analysand's need to merge with the seemingly omniscient and omnipotent self-object projected on to the analyst.

I would like here to give a practical example of how these two transference–countertransference configurations can be experienced. During three consecutive sessions with an analysand, a woman of about forty, I felt so tired that I had to fight off sleep. The 'ideal analyst' in me did not like this at all, but the fact that it happened three times made me realize that it was probably a syntonic countertransference reaction (Fordham, 1974). But what did it mean? The problem could not have been what my patient was talking about. The subjects were interesting enough, even though they were presented in a bit too much detail.

When this incidence of fatigue occurred, my patient had been in analysis with me for four years. She had come because of a symptom that was extremely embarrassing for her: she could not pick up a glass of wine, a cup of coffee or a spoon in the presence of other people without her whole arm's starting to tremble. This made her feel terribly exposed and flooded with shame; consequently, she tended more and more to avoid being with people. She was increasingly afraid and ashamed of being exposed and getting into such a state.

And yet, my patient was greatly gifted in listening to and understanding others; her empathy—a trait which Kohut usually finds lacking in narcissistic personality disorders—was very well developed. This gift must have been furthered by the fact that, from her earliest childhood on, she had been forced to develop an extreme sensitivity in order to adapt to her mother's constant expectations; it was the only way she could get at least a minimum of vitally needed attention from that obviously narcissistically disturbed woman. Later on in life she continued to give other people's needs priority over her own; whenever she could not fulfil someone's expectations, she was tormented by very intense guilt feelings.

In analysis too she tried to adapt to 'my expectations', and she tremendously idealized my 'spiritual side'. For her this idealization meant having to provide me with important dreams and interesting subject matter. Whenever she failed to do so, she felt very frightened, ashamed and inferior, and had a sense of inner emptiness. At such moments it was clear that fusion with the idealized self-object, i.e. with the so highly prized 'spiritual principle', had failed once again. On the whole, my patient showed a lively interest in the analysis, co-operated well, was intelligent and had a highly differentiated feeling for psychological connections. As she was such a tactful person, her admiration for me did not feel too intrusive. The stress laid on the spiritual was not too obviously a mere defence against the erotic component, but seemed to correspond to a genuine need in her. And so, in the countertransference thus far I had felt on the whole animated by her presence and full of ideas for possible interpretations. Occasionally, however, I found myself delivering lengthy, very knowledgeable explanations. Still my analysand seemed to feel nourished and enriched by such discussions, although she sometimes feared that on her way home she would forget all the interesting things she had learned.

As far as her symptoms were concerned, with time there was definite improvement. But we were both aware of the fact that her continuing tendency to feel easily hurt and embarrassed still prevented her from being really spontaneous. I must add here, however, that at this stage of the analysis she no longer hesitated to expose herself to a large team and even to her superiors whenever she felt she had to stand up and fight for an important *cause*. At such times she had the feeling she was borne on by some transpersonal, spiritual ideal—probably a sign of fusion with an idealized self-object. But going to a restaurant and drinking a cup of coffee with the same people still cost her tremendous efforts in trying to overcome her fears of exposure.

I could not shake off her idealizing transference and interpret it as 'mere compensation'; it was a matter of too vital concern for her. Kohut finds it important for the analyst to embody the idealized transference figure for a certain time. The analysand's disappointment that the analyst does not correspond to the ideal phantasy figure, and that has to take place gradually, stimulates the process of transmuting internalization. In Jungian terms we would say the analysand can take back the projections: the projected content is recognized as intra-psychic and can be partially integrated. My analysand too began to express some criticism towards me; from the standpoint of the therapy I welcomed her new courage.

But what did my repeated attacks of sleepiness mean? The third time this countertransference reaction occurred, I decided not to fight it off, but to discuss it in some way with my analysand. Given her vulnerability, I obviously could not state the problem directly and tell her she evidently bored me to the point of sleep. What I did ask her was if at the moment she might have the feeling that she was far away, or even isolated from me. And, in fact, she was then able to say that she had the impression she was babbling about completely uninteresting things and could naturally not expect me to be interested; consequently, she felt more and more unsure of herself. What she said meant, in other words, that when she did not have my empathic resonance she felt rejected and worthless. Further analysis of our situation showed that she found herself constantly having to fend off an ever-increasing need: a deep yearning for a mirroring self-object. This need had been deeply buried and was now slowly coming to light. It was a need to be seen and admired—that is, to experience 'the gleam in the mother's eye'. However, as it was connected with early traumatic memories of disappointment, it was coupled with fear and had had to be repressed. Therefore, all she could consciously experience at this stage of the analysis was intensified fears of not meeting up to my expectations and boring me. As my sleepiness shows, she did manage to bore me and thus to turn me into the unempathic, rejecting maternal figure; at the same time she was unable, even by the most timid of signs, to communicate to me her real need for a mirroring self-object. Our efforts at interpreting the emerging mirror transference helped her to express herself more freely whenever she felt that I had misunderstood her, hurt or rejected her. This was the beginning of further progress on the way towards self-assertion and overcoming her symptoms.

Generally speaking, it must be said here that in our society the need for praise, recognition and admiration is usually masked and can only be expressed indirectly. Narcissism is considered as something negative. As the saying goes, 'self praise is no recommendation'; one should be meek and humble in the true Christian way. Narcissistic needs often have something embarrassing about them, and most people today can speak more openly about their sexual problems than about their narcissistic ones. Those who do not hesitate to show off and are not shy in displaying narcissistic enjoyment therefore often attract typical shadow projections—a combination of rejection, envy and secret admiration. In keeping with its nature, narcissistic 'orgasm' is triggered by the beautiful self-image in the mirror, that is, by admiring applause. That is the reason why it tends to seek release not in the intimacy of a quiet little room, but in public. But 'public orgasm', if I may call it that, can only be really enjoyed by true exhibitionists; a lot of narcissistic orgies are only allowed to exist in the secret realm of phantasy. As an example of the conflict involved in narcissistic enjoyment, I can think of a relatively well-known playwright with a nearly insatiable greed for narcissistic supplies of praise and admiration, who was at the same time extremely touchy about the slightest criticism. One day a work of his was performed at a very important festival. When it had been duly applauded, he stood in the artists' box, anxious for admiring attention. And yet, when people congratulated him on his success, he was so embarrassed that he could not look them in the eye. This, in turn, was not very encouraging for those trying to congratulate him. Another playwright once told me it always took him weeks to recover from a success and the emotional turmoil it brought with it, and to find himself again. It seems to me that in such cases we can speak of what Kohut calls the discomfort caused by an 'influx of narcissistic–exhibitionistic libido' (1971).

For an analyst, also, it is not necessarily easy to cope with the boundless admiration he receives in idealizing transferences. On the one hand, such transferences tend to constellate the analyst's fears of being flooded in an embarrassing way with his own latent phantasies of omnipotence (Kohut's 'grandiose self'). On the other hand, he may feel under great pressure not to disappoint his patient's idealized expectations. Thus, the analyst may in his turn unconsciously experience his patient as a self-object whose idealizing admiration he needs intensely for his own narcissistic balance. In addition to this, it can be extremely embarrassing for the analyst to have to realize the tremendous pleasure he gets from being seen as such an admired and idealized person. This does not mean that he cannot at the same time be narcissistically hurt when the patient's disappointment slowly leads to the withdrawal of projections and the analyst finds himself no longer so deeply loved, admired and needed. However, as this is usually a good sign for the analytic process, the analyst's narcissistic needs can find a certain compensation in the form of heightened professional self-esteem.

This might be the reason why training candidates are often so reluctant about even raising the subject of the transference with their patients. They are afraid their patients might find them conceited and narcissistic; unconsciously they often confuse their possible importance as a transference figure with their personal importance. Consequently, there is a lot of beating about the bush on this matter. This is perhaps not the case for candidates of the London group, where the interpretation of the transference is 'the fulcrum of analysis' (Gordon, 1974). And yet I can imagine that it takes a lot of narcissistic investment to attain such a high level of sensitivity in dealing with the transference; keeping at bay feelings of grandiosity or inferiority must, therefore, also somehow be involved. One cannot deny how important it is for an analyst to come to terms with his own narcissistic needs and phantasies, lest they become counterproductive for his patients. In the attempt to find a *modus vivendi* with one's grandiose self, I can favourably recommend another one of Kohut's suggestions, namely the development of humour. I truly believe that tolerant humour is the best way to deal with the drive-like demands of the grandiose self. If I can accept with a good portion of humour the side in me that would so much like to be omniscient, omnipotent, world-famous and loved by all, then a great deal of inhibiting, complex-laden embarrassment can be overcome. I then acknowledge the existence of such phantasies and, to a certain extent, let them have their due; at the same time, however, I can consider them with a certain measure of humorous detachment.

It must also be noted here that in numerous places in his writings Jung shows a rather negative, even moralistic, attitude towards narcissistic needs—for example, where he says,

> The more we become conscious of ourselves through self-knowledge, and act accordingly, the more the layer of the personal unconscious that is superimposed on the collective unconscious will be diminished. In this way there arises a consciousness which is no longer imprisoned in the petty, oversensitive, personal world of the ego, but participates freely in the wider world of objective interests. This widened consciousness is no longer that touchy, egotistical bundle of personal wishes, fears, hopes, and ambitions which always has to be compensated or corrected by unconscious counter-tendencies; instead, it is a function of relationship to the world of objects, bringing the individual into absolute binding, and indissoluble communion with the world at large. [*CW* 7, para. 275]

One of the ideals of Jungian analysis is, therefore, overcoming and outgrowing this personal, touchy 'ego world' as quickly as possible in order to get onto the real, deep and numinous dimensions of the self in the collective unconscious. Analysts and also patients who have read Jung often work with this ideal in mind. They consider it less important to analyse contents that seem to belong 'only' to the personal unconscious and are seemingly unaware of the consequent danger: that these contents actually remain unconscious and intensify the shadow problem.

In Kohut's terminology the goal of this ideal of Jungian analysis would be bringing to life the compensatory structure of the self via fusion with an idealized self-object. In other words, what usually happens is fusion with an idealized 'Jung' and his ideas about the wonder world of the collective unconscious. It is true that in many cases the compensatory structure can contribute to a certain 'restoration of the self'. But often it seems rather to be a defensive structure against the primary defect. At any event, we know that people who have, for a long time, been moving in 'the deepest waters of the unconscious' do frequently still show notable signs of narcissistic vulnerability.

In this chapter I have attempted to investigate some trends in the practice of analytical psychology from the standpoint of Kohut and not the opposite, i.e. to examine Kohut's theses in the light of Jungian psychology. I think that travelling is very important, in so far as one can do so with open eyes and not with blinkers that only help to prove how much better everything is at home. Travelling makes comparisons possible, offers new perspectives that can help one to see the specific traits of one's own country more clearly. My approach does not mean that I completely identify with Kohut—at least I hope not.

There has already been one attempt at interpreting Jung's personal psychology as well as his ideas on psychology largely in the context of Kohut's concepts (Homans, 1979). Although this undertaking shed some new light on many problems, I feel it was only partially successful. My own approach is rather related to the question of whether integrating some of Kohut's ideas in analytic practice might not be helpful in refining our therapeutic tools for the benefit of our patients.

Summary

This chapter deals with some of the astonishing similarities between Heinz Kohut's theories on narcissism and many basic views of C. G. Jung. As in his last book Kohut places the self as the 'centre of the psychological universe', those similarities have become even closer and call for a differentiated comparison. Kohut seems to have arrived at his conclusions independently, by his own observations, without reference to Jung. There are many of his subtle insights which can also be used fruitfully in the practice of an analytical psychologist—as a case example tries to show. The chapter, furthermore, contains some reflections on the taboos of many narcissistic needs in our society. It finally deals with some difficulties that can be inflicted by the 'grandiose self' also upon the analyst.

REFERENCES

Berne, E. (1964). *Games People Play*. New York: Grove Press.

Fordham, M. (1973). The empirical foundation and theories of the self in Jung's works. In *Analytical Psychology: a Modern Science*. Library of Analytical Psychology, Vol. 1. London: Karnac Books.

———— (1974). Notes on the transference. In *Technique in Jungian Analysis*. Library of Analytical Psychology, Vol. 2. [Reprinted 1989, with corrections and new introduction by J. Hubback.] London: Karnac Books.

———— (1976). *The Self and Autism*. Library of Analytical Psychology, Vol. 3. London: Karnac Books.

Freud, S. (1912). Recommendations to physicians practising psychoanalysis, *Standard Edition 12*. London: Hogarth.

Gordon, R. (1974). Transference as the fulcrum of analysis. In *Technique in Jungian Analysis*. Library of Analytical Psychology, Vol. 2. [Reprinted 1989, with corrections and new introduction by J. Hubback.] London: Karnac Books.

Hartmann, H. (1964). Comments on the psychoanalytic theory of the ego. In *Essays on Ego-Psychology*. New York: International Universities Press.

Homans, P. (1979). *Jung in Context*. Chicago: University of Chicago Press.

Jung, C. G. (1963). *Memories, Dreams, Reflections*. London: Collins and Routledge & Kegan Paul.

Kohut, H. (1966). Forms and transformations of narcissism. *Journal of the American Psychoanalytical Association 14*, 243–272.

———— (1971). *The Analysis of the Self*. New York: International Universities Press.

———— (1972). Thoughts on narcissism and narcissistic rage. In *The Psychoanalytic Study of the Child, 27* (pp. 360–400). New York: Quadrangle.

———— (1977). *The Restoration of the Self*. New York: International Universities Press.

Neumann, E. (1973). *The Child*. New York: G. P. Putnam's Sons. [Reprinted 1988, London: Maresfield Press.]

CHAPTER EIGHT

The borderline personality: vision and healing

Nathan Schwartz-Salant

Herein, with a wealth of clinical material, Schwartz-Salant demonstrates the use of the concept of the 'unconscious dyad' in analysis. This leads to a sophisticated reframing of the coniunctio to suggest the multi-leveled dynamics of an interactive field. Such dynamics are specifically stated by Schwartz-Salant to go beyond the personal realm.

A further technical innovation is the idea of 'imaginal sight'. This way of relating to the patient and the clinical material makes explicit what many analysts probably do—but they do so implicitly, hence at a lower level of conscious awareness.

Schwartz-Salant's twinning of the 'logic' of the borderline patient with a particular mystical tradition serves to prevent any simplistic pathologizing. The borderline patient is presented, to a degree, as Everyman or Everywoman.

First published in *Chiron,* 1988; also forms part of a book, *The Borderline Personality: Vision and Healing* (Wilmette, IL: Chiron Publications, 1989). Published here by kind permission of the author and Chiron Publications.

The many references to the Rosarium *or the* Rosarium Philosophorum *refer to Jung's commentary on an illustrated alchemical tract of the sixteenth century. The pictures of the* Rosarium *are numbered, and the whole work, entitled* The Psychology of the Transference, *is found in Volume 16 of Jung's Collected Works. Jung thought that alchemy, looked at with a symbolic and not a scientific eye, could be regarded as one of the precursors of modern study of the unconscious and, in particular, of analytical interest in the transformation of personality.*

A.S.

The field of battle is the hearts of people.
[Dostoevsky, *The Brothers Karamazov*]

Introduction

Although experiences with borderline patients can be understood in terms of transference or countertransference projections that repeat early continual traumas (Khan, 1974) and developmental failures, this is nevertheless a faltering perspective. In this chapter I also envision my experiences in terms of field dynamics that engage atemporal forms. These field experiences are larger in scale than purely personal dynamics comprised of our mutual projections.[1] For in some mysterious way our interaction constellates, creates or discovers—no one word will do—some 'third thing'. Jung's description of the alchemical god Mercurius is apt: 'The elusive, deceptive, ever-changing content that possesses the patient like a demon now flits about from patient to doctor and, as the third party in the alliance, continues its game. . . .' (*CW* 16, para. 384).

We can say that the archetypal transference is constellated by the reactivation of early introjects in the transference and countertransference, and that this new material projects outward to yield the wondrous imagery of hermaphrodites, the combined

or double-sided objects that Jung's alchemical research illuminated. But are we simply dealing with a replay of earliest
infant–mother interactions where 'archetypal' and 'personal'
designations are of little value (Eigen, 1986a; 1986b, pp. 59ff), or
are these new processes and energy fields that are not reducible
to infant or even prenatal life? This is a crucial theoretical
crossroad, for therapists who believe that experiences in
psychotherapy replicate early failed or aborted developmental
experiences would do well to consider whether theoretical pursuit
alone is adequate to the nature of the psyche and its archetypal or
objective dimension. Often psychotherapy reveals bewildering
and bizarre introjects stemming from the patient's early childhood experiences. The therapist then identifies these through
reflecting upon fusion states and participation in projective
identification. But this approach is too limiting. An imaginal
focus is required if one is to engage the borderline person
effectively. The therapist must begin to think differently—that
is, he or she must imaginally focus upon interactive fields that
are structured by atemporal forms (Levi-Strauss, 1967, p. 198).

The interactive field can be comprehended only as 'third
presence', which often takes the form of an unconscious dyad; it
should not be viewed through a structural model of projections
that must be integrated. The object relations model is not
unimportant; its value is unquestionable. But though it is
indispensable, by itself it is insufficient. Both models are
required: the projection model that is concerned with early
developmental issues *and* the imaginal model that incorporates
the alchemical imagery of the *coniunctio* and its attending
stages.[2] We need to adopt a model that is two-sided, one aspect
pointing toward a space–time world and the other toward a
unitary world structured by archetypal processes. These two
aspects intertwine. They cannot and should not be split into
separate and opposing categories of 'personal' and 'archetypal'.
The unconscious dyad may be seen as stemming from both the
patient and the therapist *while also being* part of a larger,
interactive field. Once it is sufficiently *seen* and experienced, the
unconscious couple can eventually lead the patient and therapist
to an experience of union. This union experience is precisely what
the borderline person lacks.

Discovering the borderline patient's unconscious dyad: projections and field dynamics

'Ed' was an exceptionally intelligent and multi-talented 38-year-old man. He entered treatment for several reasons. He employed his intellectual and creative gifts only marginally in his career; in general, he was plagued by a lack of purpose and commitment to any goal. Other people were getting along in life, and he was not. A major theme in his life was an obsession with actions that others had taken toward him which he often found to be immoral; he was also absorbed with his own behaviour, of which he was a keen critic. He would spend hours alone engrossed in wondering why someone treated him as they had, or why he was so emotionally paralysed and unable to be forthright during some interaction with another person whose malevolence would later become quite evident to him.

At the outset of our work Ed seemed to be suffering from a narcissistic character disorder. An idealized transference combined with the controlling dynamics of his grandiose–exhibitionistic self was present, so that I felt compelled to have answers to his questions (Schwartz-Salant, 1982, pp. 50 ff.). My responses were usually well received, but I had an uncomfortable sense that he was trying very hard to be open to me and was merely being polite. It was soon clear that his narcissistic character formation was a defense against a deep and chaotic part of his personality. His transference did not differentiate into idealized and grandiose–exhibitionistic strands as it might have if he had had a narcissistic character.

My work with Ed demonstrates a complex interactive field (which to one degree or another is always present in the treatment of the borderline patient), that is exceptionally difficult to apprehend. In fact, my compulsion to act out a pattern of unrelatedness—by talking without much reflection—could at times nearly nullify my observing ego, and his as well. During these periods all my attempts to bring coherence or consciousness to the session only led to rôle reversals and often resulted in pain for both of us. I then felt my own pressure to 'get it right'; often I could not remain quiet. Instead, I would attempt to make interpretations, though even scant reflection would have shown me that I had only shallow comments to make. During these times, however, I was not disposed to self-reflection, but would proceed with my commentary, all the while feeling dull-witted and hoping that what I had to say would be accepted. As Ed was intent upon being truthful, he did not accept this behaviour from me. He had suffered too many years of being tortured by frustrated mental and creative gifts and previous unsuccessful therapeutic experiences to allow our work to fail, too.

Often, I felt that Ed was the truth-seeker, whereas I was the liar, just barely able to survive. Survive what? That is not easy to describe, but I can say that soon after our work began and the strength of his narcissistic transferences diminished, our unconscious psyches became meshed together in such a way that a searing and tormenting energy field was established that nearly destroyed my capacity to think and reflect. Each time Ed arrived, I would have a brief period of optimism and feel that we might establish a good connection and proceed with our work. I would then become emotionally and physically limp, and it would be difficult for me simply to remain embodied and be with him. Instead, I usually felt obliged to talk, and thus to *act* rather than *be*. Often I could not tolerate the absence of meaningful content between us, and sometimes I was frightened of this man. At times, I felt that he might strike me, but my more usual afflicted state was one in which I believed that he was the one dedicated to the truth and that I was a fraud. This stance was unchallenged by Ed's torment about being the subject of his own lies, especially the denial and distrust of his perceptions.

For over a year we could barely relate to one another, though there were many desperate attempts to create a sense of connection. During this period, my work with Ed primarily consisted of my showing him that I could survive amidst his attacks. Every word I used, each tone of expression I chose, came under his scrutiny. During this process, Ed began to form a growing alliance with me. One day, he spoke of some reading he had been doing and, to my surprise, asked about the nature of our unconscious couple. This represented a crucial shift in his psyche toward an attitude of more cooperation in the therapy; I was then able to reflect imaginatively upon what might be structuring our interactive field. I arrived at a hypothesis that made sense to both of us: that a couple who did not want union was our major obstacle. The state of non-union (depicted, for example, in picture seven of the *Rosarium,* 'The Extraction of the Soul', *CW* 16, para. 476) is described by Jung as a loss of the soul, and has a similar impact to that of a schizophrenic dissociation. Our *soul-less* interaction manifested in ways that seemed to catapult us into completely different universes. At such times, I would believe that we were actually relating well to each other, yet we were actually not communicating at all. Upon reflection it became clear that my interpretations were strained; I wasn't connected to him and had been speaking to avoid the pain of emptiness, despair and a feeling of impotence. In fact, the level of dissociative intent was so profound that we each might as well have been talking to ourselves.

The *Rosarium,* commenting upon picture seven, offers the following recipe for healing this disconnected state:

> Take the brain ... and grind it in most sharp vinegar, or in children's urine until it is obscured, and this being begun again as I have written it, may again be mortifed as before. . . . He therefore that maketh the earth black shall come to his purpose and it shall go well with him. [McLean, 1980, p. 45]

Notably, the *Rosarium* also adds that in searching for this black earth 'many men have perished' (ibid.).

'Grinding the brain in sharp vinegar' is by no means a poor metaphor for the way I functioned with this man, and he with me. Many of his nights were spent trying to recover from sessions that destroyed his ability to think and left him totally confused and enraged. The *Rosarium* implies that there is a purpose to the tormented states of mind that afflicted both of us. This purpose is suggested by the creation of the hermaphrodite (picture ten, 'The Rebis', *CW* 16, para. 525). The alchemical Rebis is a combined male–female object and represents the creation of a fertile and stable interactive field. But illustration seven, 'The Ascent of the Soul' (*CW* 16, para. 475), warns of a great danger—perhaps the death of the therapy, and perhaps activation of the patient's tendencies towards self-destruction, a possibility that always exists with the borderline patient when levels of extreme dissociation and despair are engaged. In Ed's and my work together, there was some ground for believing that the states to which we were subject had some purpose; it was equally clear that our *nigredo* would not become fruitful if our therapy process were to be dominated by acting-out and unconsciousness.

Over the course of many trying sessions that took place within a period of approximately two years, the nature of our problem began to emerge. Our interaction was structured by an unconscious couple dominated by a drive for non-union; each half of the couple desired to destroy the other through lies and malicious envy. At the same time, the parts that comprised this couple were stubbornly and inextricably bound to each other. Thus our interaction was dominated by the characteristic borderline quality of simultaneous drives toward fusion and separation, which together produced great confusion.

As a very young child Ed had experienced his parents in ways that resembled the dynamics of this dyad. He recalled feeling persecuted by his parents' false implications that they actually *saw* him and had his best interests at heart. Over and over again, he would be perplexed by their antagonistic behaviour towards one another and their destructive fraud and deception towards him. Apparently, they had functioned as a double-sided object, each half contributing to this persecuting dyad. The young, extremely intelligent and sensitive child would earnestly lecture them on their behaviour and would be repeatedly upset and unhinged by the accumulating knowledge that he had had no effect at all, except as it rebounded onto him in the form of his father's rage or his mother's martyrdom.

This unconscious parental dyad had been split off from his otherwise normally functioning personality in order that Ed could survive. Consequently, he developed the typical borderline split between a normal-neurotic and a psychotic personality—a split that was also a fusion state. James Grotstein writes:

> In approaching a psychoanalytic conception of the borderline I should like to offer the following understanding: What seems to give the borderline personality (and borderline state) its uniqueness in differentiating itself from psychoses on one hand and neuroses on the other is not so much its midplace on the spectrum but is instead a qualitative difference. This qualitative difference is characterized, in my opinion, by the presence of a psychotic personality organization *and* a normal or neurotic personality organization which have undergone a unique interpenetration with each other so that a new amalgam emerges which can well be stated as 'psychotically neurotic' or 'neurotically psychotic'. It is as if a collusive symbiosis exists between these two twin personalities which

allows for an unusual tenacity, stability, and cohesion compared to psychotic states generally. [1979, p. 150]

When Ed's defensive-idealized transference waned, his psychotic
parts (largely conveyed by the unconscious dyad) entered the
therapy process and nearly usurped it. This led to what could be
called a transference and countertransference psychosis; its
intensity was extreme. Yet unless therapy contains a transference psychosis (and a countertransference psychosis as well,
though hopefully to a lesser degree), there is little chance of
healing the borderline person. By countertransference psychosis I
do not imply the therapist's blatant loss of reality or decompensa-
tion, but rather the emergence of parts of his or her personality
that are unintegrated, thus having an autonomy beyond the
organizing domain of the self. These 'mad parts' of the therapist
can take over the therapy in subtle and diverse ways—the patient
may introject them and begin to act quite mad, even to the point
of engaging dangerous situations in the outer world. For
example, after a therapist had seductively shared his personal
material with a borderline patient, the patient dreamt that he
was being driven in a vehicle by a madman. The patient's
outer-life situation reflected this psychic state: as a result of his
irrational behaviour he was nearly fired from his job. This
sequence was a consequence of the therapist's denial of his own
psychotic parts—unintegrated and compulsive qualities of his
personality—which he was 'sharing' in the hope of creating a
'holding environment'.

To convey the extent to which Ed and I were dominated by an
unconscious dyad, I will relate material taken from sessions that
took place two years after our work had begun. At this time, Ed
dreamed that he was gently embracing two women, one black, the
other white. I understood this to be the image of a combining
state, which I, too, could now carry in projection because there
had been sufficient reparation on my part for previous analytical
errors (for example, talking too much and acting rather than
being embodied). I felt that he thought me more reliable than
heretofore; it seemed to me he was no longer obliged to split me
up into 'good' and 'bad' parts, which he had to scan from both a
conscious and an unconscious perspective.

The dream of the two women was soon followed by another in which he and another man, whom he associated with me, were flying in an aeroplane very close to the ground in order to gain a view of the earth below. At first, the other man was guiding the vehicle, but then the patient was taught by the man to guide it himself. This dream seemed to indicate that the therapy was now based on mutual cooperation. Indicative of the potential of our interactive field was the emergent image of a fruitful coital couple. The dream image of the aeroplane symbolizes a vessel; as this vessel hovers near the earth, we can say that the image indicates both spirit and a capacity for a solid therapeutic alliance. Such understanding had been sorely lacking during the prior two years; Ed had suffered as a consequence and had taken great pains to make me understand that I was *the* cause of his great distress.

Soon after this dream, I was surprised to find Ed once again in a state of extreme agitation and doubt about my role as therapist and about the therapy itself. Yet this was no cause for surprise. My desire to see our process progressing and free of Ed's searing criticism was a tendency that, he said, 'drives me crazy'. His comment led me to examine why I was driving him crazy, and whether or not I wanted to do such a thing to him. To use his phrase, which I found unpleasantly apt: why was I (again) 'operating in bad faith?' But, before the examination could proceed, a row occurred that left both of us in a state of doubt over whether or not it would be possible to continue therapy.

I will be specific about the session in question. Ed arrived on time, and even before sitting down asked me a question about a previous remark I had made. His question felt like an attack, although it was not expressed angrily; I became very defensive. But my response was far stronger than usual; I lost sight of my defensiveness as I felt my body fill with an agitation that was disintegrating in its affect. It seemed that my insides were under an attack of global nature. I was anxious, inwardly shaking; at the same time I found myself trying to act as if everything were okay. In effect, I was denying the state of non-union that existed both between us and within myself. Clearly, I was behaving in a borderline way. I had previously experienced this state with him, though not so intensely as in this experience. The accusation of operating in 'bad faith' always appeared as a reaction to this kind of behaviour. The seriousness and prominence of this accusation gradually increased during the course of the therapy.

The session I am describing cannot be understood without a clear comprehension of the evolution of this theme. In this instance, the illusion that a viable and helpful connection now existed between Ed and myself was part of the underlying deceit; the fact was that in significant ways I did not want an emotional contact with him. The awareness of my desire *not* to have any form of union with Ed was slow in arriving; in retrospect, I am both chagrined and astonished at the ingenuity of the tactics I employed to avoid this discovery. Certainly, a subjective counter-transference was present, but much more was operative in this interaction. There was a field-quality inherent in our process in which non-union was the main ingredient.

One of my unconscious strategies to avoid contact with Ed was to remain anxious. My fear of the malignant energy field, evoked by our mutual presence, would thereby allow *him* to take the lead in understanding any material the therapy process was engaging. When I was at my worst, I would present Ed with an extremely toxic double bind by denying the madness between us and electing to see him (and, by implication myself) as possessing strength and adeptness, qualities carried by the normal-neurotic self. I often found myself dull and unable to think clearly. Worse, I would find myself immersed in an imaginative and creative void, a leaden state that combined heavy Saturnian authority and the compulsion 'to know'. In contrast, Ed would seem bright, sharp and intelligent. It was as if his ownership of these qualities meant that they were unavailable to others—specifically, to me. I would submit to the sense of having lost all acuity, all creative energy. In any other case I had at the time I would have capably employed these countertransferential reactions syntonically and unearthed an 'other side' of chaos, despair and helplessness; in this case, I did not. Nor did I recognize that Ed needed me to be able to think with him, if not for him. I later came to realize that there was a *choice* involved in this profound countertransference, though this choice was not evident to me at the time. Leon Grinberg has described the course of this countertransference as follows:

From a structural point of view, one may say that what is projected by means of the psychotic mechanism of projective identification operates within the object as a parasitic super-ego, which omnipotently induces the analyst's ego to act or feel what the patient in his fantasy wants him to feel or act. I think that this, to some degree, bears comparison with the dynamics of hypnosis as described by Freud. According to Freud, the hypnotizer places himself in the position of the ego ideal, and hypnotic submissiveness is of a masochistic nature. Freud further holds that in the hypnotic relation a sort of paralysis appears as a result of the influence of the omnipotent individual upon an importent and helpless being. I believe the same applies to the processes I am discussing in that the analyst, being unaware of what happened, may later rationalize his action, as the hypnotized person does after executing the hypnotic command. By means of the mechanisms of obsessive control, the inducing subject continues to control what he projected onto the induced object. The subject's omnipotent fantasies thus acquire some consistency, as they seem confirmed by the object's response. [1977, pp. 128–129]

In time, I began to shake myself out of this hypnotic involvement with the patient and was able to recognize this state of non-union. This emerging awareness, combined with Ed's concerted efforts to contain me, resulted in redeeming the therapy.

I have emphasized that I 'chose' non-union because I have no doubt that a choice was involved, although I was unaware of it at the time. But the fact that a choice existed meant that a moral issue was involved: I had lied to Ed about understanding him, and about being in the same psychological universe with him. I must emphasize the aptness of his complaint that I was acting in bad faith; the recognition of its truth was shocking. My self-image had been that I was a person who deeply wanted union—indeed, who held it in the highest esteem.

It was against this background that I was finally able to recover my bearings in the therapy. It was abundantly clear that transferential elements were involved and that my behaviour was a representation of Ed's interaction with his mother and father, and particularly with the parental couple that their psyches evoked: a couple in intense, antagonistic disunion, each out to destroy the other through envy and hatred. My bad faith

and lies reflect his parental experience. The state of being
overwhelmed and barely able to retain my thoughts replicates his
feelings when his parents continually denied his perceptions. His
parents also represented deceitful behaviour, of which he was
certainly capable—indeed, he could treat his friends and
acquaintances with the very lack of truthfulness that he found so
distressing in others. But I, too, was driven to behave in immoral
ways; and while I can attribute this compulsion to countertransferential acting out, which it certainly was—especially the
resistance of experiencing despair—something else was involved.
We were both participants in a process that was not merely a
repetition of past history but was also a creation in its own right.

In my therapeutic work with Ed I was often thrust into a
masochistic position.[3] In part, this was a matter of choice, based
upon my belief that the borderline person *sees* what the therapist
does not wish to be seen. By acknowledging Ed's perceptions (for
example, that I had *chosen* to act in ways injurious to him), I was
obliged to recognize unconscious shadow aspects of my personality that I had allowed to guide my behaviour. This helped him to
begin to gain faith in the correctness of his perceptions. I could
easily have dismissed his complaint as a paranoid distortion
which was picking up a shred of truth. This perception would
have been comforting to me, but very undermining of Ed.

I also wish to note that there were times, though perhaps too
few of them, when I reacted to Ed in ways that were not
masochistic. For instance, at times I expressed how much I hated
the way he was treating me, especially his criticism of my words
and behaviour, which he mercilessly scrutinized as being careless
and incompetent. This expression of hatred was possible—and
was not assaultive—when I could feel how much his attacks (even
though they may have been premised upon truth), were painful
and frightening to the small child within me. I was standing up
for this child when I could talk about my hatred without
attacking Ed. Indeed, this direct response was a relief to Ed, for it
showed that I was real and perhaps even trustworthy, despite the
fact that a good deal of what occurred between us was dominated
by an intense drive to disrupt contact.

The clinical material that relates to this patient depicts some
of the more difficult aspects I have encountered when treating the
borderline person. It is impossible to separate clearly the personal

transference and countertransference from the archetypal field dynamics that are so richly constellated within these levels of treatment. The therapist treating the borderline patient must acknowledge the experience of non-union. He or she must also be capable of accepting its existence and of respecting it as a state that holds meaning beyond what can be gleaned from the immediate experience. Hence, therapy will depend to large measure upon faith and a capacity to repair the errors incurred while defending against the pain of non-union.

Ed and I seemed to engage a transference couple that desired non-union and was so split from awareness that neither of us had any idea at all what the other was saying. Some other active force placed us in what felt like separate universes. Was he responsible? Was I? Was he out to defeat me, or to see whether I could be tricked by his duplicity? For example, would I obligingly act as if things were going well just as he often did as a child when he had to split from his real perceptions and try to believe instead that his parents were doing the best they could? And was our interaction doomed because of its destructive nature, or, as the *Rosarium* suggests, was it somehow a process through which a new self was being formed? Often our therapeutic endeavour seemed possessed by a demonic, trickster-like force that toyed with me as if I were its infant.

How can one understand this demonic force? Can it be reduced merely to the component of envy—that is, *my* envy attacking our connection by 'misunderstanding' him? Or, was I acting out his introject of parental envy? Such interpretations have value; other equally 'valid' interpretations could also be made. But if we do not also possess an archetypal viewpoint, we are likely to overlook the essential fact that something of a significantly different nature has been operating—an archetypal process much larger than the two of us.

A subsequent session revealed other aspects of our unconscious process. Ed began with a question: 'What is your relationship to my inner couple?' It seemed as if his plight was encapsulated in this question, and I acted as if there were no time to lose, feeling pressed and harried to 'get it right'. I began to lecture him: 'The inner couple is also an image of the relationship of your consciousness to the unconscious. If the couple is in disharmony, you will be in disharmony as well.' To this assertion he bristled, as usual, with the insistence that I was being as impersonal as a textbook. And he was right, of course. There were other instances of my intellectualized attempts to answer his question during this session; all were spun from my haste and a refusal to take the time to sort out what he was saying—to understand truly instead of pretending to understand. My behaviour had perpetuated my erroneous belief that I was connected to him. We also exchanged roles: at times I would feel the need to slow down and be utterly precise, whereas he would gallop along, moving too quickly for me to be able to understand him in a full, grounded way. Suddenly, Ed returned to the question: 'What is your relationship to my inner couple?'

The fact that I was feeling somewhat depleted helped me to orient myself in a way that I knew might be helpful—back towards what had been happening between us in the here-and-now. I allowed myself to become more centred, more fully embodied, and I surrendered much of my control. Only when I finally succeeded in returning to my own feelings was I able to recognize that I had been afraid of being physically harmed. My fantasy had been that I had better get the right answers or he would hit me.

Then I began to realize that I had been experiencing and re-enacting Ed's early life with his parents, for when he failed to create harmony between his parents, he would be in great danger of being hit. He experienced his parents' disharmony and antagonism as dangerous both to the family unit and to himself, and he had to set it right, lest he be attacked. His solution was, in effect, to attempt to force his mother and father to behave differently—both towards one another and also towards him. It appears that I had been acting out an introject of his child-self as it compulsively attempted to create union. In this particular case, the urgent demand was that I create harmony between us by answering the question about his inner couple. And the compulsion to do so overrode the underlying awareness that a basic lack of connection—a prevailing non-union—was the dominant factor in our relationship.

I expressed these thoughts to Ed, and this interpretation proved somewhat effective in leading us to a deeper understanding. He suggested the possibility that he was attacking me for acting in disunion with myself, adding that I could be seen as

representing both his own couple in disunion *and* his child-self
frantically attempting to change the situation. Alternatively, I
could be seen as a person who incorporated the potential to evoke
the disharmony that he found so devastating. Whenever I would
evoke disharmony by being out of harmony with myself, Ed
would become very nasty and have the urge to hit me. The
verbally abusive negative inner couple (his parental images in
their state of disunion), which were constellated in me, severely
affected him.

There was a definite improvement when we became able to
objectify the interactive field in terms of a couple engaged in
battle while paradoxically desiring no contact at all. We were also
able to observe this same couple as persecutory of the small child
within each of us. Containment for these persecutory affects grew
as we became able to identify the couple imaginally. Perhaps this
containment is the element that enabled the therapy to continue
and even reach the point at which our interactive field was able to
transform into a unified field and a working alliance. At that
point, the significance of transference and countertransference
dynamics diminished, and Ed could begin to make substantial
changes in his life. In the *Rosarium* (*CW* 16), picture seven is
followed by a regenerative state depicted by falling dew. The
soulless couple, washed and revitalized by the dew, is eventually
renewed in the form of the Rebis, the hermaphrodite (picture ten).
The hermaphrodite represents the creation of a linking structure,
akin to what Jung calls the 'transcendent function' and what
Winnicott calls 'transitional space'. As a result of our linkage, the
therapy gained a playful and explorative quality that had
previously been absent. In an important sense, Ed's individuation
process began anew at this juncture, and the significant
life-changes that he was able to make further contributed to his
growth.

The following example illustrates how an unconscious dyad
structures not only the interactive field, but also one's mind–body
experiences. It also reveals how the therapeutic apprehension of
the unconscious dyad in its form of non-union can lead to a field of
union.

'Mallory', a 35-year-old woman, began a session by telling the
following dream: 'In an ancient stone atrium I was doing an erotic
dance with an eighteen-year-old boy. He knew more than I ever

will.' I sensed that she wanted me to be excited about the dream and felt awkward about having absolutely no response at all. I reflected upon the previous day's session, which had dealt with Mallory's fears that I would be angry with her because she was emotionally distant. I felt disconnected from the dream; it also felt dismissive to sidestep my thoughts about yesterday's session. I attempted to link these feelings by saying, 'Since the dance with the boy and the stone atrium seem to be such positive symbols, perhaps you had the dream to affirm how vital it is to stay on the track of what happened yesterday, and to encourage you to not withdraw out of fear of my anger.'[4] To this Mallory replied, 'You'll have to help me, I don't know where to go from here.'

Suddenly I felt dull and flaccid, as if all sense of structure, all alertness, had vanished from my body. I was mentally engaged and expectant, waiting for something to arise either from her or from me. But I could not readily contain the dull and flaccid feelings, and almost immediately began to recount yesterday's experience, recalling how frightened Mallory had been. With this, her countenance changed abruptly, and she bitterly reproached herself: 'I never do it right. You're cold, angry with me. I can feel it.' I had difficulty at that moment distinguishing 'me' from what felt like a 'them'—that is, her parents.

It was clear that something important was going on, and I realized that Mallory might be using the session to repeat a family pattern. I asked, 'Where are you with your parents now?' 'I'm at the dinner table, she is to my left, he to my right. I'm terrified, constantly alert, scanning for danger. I have to be, I have to make sure everything is okay. She's a bit drunk and stuffing herself with food; he is passive, simply waiting. But I know he will explode at any moment. I have to prevent this somehow, but I don't know how. I try to humour them; it barely works. I know his anger will eventually come out, he'll explode. Then she'll withdraw and be a martyr, terrifying everyone with her martyrdom. He'll then be frightened, and her martyrdom will turn to anger against me.'

With this information, I could play with the following possibility: when I had initially heard Mallory's dream, my silence had stemmed from the fact that my mental processes had replicated her silent father's dullness; and my awkward and flaccid body feelings probably resembled those of her drunk mother. I was somewhat intimidated by this patient's capacity to put me into such uncomfortable states. I did not feel any recognizable anger, but it was difficult to allow myself even minor feelings of irritation in working with this patient, because I feared they might trigger a paranoid reaction that could lead to a delusional transference certain to doom the therapeutic work. This aspect of our interaction was a mixture of mutual neurotic and psychotic parts. I had split off from the rage I was feeling and as a consequence did not adequately embrace the nature of the couple I had introjected; instead, I avoided the anger embedded in my dull state by absorbing it, behaving like her martyred mother. I recognize that I could have interpreted this state as a response Mallory might naturally have anticipated. But Mallory's paranoid, scanning field was too intense to have hazarded such an interpretation.

My mind and body seemed in general to represent Mallory's inner parental couple. The parts of the couple were split from each other and also at war; my mental and somatic selves reflected this state. When I was well-connected, Mallory would feel at ease. She would keep me centred by telling me stories about her life. At such times, Mallory was able to create in me a unified inner couple that did not terrorize her. But this endeavour was always strained by her foreboding that the future would bring further persecutory states. By 'fixing me' Mallory could only temporarily avoid the battle that would certainly come. Just as her parents would fight with each other in spite of her best efforts to entertain them, so my two natures would eventually fall out of harmony. On one level they already had, for the unity Mallory had been able to achieve was only accomplished through our mutual splitting—she from her fear, and I from the tension and anxiety that was always nearby.

The feeling-tone of the session would immediately change when these moments of disunity occurred. If I did not know what to say or do, or if I felt muddled, Mallory would think I was angry with her. She would experience me as if I were her father at the dinner table. 'What's wrong?' she would ask; she would then feel that she could not 'fix' me, and would become very frightened and would complain that she 'never does it right'.

When I was able to become aware of how my own unconscious was being influenced and structured by Mallory's internal

parental couple, several advantages accrued. First, she partici-
pated in a corrective emotional experience, in the sense that she
could experience me as embodying her parental couple but could
see that I did not retaliate. I also required less 'fixing' than they
did, especially as I grew more conscious and did not act out the
splitting process, thereby losing sight of the opposites. Mallory
now had the possibility of freeing psychic energy that had
hitherto been in the service of an incessant scanning process that
had remorselessly energized her negative parental couple.
Secondly, by Mallory experiencing how I could maintain my own
mind–body union while she was in disunion, she gained the
possibility of introjecting a more harmonious dyad.

In the sessions that followed, we had a sense of connection, of
working well together. Mallory said that it 'felt good, but what
about the other stuff?' She meant, of course, the disunion we had
previously experienced and was also referring to her fear of my
rage. I noticed that she was scanning me, for I felt its pressure, as
if her *vision* had a substantial quality that exerted a force. I
encouraged her to express what she saw, and she reported that I
was defensive. It was a struggle to accept her finding, and I asked
how she recognized my defensiveness. Mallory responded by
saying, 'Maybe you're worried about something.' I was aware of
an inner tightness and had a sense that I was withholding my
feelings. Mallory wondered aloud if these feelings were sexual,
saying, 'that's usually the root of things'. Here was something
new and important, for Mallory had dared to imaginally see me
and express her feelings about me.

The borderline person concretizes imaginal perceptions
inwardly. For example, at the beginning of a session, he or she
might perceive the therapist as being tired and withdrawn but
will say nothing about it. After some contact has been made in
the session, the patient, provoked by an inner attack, might
comment on how he or she is being 'too much of a burden for you,
or for anyone'. The patient's vision, which may be regarded as a
psychic organ or structure that the person refuses to acknowledge, will become demonic if he or she cannot dare to
communicate through it.

Mallory had dared to share what she had seen; I could then
respond to her vision by indicating where her perceptions were
accurate and also by indicating areas that were beyond her

perceptual lens. Thus, her imaginal perception was tested, and she was able to depart from a feeling of omnipotence—namely, that what she saw was *the* truth. On other occasions, Mallory split from what she could *see* by relegating her accurate perceptions to her own madness. What one *sees* is often very disturbing. In fact, a person's imaginal perception is usually denied early in life because what is perceived by the child (for example, a parent's hatred) is too searing to absorb. Many borderline persons begin to integrate split-off psychotic parts when they become able to dare to see that they had been hated by their parents. Being able to share one's imaginal perceptions is extremely important, though this ability is rarely available to the borderline person. Instead, as dreams often reveal, the imagination usually becomes mired in matter. The dreamer may attempt to jump across a stream and will be able to get only halfway across, or try to enter a room, only to encounter a lead-sealed door. There are endless variants of such themes, in which the linkage of two different states is severely hindered.

In Mallory's case we continued to explore her scanning process, noting everything she *saw*. She began to experience the virtues of her *sight* and came to enjoy the fact that it could be a relational tool rather than merely a defensive one, one that operated like a kind of psychic warning radar. She could also experience how my *seeing* her, as well as she *seeing* me, had the effect of enlivening our interaction. This, in turn, produced the experience that something autonomous was coming to life between us: a sense of union with a characteristic rhythm that both joined and separated us. In following sessions, Mallory and I began to grasp aspects of her negative inner couple and also began to experience the release of a positive couple that began to structure our interactive space.

The *coniunctio* is not only an event but a pattern; disharmonious aspects of that pattern soon began to emerge with Mallory and myself. In the session following the union experience something was askew; the positive couple was absent, we were not working well together, and it felt terrible. In an effort to resume our good connection, I actually said: 'What about us?' No longer passively scanning with paranoid defenses, Mallory immediately sensed what was 'off' in my remark. 'The *us* feels slimy,' she said. 'That's how my father was, but he would always deny it. It was never in the open. If you had said, "How about you and me?" it would have been different—clear, honest. The *us* feels terrible!' This remark led to our awareness of the existence of an incestuous couple. This couple also appears in the *Rosarium* following the *coniunctio* (*CW* 16, para. 468). Our *coniunctio* had served to attract more unconscious material and to perpetrate the kinship quality between us. It also led to another stage in Mallory's integration of her *vision*.

Integrating one's imaginal sight—that quality which is usually split off and has taken up domain in the patient's psychotic part—is often accomplished only after the therapist *sees* this *sight* operating in the patient; in effect, it is as if the therapist is being spied upon. For example, after I had worked with a male patient, 'John', for six months, I recognized that while he constantly scanned me, he also idealized me and sacrificed his vision, or attempts at vision, to that idealization. Usually, the scanning was a very subtle background phenomenon, which was barely perceptible unless I made an extra effort to be embodied and emotionally present. But his idealization induced me to bask in the self-approving light of what a good therapist I am, rather than reach out to contact him sufficiently to perceive that he *saw*.

Once I was able to focus upon his background scanning process, John began to speak about his fears of women. The world, he claimed, is 'a batch of piranhas'. I was not included in this assessment, however. I was different, safe. Indeed, how else except by idealizing me could he face his fear? John asked if the piranhas were real, then quickly affirmed their reality and their power to fracture his sense of identity. It became clear that his idealization separated me from destructive energies and allowed him to split from his negative inner images. Any attempts John made to confront these negative images had an 'as-if' quality that conveyed the falseness of his effort.

John volunteered that each time I saw him scanning me he felt a physical tension in his chest, stomach and throat and would feel the reality of inner persecutory attackers. When I did not employ my imaginal sight, his splitting defenses of idealization would remain intact. When I would communicate this idealization strategy to him, its defensive function would temporarily abate, only to be replaced by a masochistic defense. John would agree with everything I said and even add further examples to help me prove my point. He would explain that my reflections made him very anxious. It was clear that in these strenuous efforts to keep me 'ideal' he was splitting from what he really *saw*—namely, the knowledge that I often did not *see* him or the intensity of his fear. Over and over he would complain that his smooth exterior hid his true feelings from everyone *except from me*; only I knew that he was really very young and afraid. He would simultaneously attack and soothe me: he would tell me that I did *not* see him, but would continue to split from his own perception by insisting that I was different from other people.

Imaginal sight is like active imagination, *but when using imaginal sight in the here-and-now of therapy it is essential that the unconscious of the therapist be constellated through his or her countertransference.* For example, only after I had become conscious of my splitting tendencies and of a somewhat flattened affect that did not engage John's psychotic parts could I begin to make use of this countertransference reaction. By consciously submitting to this induced countertransferential state and becoming embodied, I could allow imagination to lead me to perceive his background scanning.

The imaginal realm does not necessarily manifest through visual images; feeling and the kinesthetic sense are also natural conduits. Possibly the nature of the imaginal act is coloured by the therapist's inferior function, so that one therapist will see 'visibly', whereas another will see 'feelingly'. In any event, the process requires that the therapist allow himself or herself to be affected by the patient's material without having to resort to interpretation, which would at best prove to be a defensive manoeuvre.

Imagination is an act born of the body. It arises out of a matrix of confusion and disorder. Faith, rather than the mastery of understanding, is its midwife.

Madness, religion, and the self in borderline states of mind

The borderline patient has a core of madness that must be uncovered if successful treatment is to be achieved. The patient's self, or soul, is enmeshed in psychotic mechanisms of splitting and denial. This true self might be represented as a child living in filth, or locked up, or petrified, or frozen in ice. There are countless images that depict this state. The following clinical material is drawn from my work with 'Amanda', a 48-year-old borderline woman. Amanda's psychotic parts could only enter the therapy after I was able to end her obsessional control, which manifested by her reading to me from a notebook. Her explanation for this controlling behaviour was that she might 'otherwise lose her thoughts'. In daily life Amanda functioned quite well; to a large measure her madness intruded into an otherwise competent, functioning personality only during therapy sessions. A relatively condensed psychotic transference, in which delusional processes are contained by a sense of alliance, is highly desirable in treatment (Grotstein, 1979, p. 173).

Amanda's confusion was dominant in our therapy process; this confusion was disorienting for both of us. As a three-year-old child Amanda had suffered an overwhelming trauma: her father had left the family.[5] He had never said goodbye to Amanda, ostensibly because the family felt that she would be better off without so explicit a closure. Yet her father had been her only source of love and comfort, as well as the only barrier between her and her mother and grandparents, whom Amanda experienced as cold, aloof and harsh. She recalled an early memory of her mother sending her to play outside on a rainy day. Her mother had dressed her in new white shoes but had then scolded her for getting them dirty. This memory is a paradigm for her early individuation experiences: separation from her mother was undermined by the implicit demand that she remain fused with her mother's narcissism. This included the demand that she appear to be perfect. With such a maternal background Amanda had only minimal positive internal resources. She thus had little support to help her contain the intense anxieties that erupted when her father abandoned her. She had lost her only love object.

This incident had been so traumatic for Amanda that no therapeutic work on her relationship with her father could occur for several years. Up to that time, Amanda had never mentioned him. Eventually, she began to refer to him as a 'nice person'. She would also say that 'he preferred my mother'. Even though he returned to the family fold after a nine-month absence and was present in her life for the next 40 years, there was almost nothing she could find to say about him; her mind would become blank.

Gradually, Amanda's abandonment fears entered the transference, and session endings became very painful for her. Between sessions Amanda's image of me was often effaced, but occasionally she was able to suffer my *absence* consciously, rather than by splitting and becoming manic. It became possible to begin the reconstruction of what had happened in her inner world when her father had left. One memory she was able to salvage was that she 'became hysterical and hid under the bed' after she discovered that he had left. Her conscious memories of this event began and ended here, however; even this recollection felt uncertain. In fact, all of Amanda's recollections had a strange uncertainty to them. Our reconstruction of what may have happened upon her father's return nine months later includes the hypothesis that Amanda believed that the returning father was an impostor. Moreover, she had, in effect, created an inner, idealized father who would someday return and truly loved her. In the transference, Amanda split me into several 'fathers', including both the impostor and the idealized father. The latter existed only outside the therapy sessions in her imaginary conversations with me.

A severe reality distortion occurred when Amanda's father deserted her: she denied her love for him and his very existence. Since Amanda's positive inner world was of such little worth, she could not mourn his loss. A delusional inner world came into play, one that was structured by both the idealized father and its negative split-off polarity, the impostor father. She did not experience either of these images consciously; life with real father continued as if he had never abandoned her. Amanda would say that he was 'nice'. Inwardly, however, her perceptions were dominated by severe distortions: her father was/was not the man who had returned to her—that is, this was neither her real father, nor an impostor.

In the transference I was initially regarded as the impostor to whom Amanda had to learn to relate. This took the form of her insistence that I list the rules of patient behaviour. 'What should patients say or do with the therapist?', Amanda would ask. I was depersonalized by her, but not completely. She was always able to maintain a sense of humour, which represented her observing ego; at the same time, she was extremely serious.

When I succeeded in interpreting her splitting, she suffered the loss, outside the therapy sessions, of my image; a painful deadness eclipsed her imagination. 'Out there you don't love me any more', she would say. A long period of depression and acute suffering of abandonment feelings ensued. At these times, Amanda's psychotic parts would become enlivened, for she could not be sure the real 'me' would return.

After working with Amanda's abandonment feelings, it became clear that yet another 'father' existed—one who carried the depth of her abandonment experience. This 'father' was identified with money, although the very mention of this theme released an almost immediate hysterical flooding. She recalled that her father had left the family home because he hadn't been able to earn a living that matched family standards. Amanda's understanding was that her mother and grandparents had kicked him out because of his financial dereliction. In her unconscious, money was the root of all her loss. In daily life Amanda would do everything she could to 'forget' how much money she had. An inheritance she received was traumatic because it forced her to think about money; her only recourse was to hide the money in a bank account and forget about it completely. To invest it, or even to draw interest from the principal, was beyond her capacities. Money had little reality for her other than its connection to abandonment.

For many months the mere mention of money invoked such overwhelming abandonment feelings that the continuity of memories and insights was disrupted. After my persistently confronting this issue during many therapy sessions, Amanda's capacities to deal with money issues gradually began to improve. With her growing capacity in this area a fog seemed to clear; the fact that money was unconsciously identified with the father who had deserted her became a more stable psychic reality. We could then recognize 'three fathers': the impostor father, the idealized father, and the abandoning father, represented in Amanda's psyche by money.

Amanda's splitting in therapy sessions lessened, but it still served to dull her pain; she remained extremely confused. A 'blanking out' of her mental processes often occurred. As she put it, 'The head doesn't work.' Each thought or memory would immediately produce others, so that a multiplicity of centres was created; each would compete for her attention and thoroughly confuse both of us. Amanda would then reject all my attempts to explain what was happening. These experiences truly reflect Harold Searles's statement:

I often have the sense that one or another patient is functioning unconsciously in a multiple-identity fashion when I feel not simply intimidated or overwhelmed ... but, curiously and more specifically, *outnumbered* by him. [1979, p. 448]

These qualities of confusion, splitting and reality distortion all form parts of the borderline person. Rarely is there a total distortion of reality, although the behavioural stance often possesses an autonomy that is like a state of demonic possession. The quality of near-psychotic behaviour is often stressed in the literature on the borderline personality. But there is also a strange kind of order in this 'possessed' behaviour. We can begin to glimpse it in this clinical material as we consider the way in which Amanda often rejected interpretations.

Amanda would say something like, 'that's not quite it', or 'maybe'. Her response was always frustrating because I had usually put a great deal of effort into trying to create some coherence for her as well as for myself. As a result of her denial I would often become irritated. At times, this reaction would be quite strong; it was often clear that projective identification was involved. This led me to attempt to examine her anger with me for 'disappearing outside of the sessions'. Such interpretations were somewhat effective. But this enterprise did not reach Amanda's psychotic parts.

It should be noted that when Amanda gave me such conditional answers, though I was irritated, I did not feel that my interpretations had been totally negated. In fact, Amanda was often at her best at these moments, and her mode of rejection rarely displayed a strong intention to defeat me. If my interpretations were grossly inaccurate, she would become confused. Then 'other thoughts' would fragment her attention, leaving both of us in a muddle that also obscured her anger towards me. But when my interpretations were relatively sound, they elicited a reaction in her that revealed a level of depth that was not usually apparent. If, regarding an interpretation, I asked the question, 'Does that seem right?' Amanda would reply, 'Not exactly.' If I asked, 'Is it wrong, off the mark?' she would answer, 'No, not completely.' At these moments, it seemed that she was *using* my interpretation to get close to something. But what? Apparently, Amanda was able to find value in the same interpretation that she was negating. What I said was considered by her to be neither true nor false. She would suspend choice, but not for defensive purposes. A process was at work inside her that could only express itself by her suspending choice. I discovered that if I 'hovered' in the suspension without trying to amplify the interpretation, she would often remember a detail from the past or have a new insight. She would have to balance each statement she made with a second statement that revealed the confusion or incompleteness of the first. There was no possibility of saying, 'This is right,' but only, 'It is neither right nor wrong.'

The French psychoanalyst André Green, whose thinking has influenced my approach to this clinical material, has described the borderline person's 'logic' as follows:

> According to the reality principle, the psychic apparatus has to decide whether the object is or is not there: 'Yes' or 'No'. According to the pleasure principle, and as negation does not exist in the primary process of the unconscious, there is only 'Yes.' Winnicott has described the status of the transitional object, which combines the 'Yes' and the 'No', as the transitional is- and is-not-the-breast. One can find precursors of Winnicott's observations in Freud's description of the cotton reel game and in his description of the fetish. But I think that there is one more way of dealing with this crucial issue of deciding whether the object is or is not, and that is illustrated by the judgment of the borderline patient. There is a fourth possible answer: *Neither 'Yes' nor 'No'*. This *is* an alternate choice to the refusal of choice. The transitional object is a *positive refusal*; it is either a 'Yes' or a 'No'. The symptoms of the borderline, standing for transitional objects, offer a *negative refusal of choice:* Neither 'Yes' nor 'No'. One could express the same relation in experiential terms by asking the question: 'Is the object dead (lost) or alive (found)?' or 'Am I dead or alive?'—to which he may answer: *'Neither Yes nor No'*. [1977, p. 41]

When in acute distress, the borderline patient can never be certain whether the therapist is truly present in a flesh-and-blood sense. One could also say that the patient is uncertain if the therapist is alive or dead. This state of uncertainty always exists in the patient's unconscious and manifests itself in bewildering ways when splitting defenses fail to dispel abandonment anxiety.

Hence, the patient can never answer the question: *Is the therapist alive or dead?* as it would appear meaningless and confusing to do so. Moreover, if he or she were to be asked: *Is the therapist both alive and dead?* the patient would continue to be confused, for it would mean that the therapist was a transitional object, that is, something both created and found.

The patient cannot experience the creativity of transitional space while in a state of confusion. Indeed, the possibility of 'play' is usually absent for the borderline patient. The therapist, who tends to become so embroiled in countertransference reactions that his or her foremost desire is simply to survive each encounter, often feels either depressed and dull, or manic; like the borderline patient, the therapist will then *act* by using commentary to fill space rather than undergo an experience of *absence* (Green, 1977, p. 41). This state is a difficult one to bear; to be able to sustain it requires the supporting faith that if one delays action and simply waits, the patient will not become destructive, and the psyche will become enlivened. At crucial moments in the therapeutic process, the therapist's supreme act of faith in relation to the borderline patient is to trust that this patient will not 'kill' him or her. To render the therapist ineffectual and mindless would be one way in which the patient would effect such a 'killing'.

In Amanda's material it was not a matter of my interpretations becoming more cogent, or of my needing to augment and deepen them. Instead, what was needed was that I be able to register and accept Amanda's sense of paradox. This sense of paradox was only able to manifest itself when I could remain in an embodied and receptive state amidst the experience of absence. Her dialogue would now be sharply in contrast with her more usual confused and fragmented state of mind. For fleeting moments I would be privy to a depth in her that was normally hidden by her splitting defenses and an infantile ego that 'just wanted to feel good'. Thus, Amanda's remarks carried with them an awareness that my interpretations were only partially satisfactory. Her response to my interpretations was that they were 'not correct' *and* 'not wrong'. However, on a deep and subtle level it was not a question of whether or not a statement was right or wrong but rather that it was *neither* completely right *nor* completely wrong.

The subtleties of madness are often only perceived through feeling and observing our own states of confusion. In the case under discussion, more overt forms of madness also began to be uncovered. Some of these forms were not very subtle, and their perception merely required an empathic observer who would be sensitive to the patient's shame at carrying such fears of madness. For example, Amanda revealed a considerable paranoia when she expressed fears that her money would be stolen by the bank, or that her checks were only the bank's way of cheating her. She was also persecuted by fears that her grandchildren would be stolen from her while she accompanied them to school. But Amanda's more subtle forms of madness, in which confusion and reality-distortion coexisted as part of a 'neither-yes-nor-no' logic, were more difficult for me to decipher; this was so because of my tendency to deny the existence of these states.

There are a number of reasons for the therapist's having countertransferential reactions of confusion and irritation. Firstly, the therapist is not being asked to add or subtract content from what he or she had said, although that wish may be implicit in the patient's communication. More important is the frustrating sense of coexisting opposites: one has the feeling that he or she is both approaching *and* at the same time failing to apprehend the patient's process. This process is not a sum of distinct parts; it can be known only in its wholeness. Generally, the borderline person hates partial interpretations; the therapist often feels persecuted for not being perfect and may even complain (sometimes aloud to the patient!) that he or she is always being criticized. Often, the therapist's best efforts are diminished by the patient's outright anger and rejection.

Amanda's splitting began to diminish further when she became able to experience her abandonment anxieties; our confusion lessened, and her imagination slowly began to function. Gradually, she began to be able to 'find me' outside our sessions. I was becoming more of a 'real' object and less an 'idealized father'. The therapy became lively, though the outside world (in which she functioned well but took little interest) remained a place of psychic deadness. All of Amanda's interest was concentrated on returning to the therapy.

Amanda's external object relations were becoming more realistic. Her husband, who for years had carried an idealized projection and had betrayed her through affairs with other women, came gradually to be seen more realistically. Previously, his inner deadness had persecuted her, but once she came to know and respect her own angry feelings, she was able to rail at his lack of relatedness. Gradually, and without necessarily liking it, Amanda could begin to accept him as he was. There was also a substantial improvement in Amanda's relationship with her mother. This change accrued as a result of her learning to recognize when she was angry with her mother. At first she could feel this anger only with therapeutic help, and it would often take many days to do so. Gradually, the interval between incident and anger decreased until finally her inner response coincided exactly with the outer provocation. Amanda began to confront her mother more assertively and was actually able to forge a better relationship with her. The gradual emergence of a functioning self was epitomized by her greatly diminished tendency to split; her imaginative capacities grew, and she became more willing to find value and meaning in the pain of her abandonment anxieties.

This new split between the affectively dead external world and the lively therapeutic world represented not only a good/bad dichotomy but also an entrance into the Kleinian depressive position that she now experienced in relation to her father. Our process prior to this development had largely taken place within a paranoid–schizoid realm where splitting and persecutory affects dominated. As the process moved to a level of the depressive position, Amanda's hatred of me as the transference father was displaced into the full outer world, and her love of me, as the transference image of the once-loved father, was more fully experienced in our work together. This splitting was, however, more manageable than it had been formerly, and interpretation could now be more effective. What she was facing was the split between love and hatred, and with great trepidation she began to express her hatred to me. Its first appearance took the form of a jocular remark: 'Out there I hate you.' Over time she could begin to join with the affect while in my presence.

This new-found courage had a continuing positive effect. Her capacity for the play of imagination had previously been severely limited, and she had been especially prone to split her emotional life between feelings of love and hate. This splitting now diminished, and Amanda gained an imaginative capacity that could be communicated to me and was more complex than her previous flow of fantasy that had circulated around the idealized father-projection. This distinction is important and registers the difference between what alchemists called true and fantastic imagination (*CW* 12, para. 360). The borderline person often experiences either an imaginative lacuna or else a torrential flow of imagery and affect in countless passive fantasies *that void experiencing feelings*. The false imagination functions to split a person from his or her feeling; it also furthers mind–body splitting and often manifests in somatic complaints. But true imagination, according to the alchemical metaphor, is far more realistic; it engages feelings and nurtures the growth of consciousness and the awareness of the suffering of one's soul.

There is one other important issue that should be mentioned in relation to this case. About a year before Amanda's abandonment anxieties and imagination became the focus of treatment, she dreamed of a small girl who was frozen in ice. The ice began to thaw, and the child began to come to life. This dream was itself a critical juncture in our work, and it was preceded by a strange occurrence. At the close of a particular session, Amanda suddenly turned around and spoke to me in French, which she had never done before. In the next session Amanda asked me about 'sub-personalities', since she had realized that 'another person' had spoken French to me. We discovered that this 'personality' carried her sexuality for her. For the first time, an erotic feeling existed between us. I believe that the 'sub-personality' in her dream material was the first appearance of a self structure, especially because its appearance had a synthesizing effect that overcame dissociation. This 'personality' had previously been split off and had existed in a frozen, schizoid state.

The loving and erotic quality between us remained for several months, then vanished with the emergence of her abandonment anxieties and depression. It appears that in order for the self in this patient to embody and become part of space-and-time life, she first had to be able to experience and suffer acute feelings of abandonment. Schizoid self-parts are always present in the borderline person, and their integration is essential if a sense of self is to emerge.

The borderline person's emerging self will make use of the therapist's interpretation in a bewildering way. When an interpretation is accepted, he or she will often return to the next session with material that seems to deny it. The therapist may feel confused or angry and will often tend to *act* through intervention or withdrawal. 'Acting', as André Green says, is 'the true model of the mind. ... Acting is not limited to actions; fantasies, dreams, words take the function of action. Acting fills space and does not tolerate the suspension of experience' (1977, p. 41). The therapist may feel as though the patient has denied what has previously been communicated, but this 'perception' actually serves to block perception in his or her own emerging state of confusion and incapacity to tolerate *absence*. That is, we feel attacked by the patient because of our limited capacity for self-experience, and our incapacity to experience the *absence* of the patient; we flee to the safety of feeling hurt, rejected or angry.

At this point it would be worthwhile for us to examine the discrete parts of this process. If the therapist is unable to contain the pain of the patient's *absence* and says something like, 'But last time we came to an understanding that you now seem to be totally denying,' the patient might say, 'What have I said to indicate that?' The therapist may then feel angry because his or her sense of reality has been attacked. Yet the therapist had misunderstood the patient's communication and had seen it to be a negation of his or her interpretations, whereas in fact the therapist has made an assumption that an agreement has been reached. This assumption has been made in order to dispel his or her own confusion and to avoid undergoing the suspension of experience. At the point where the patient might say, 'What have I said to deny what we did last time?' the feeling of confusion will often dissipate, leaving the therapist with the sense that he or she has acted badly by assuming that the patient had denied previous insights.

At this point it will seem to the patient that he has been merely reflecting, and in so doing setting aside what had transpired. Yet the therapist has taken this 'setting aside' to be an attack on the work of the last session; he or she may view it as a 'negative therapeutic reaction'. In fact, the patient has been trying to make use of the interpretation *by temporarily denying it*.

This act can appear to be a complete denial. The therapist's narcissism is attacked, since he or she wants a given interpretation to be definitive, not merely a stepping-stone to a deeper level. What must be understood is that the patient is attempting to disengage from the therapist's narcissism by employing this 'neither/nor' logic. To do this is terribly risky, for it means that the patient is beginning to show more of the true self and is thus daring to ignore the therapist's narcissistic needs.

The negative logic of the borderline patient so aptly described by Green can also be understood conceptually through the system of the *via negativa* of the fifteenth-century cleric and mystic, Nicholas of Cusa. The *via negativa* is a metaphysical system that provides a mode of perceiving both the nature and the goal of the borderline person's use of negation as a path to self-emergence. In this system, every positive statement stands in opposition to another that demonstrates its finitude or incompleteness; thus, each statement yields another that can be added to the previous one. God, the unknowable object of this dialectic, remains unified; He is a *coincidentia oppositorum*. Hence, the state in which opposites are united, and painful and deceitful splitting may at last be overcome, represents the unconscious goal of the borderline person. To reach the goal, however, a journey through a territory of madness is demanded. This domain of madness is one in which the inner life suffers fragmentation and confusion; in other words, it is the complete antithesis to unity and the harmony of opposites. Moreover, madness itself seems to guard against the psychic intrusion of others. Madness is a process belonging to a self that has survived persecution, and which, however weakly, manifests in paradox—the fulcrum of the borderline person's peculiar logic.

Moreover, the therapist can err by failing to embrace the 'neither/nor' logic of the borderline patient. He or she may attempt to understand the meaning of a patient's communication by interpreting feelings encountered in the countertransference. For example, 'The anxious feelings I am having with this person inform me that he may be dominated by abandonment anxieties.' This is what Frederick Copleston describes as the level of the senses, which simply affirm (Copleston, 1985, p. 237). Or, the therapist may try to gain knowledge of the patient by determining what *is* or *is not*; for example: 'She is in a manic state, but this may not be the core issue; instead, the mania may be a defense against her abandonment depression.' Copleston refers to this form of reasoning as one in which 'there is both affirmation and denial' (ibid.). What is required is that one face the madness; *the therapist must learn to continue to be, without necessarily knowing*. In this way, one respects the unknowable.

In Nicholas's thought, sense-perception corresponds to what Green has called primary process thinking, and discursive reasoning (*ratio*) corresponds to the reality principle. The borderline person's logic, which follows the model of *neither 'Yes' nor 'No'*, corresponds in Nicholas' system to the *intellectus*.

> Whereas sense-perception affirms and reason affirms and denies, intellect denies the oppositions of reason. Reason affirms X and denies Y, but intellect denies X and Y both disjunctively and together; it apprehends God as the *coincidentia oppositorum*. This apprehension or intuition cannot, however, be properly stated in language, which is the instrument of reason rather than intellect. *In its activity as intellect the mind uses language to suggest meaning rather than to state it.* ... [Copleston, 1985, p. 237—italics mine]

One can never *understand* a person's mad parts, *but one can know that one does not know.* Any understanding that translates the state of madness into a discursive process (such as causal sequences of failed developmental stages) fails to grasp the nature of madness and also fails to provide a symbolic sense of containment for the borderline person. Such reductive thinking turns the borderline person's madness into a *thing* to be ordered, instead of admitting it to be as vital and alive and characteristic of self as the person's other more readily acceptable qualities. The reductive method cannot circumscribe the phenomenon of madness, which is beyond the province of rational knowing.

The only *knowing* that is useful in the treatment of borderline disorders is the knowing that is reached through a negative logic. The patient's madness has the capacity to distort and destroy his or her own and the therapist's perceptions in such a way that seemingly benign interactions, or interpretations that were formerly accepted by the patient and have been introjected, turn into persecutory objects. But it should be clear that this change from the benign into the persecutory is not the result of the patient splitting from abandonment anxieties, since abandonment experiences are *neither the cause nor not the cause* of the person's madness. We need to be able to tolerate the suspended state of *not knowing,* and at the same time not negate the attempt to know. This form of waiting can provide a deep experience of a person's psychotic parts, as well as a mode of gaining familiarity with them, even if it is not possible to become truly comfortable with the feelings of oddness and terror, absence and mindlessness that they are apt to provoke.

Madness: *personal or impersonal?*

Is the madness one experiences in another person personal or impersonal? Certainly, it can feel like a soulless thing that terrifies subject and object by its very absence of form and clear affect and by the void of experience that is part of it. For madness is imbued with *absence* or *blankness* rather than the affirmative presence of any *thing.* In therapy, the madness one begins to see seems like an alien Other that has nothing to do with *the patient with whom one wishes to be.* Certainly, it is difficult to accept the mad parts a patient brings into the room. To avoid these parts, we tend to cling to explanations of projective identification dynamics and to manufacture interpretations that may even include the therapist's fear of being abandoned. But these choices all are defensive strategies to fill a void, an absence of experience, a core where thought and experience do not exist.

It is easy to think of madness as matter to be organized. A therapist may communicate the following: 'You are fleeing from an abandonment anxiety and fear that I, too, will abandon you in the process.' This rationale may be true, but it is also defensive, a way of avoiding the absence and blankness that can characterize madness. Yet the patient, assaulted by 'well-intentioned' interpretations, quickly flees into extreme states of mind–body splitting, and the therapist's intrusion goes unnoticed. Indeed, the patient is as happy as the therapist to have something to cling to—in this instance, the interpretation of an anxiety state. The patient's anxiety becomes a *thing* to be ordered and understood. It becomes a substitute for madness and reduces it to an impersonal energy.

How can madness be considered to be personal? Can I, or need I, love my patient's madness? The image of St. Teresa drinking the pus of her sick patients seems relevant in its excess. How can this madness, which often succeeds in turning both people into automatons, be part of one's humanity? To bear a saintly attitude towards it, to be the 'wounded healer' or the doctor who wears the mantle of the suffering patient, will not be experienced by the patient as embracing and containing the patient's process. Indeed if the therapist identifies with this saintly image of the wounded healer, a disjunction between patient and therapist will be certain to occur.

A quite different situation emerges if the therapist is able to succeed in encompassing the phenomenon of a patient who now reveals *his or her* madness. The patient has been terrified of exhibiting this madness. The realm of madness is a no-man's land, a place where meaning, imagery, and all relational potential is destroyed.[6] When the therapist is able to comprehend madness as an aspect of the patient and becomes able to experience the patient and the patient's madness in a personal, human way, a change can occur: as one enters into the alien territory of the patient's madness, one's personal orientation fails. A solely personal relationship to this phenomenon cannot fully contain it. One has the feeling that madness must be apprehended through a more comprehensive perspective. As a larger container for madness is allowed to develop, a sense of an impersonal dimension becomes prominent. The patient's madness begins to seem autonomous; it can appear like a machine or a deity, a separate force that not only rules the patient, but can also rule the encounter between patient and therapist. The impersonal/archetypal perspective can become too extreme and stray too far from human levels. One must then return to the smaller personal framework, though this soon feels too confining and again requires expansion.

Thus one's perception of madness oscillates between personal/impersonal, or personal/archetypal polarities. I cannot say that I relate to the patient's madness in a personal way, but neither can I say that I relate to it in an impersonal way. Yet if I say that the relationship is both personal *and* impersonal, I have abstracted

my experience in an intellectual way that destroys the experience
of madness. I resist destroying the strange and even awesome
way in which personal and impersonal qualities are coupled—a
coupling that seems to become manifest only when the phenomenology of madness *as part of the patient* is deeply engaged.
What I can say with certainty, however, is that the patient's
madness is *neither personal nor impersonal.*

This distinction between the personal level and an impersonal
transcendent level is also revealed when the mystic is asked the
question: Is the God you experience personal or impersonal? The
mystic will answer that the god-experience is intensely personal.
Once this observation has been voiced, it will seem incorrect; the
mystic will then speak of God as sublimely Other, and say that
his or her experience belongs to a realm that is intensely
impersonal. It will not do to say that the god-experience is both
personal and impersonal. To do so would bind and falsify the
experience. One can only say that the god-experience towards
which the mystic's soul reaches is neither personal nor impersonal.

The mystic's paradoxical expression embraces his or her
experience. The borderline person's *neither Yes nor No* rarely has
the fluidity of paradox but instead caricatures it. The mystic's
paradox communicates a sense of wholeness, whereas the
borderline patient's paradoxical logic—when its elusive and
underlying truth is not apprehended—can trigger feelings of
emptiness and confusion in the therapist.

The borderline person's *neither Yes nor No* seems to cancel
whatever has been achieved. For example, a session may
approach clarity, and confusion will wane. The following session
may begin with an attack. The patient's attack is his or her way
of guarding against the therapist's tendency *not* to see in a
paradoxical way. What the patient would wish to say to the
therapist—if the therapist has not eliminated all possibility of
communication by precipitous talk or action—is that the insights
gained in the previous session are neither correct nor incorrect.
By attacking the therapist, the patient is simply expressing an
inability to grasp the paradoxical nature of the therapeutic
experience. If the therapist can suspend action and create a space
for confusion and an absence of knowing, *then* the patient may be

able to say that a previous interpretation was neither complete nor incomplete.

The soul of the borderline person and Nicholas of Cusa seem to have a common approach to the *numinosum*. It is as if the person were saying, 'You cannot fully know me. I am beyond any rational comprehension. You can only know that you do not know. If the knowing you possess is authentic and hard-won, I will allow you to approach my soul, but only if you always know you do not know. Your need to know and your arrogance are the greatest threat to me, as is your being anything less than your best as you try to understand me.' As one approaches the soul of the borderline person, one crosses into the territory of madness. Jacques Lacan has written: 'Not only can man's being not be understood without madness, it would not be man's being if it did not bear madness within itself as the limit of his freedom' (1977, p. 215). Unless one can delve into the borderline person's madness, one will never be able to understand him or her.

The borderline person's madness accrues from experiences of extreme pain, confusion and bewilderment. To a degree, madness is created—though it is also an *a priori* state, like the chaos of myth and alchemy—by denial, splitting, projective identification and identification of the ego with archetypal images. Madness defends against the pain of being hated, scapegoated and attacked by parental guilt and envy for any individuation effort. Madness also serves to dull the experience of pain. The soul, in its exit from the territory of madness (when, for example, it is being *seen* and *daring to be seen*), is always attended by the pain that accompanies the process of overcoming splitting.

The borderline person often acts in ways that appear mad because the pain is so deep and the risk of having it touched *so* great that all avenues to his or her soul are full of roadblocks, detours and warning signs of danger. The borderline person is always testing, for example, by asking an 'attacking' question. When the borderline sector in any individual is approached, the danger light goes on. The *coniunctio,* with its capacity to heal splitting, always touches upon the insufferable pain endemic to it. This pain and its attendant madness is at the core of the borderline person. The patient will "go on alert" in order to ascertain whether or not the therapist realizes and is capable of handling the depth of his or her pain and sensitivity. If the therapist asserts his or her understanding, while the patient sees this assertion to be incomplete if not false, then a detour must be made until the risk is diminished. These detours engage madness and lead to 'nothingness'—a state of suspension and waiting; the patient watches to see if *this time* his or her pain will be apprehended and understood.

Borderline and religious experiences

Is there a relationship between the thought processes of the borderline person and genuine experiences of the *numinosum* as in mystical experiences or in Nicholas of Cusa's *via negativa*? In genuine mystical experience a union with the divinity is known as a *complexio oppositorum*. The soul's immersion and then separation from God is a reality, and that union then lives on *in the soul of the mystic*. But for the borderline person *loss of union* is the critical issue. Whatever union experiences with the *numinosum* may have existed, especially during the first months of life, and whatever union experiences in later developmental stages may partially have taken place, the borderline person has not been able to own or incarnate them sufficiently.

Often, the borderline person may serve as a link to the *numinosum* for other people—for example, he or she may be psychic, or be a therapist who is a borderline person. The *numinosum* may be alive and remarkably healing for others when the borderline person serves as its conduit. But it has not incarnated *for the person*. When he or she is alone, the *numinosum* disappears; it is no longer experienced as a healing Other, but constitutes instead a reminder of painful absence and abandonment that can barely be tolerated. Somatizations and mind–body splits eliminate the capacity to differentiate feelings and to experience conflicting opposites; a bewildering simultaneity of contradictory feeling-states occurs.

There is a link between borderline states of mind and a genuine experience of the *numinosum*. The manifestation of borderline states of mind within religious experiences is well known. For instance, St. John of the Cross suffered from a terrible sense of emptiness and depression. In his experience of 'The Dark

Night' his mind was often blank and his thoughts fractured; he lived in despair, feeling abandoned by God and by people. He had profoundly difficult experiences that caused him severe suffering. He was ostracized by his community and imprisoned. Yet, he was also able to remain calm, even serene, in the belief that all of his suffering was for the purpose of purification through which he might receive God (Williams, 1980, pp. 159–179).

The story of St. John's life evokes diagnostic reflections over borderline phenomena. The workings of John's 'psychotic twin' are evident in his mental blankness. The persecutory anxieties he suffered are manifest in the responses of the world elicited by his behaviour. Borderline persons generally thrust their madness into the environment. John's severe states of abandonment are characteristic of the borderline person, as are his feelings of emptiness and his proclivity for seeking pain. Moreover, John's vision of suffering as a way to God might be seen as a symptom of good/bad splitting and manic and omnipotent defenses; these states would then be viewed as defenses against his feelings of worthlessness. John may have been a borderline personality, but his influence upon spirituality and his understanding of complex meditative states of mind has made him an invaluable source of wisdom.

But one does not need to examine borderline logic and its relationship to various mystical systems to recognize the link between borderline phenomenology and religious pursuit. Consider *The Diagnotic and Statistical Manual of the American Psychiatric Association, Third Edition* (DSM III),[7] which offers the following eight diagnostic criteria for the borderline personality disorder:

1. impulsivity or unpredictability in at least two areas that are potentially self damaging, e.g., spending, sex, gambling, substance use, shoplifting, overeating, physically self-damaging acts;
2. a marked pattern of unstable and intense interpersonal relationships, e.g., marked shifts of attitude, idealization, devaluation, manipulation (constantly using others for one's own ends);
3. inappropriate, intense anger or lack of control of anger, e.g., frequent displays of temper, constant anger;
4. identity disturbance manifested by uncertainty about

several issues relating to identity, such as self-image, gender identity, long-term goals or career choice, friendship patterns, values, and loyalties, e.g., 'Who am I?', 'I feel like I am my sister when I am good';

5. affective instability: marked shifts from normal mood to depression, irritability or anxiety, usually lasting a few hours and only rarely more than a few days, with a return to normal mood;

6. intolerance of being alone, e.g., frantic efforts to avoid being alone, depressed when alone;

7. physically self-damaging acts, e.g., suicidal gestures, self-mutilation, recurrent accidents or physical fights;

8. chronic feelings of emptiness or boredom.

But these criteria are also a profile of the Old Testament creator Yahweh, who certainly possessed at least five of the stated criteria! He was impulsive and unpredictable in ways that were self-damaging. His relations with his people, with Israel, were unstable and marked by idealization and devaluation. His anger was intense and often uncontrolled, and he could behave ruthlessly and with complete disregard for his chosen people. He destroyed his own creation with a flood. His identity was diffuse, for he needed constant mirroring. His moods often changed capriciously.

Diagnostically speaking, Yahweh is a borderline personality. This fact is instructive: Yahweh may indeed be a borderline personality, but he is also the supreme light, the source of the *numinosum*. In the Old Testament, Yahweh has a personality that includes not only numinosity, creativity and wisdom beyond that of any mortal, but his personality *also* includes borderline characteristics. Perhaps it is not possible for a human being to bear a creativity that touches a divine level *without his or her also suffering borderline states of mind*. In the figure of Yahweh, light and the dark are united, albeit in a bewildering fashion. But the combination of the positive *numinosum* with borderline characteristics is a mark of the creative genious of the Old Testament. This should not be forgotten amidst our efforts to separate light and dark qualities of the *numinosum* from each other, an essential task that must be performed in order that the light may incarnate.

The therapist learns to *see* the dead or blank self of the borderine person and to survive persecutory attacks upon any form of linking and the suspension of mental processes that its 'neither/nor' logic induces. Although it is important to uncover chronic states of abandonment in working with the borderline person, this task is only a first step along the path of encountering states of mind characterized by blankness and mind-destroying fury. *The torment of abandonment may thus be seen as a rite of passage for an incarnating Self.* But abandonment issues do not sufficiently explain the borderline condition. To focus upon them at the expense of engaging deeper levels of the *numinosum* results in creating the capacity for repression but does not facilitate the embodiment of the self as a centre that is in contact with the *numinosum*.

Treatment

The following reflections on the borderline psyche and treatment considerations derive from various sources. These are Bion's concept that there are both normal and psychotic parts to every personality, Jung's researches on alchemical symbolism, my own clinical experience of the *numinosum* manifesting in positive and negative forms, and my emphasis on the importance of the unconscious dyad. The psychotic part of a person may be thought to contain the image of the child, who represents the true self or soul. This child image often appears in a depleted or helpless state; it is a *dead self* not unlike the dead Osiris, who languished in the Underworld and was attacked when he dared arise. Another image representing the psychotic part is of a couple who are fused, yet in a state of radical disunion. This couple violently rejects separation, yet the parts of the couple are at the same time without any genuine contact. I have found, in my clinical work with patients, that the unconscious couple often assumes a violent form, with each member striving to attack the other; the female part often has a powerful phallus, and the male part is engulfing and mutilating. This unconscious couple often manifests in interpersonal relations and causes confusion or a sado-masochistic interaction between therapist and patient. But this interaction is a defensive operation engaged in by both patient and therapist to prevent them from experiencing the actual nature of the unconscious couple, which is especially hateful towards the soul. The couple, locked in a deadly and cruel combat, is actually a single, double-sided object (Green, 1977, p. 40), which is deeply antagonistic to the child held captive within its territory.

Thus the psychotic part of a person contains the soul as well as an extremely persecutory dyad, a couple existing 'before the creation' and prior to the separation of opposites. The dynamics operating within this dyad are complex, but Jung's researches into alchemical symbolism provide some guidance for an understanding of them. Should we regard the extremely destructive affects that accompany the psychotic part of the individual as a result of developmental traumas? Or might these destructive affects instead be a consequence of union experiences that include but are not simply reducible to historical antecedents? Jung amplifies alchemical texts that illustrate how union experiences at first create very destructive contents; in alchemical language these contents are called thief or devil, and often they assume such animal forms as the rabid dog, snake, basilisk, toad or raven (CW 14, para. 172). The borderline person's shadow, which houses these destructive contents, will commonly appear in the form of the renegade that seeks to destroy anything positive or life-giving. Another prominent shadow configuration is the seductive death demon (which Neumann calls uroboric incest), who lures the soul into a regressive fusion and plays upon the soul's memories of its original experience of the *numinosum*.

It is important to have a dual understanding of these shadow elements. On the one hand, they can be perceived as part of an introjective structure, born from the patient's ongoing need to deny the horror of his or her early perceptions. A kind of inner fifth column is thereby created—what Bion represents as the *fiend* that lies (Meltzer, 1978, pp. 106ff.). This image of the fiend is clearly identical to the devil, who carries the destructive function in many religions. On the other hand, *extremely destructive states of mind can be created through the experience of union*; these dark creations attempt to destroy the memory of the union experience, and they shred the patient's recall of the god-experience. The so-called negative therapeutic reaction is susceptible to containment when both patient and therapist become conscious of the fact that a union experience, though barely perceptible, has previously occurred. Such union experiences are registered in dreams and may also be experienced as processes between two people.

The union experience is of special significance when one is working with the borderline person. Through it, the therapist introjects the person's previously split-off, helpless self, which, as I have noted, commonly takes the form of an injured or tormented young child. Such union experiences, including their resulting demonic products, can bring to light the patient's constant inner struggle—a battle between life and death in which the opposing forces are God and the Devil. When this conflict is unconscious, it is manifested in sado-masochistic dyads that structure the patient's inner life and relationships. This sado-masochistic style creates a relatively safe territory for the patient, even though he or she must pay dearly for it. The toll is taken in terms of relational failures and an undermining of creativity and all forms of self-assertion.

When the truly demonic parts of a person become conscious, a new stage is set, one in which death through suicide, illness or accident becomes a serious concern. At this stage, the therapist will often wonder whether the patient's previous unconscious use of splitting devices were not a better state of affairs! But if the patient can be helped to confront the death-drive within the context of union—that is, by seeing its relationship to positive experiences—he or she may discover new self-images and thus a reason for living. In alchemy, forms that are dangerous at the outset (such as the 'rabid dog' and the 'thief') later become protective of the 'child', which represents the new self. In some mysterious way, demonic aspects may be necessary for the destruction of structures in the old personality that have outlived their usefulness.

Throughout this process, a grave danger lies in the therapist's need to be in control, for if this need is not surrendered, he or she becomes aligned with the 'old king', who rules the normal, competent personality. This neurotic need may severely undermine the healing process by creating more splitting in the patient and between patient and therapist. *One needs the patient's help,* otherwise the healing process cannot stand against the powerful forces of death and destruction that emerge from the psychotic parts of both patient and therapist.

To be able to *see* that the psychotic part is also the link to the *numinosum* in the borderline person is crucial for the initiation of the healing process. But once the person's madness begins to be more fully uncovered and mutually acknowledged, then the *numinosum* may be directly encountered as the transcendent Self. I believe this experience is what Grotstein calls the 'background object'.[8] One would hardly expect to discover the *numinosum* amidst the confusion, splitting and denial that can dominate treatment. But the *numinosum* is nevertheless present. This transcendent Self is not created through interpersonal relations, but rather an *increatum* (an *a priori*), and the patient's birthright. When the *numinosum* incarnates, healing is nearby.

But the forces of death or destruction must never be underestimated. The devil works at this stage of potential healing as a trickster, luring the therapist into thinking that all is well and often seducing him or her away from an encounter with the patient's madness. Once the *numinosum* becomes part of the patient's (normal-neurotic) functioning personality, we enter a phase in which the patient aligns with life and against death.

The linking of the normal-neurotic to the psychotic part of the patient is a crucial treatment issue. I have underscored the importance of imaginal sight in this process. Also, the therapist must remain vigilant; he or she must be careful not to split the person into separate functioning and psychotic parts. The patient's splitting and denial can be so strong that the 'normal' part may be favoured by the therapist. Both parts must, instead, be seen as fragments of a whole.

Discovering the existence of the unconscious dyad and entering the imaginal process it engenders can lead to the transformation of the interactive field, so that an ability to play and an experience of the transcendent function (*CW* 7, para. 121) can emerge. This transformed space is crucial because it allows a possibility of linkage between the normal and psychotic personality that cannot be achieved through acts of interpretation (Grotstein, 1979, p. 175).

The borderline person lacks a transcendent function. This is not to say that a link between conscious and unconscious does not exist—in fact, the person may have a channel through which the unconscious may be freely brought to consciousness. According to André Green and others (see Meissner, 1984, pp. 55ff.), borderline persons do not manifest *functional* transitional phenomena:

> Borderline patients are characterized by a failure to create functional byproducts of potential space; instead of manifesting transitional phenomena, they create symptoms to fulfill the function of transitional phenomena. By this I do not mean to say that borderline patients are unable to create transitional objects or phenomena. To say such a thing would be to ignore the fact that many artists are borderline personalities. In fact it can only be said that from the point of view of the psychic apparatus of such individuals, transitional objects or phenomena have no functional value, as they do for others. [Green, 1977, p. 38]

The borderline person has little capacity to play with the unconscious, to affect it by consciousness or to allow the conscious personality to be affected by the unconscious. Instead, the unconscious will pronounce itself by presenting the patient with extremely concrete associations to dreams which rarely lead to other associations; or with a random flood of ideas, or, conversely, with a total incapacity for free association or imagination. The borderline person may be a psychic or a creative person of great gifts, yet he or she is usually only a 'receiver' for this information and can rarely interact with it in a meaningful way. Borderline persons can often use their psychic gifts to help others but can do little to aid themselves. Subject to the unconscious, they feel completely helpless when confronted with its contents. Therefore, creation of a transcendent function is especially crucial for the therapy of the borderline individual.

I suggest a model of a psychotic part that contains a parental couple that is a single object (a negative state of the hermaphrodite) and wherein the soul is terribly afflicted by the death-force that incarnates as the renegade. Yet, by imaginally working with the unconscious dyad manifesting between patient and therapist, a transcendent function can emerge that will link the normal-neurotic and the psychotic parts of the patient. Throughout the process, vision will be severely curtailed unless there is a profound recognition of the *numinosum*. That uncreated element—often perceived in the background, or fusing with the normal personality to create a polluted state—must be seen as the patient's birthright and an essential source of healing.

NOTES

1. The following statement by Claude Lévi-Strauss describes an approach to psychic material that precisely mirrors Jung's model, and, indeed, my own: 'Many psychoanalysts would refuse to admit that the psychic constellations which reappear in the patient's conscious could constitute a myth. These represent, they say, real events which it is sometimes possible to date. ... We do not question these facts. But we should ask ourselves whether the therapeutic value of the cure depends on the actual characterization of remembered situations, or whether the traumatizing power of these situations stems from the fact that at the moment they appear, the subject experiences them immediately as living myth. ... The traumatizing power of any situation cannot result from its intrinsic features but must, rather, result from the capacity of certain events ... to induce an emotional crystallization which is molded by pre-existing structure ... these structural laws are truly a-temporal' (1967, p. 197ff.).

2. André Green's discussion of what he calls 'tertiary processes' is pertinent here. He defines these processes as 'not materialized but made of conjunctive and disjunctive mechanisms in order to act as a go-between of primary and secondary process. It is the most efficient mode of establishing a flexible mental equilibrium and the richest tool for creativity, safeguarding against the nuisance of splitting, an excess of which leads to psychic death. Yet splitting is essential in providing a way out of confusion. Such is the fate of human bondage, that it has to serve two contrary masters—separation and reunion— one or the other, or both' (1977, pp. 41–42). Green's 'tertiary processes' occur, I believe, in the interactive fields I am describing. This process, as he says, links 'conjunctive and disjunctive mechanisms', or, in our terms, the separating and conjoining aspects of the *coniunctio*. We also recognize the need for interpretation which always involves some degree of splitting.

3. For an important discussion of masochism by Gordon see chapter twelve in this volume.

4. This interpretive attempt was clumsy and useless to the patient; it was stated to relieve my own discomfort.

5. In this discussion I have not focused upon the patient's maternal experiences, which certainly contributed to her splitting defences. My impression is that they may have had lesser developmental significance than abandonment issues with her father.
6. See M. Eigen's *The Psychotic Core* (1986b) for a masterful discussion of psychosis.
7. The criteria for borderline personality listed in the updated version, DSM III-R, do not change the argument that follows.
8. He writes that this 'corresponds to the most archaic organizing internal object which offers background support for the infant's development. ... it is one which is awesome, majestic, unseen, and behind one. It "rears" us and sends us off into the world. In moments of quiet repose we sit on its lap metaphorically. In psychotic illness and in borderline states it is severely damaged or compromised' (1979, p. 154n).

REFERENCES

American Psychiatric Association (1980). *Diagnostic and Statistical Manual of Mental Disorders* (Third Edition). Washington, DC: APA.

Copleston, F. (1985). *A History of Philosophy,* Vol. 3. New York: Doubleday/Image.

Eigen, M. (1985). Toward Bion's starting point: between catastrophy and faith. *International Journal of Psycho-Analysis* 66:2.

———— (1986a). The personal and anonymous 'I'. *Voices.* Vol. 21, Nos. 3 & 4.

———— (1986b). *The Psychotic Core.* New York: Jason Aronson.

Green, Andre. (1977). The borderline concept. In P. Hartocollis (ed.), *Borderline Personality Disorders.* New York: International Universities Press.

Grinberg, L. (1977). An approach to understanding borderline disorders. In P. Hartocollis (ed.), *Borderline Personality Disorders.* New York: International Universities Press.

Grotstein, J. (1979). The psychoanalytic concept of the borderline organization. In J. Le Boit & A. Capponi (eds.), *Advances in Psychotherapy of the Borderline Patient.* New York: Jason Aronson.

Jung, C. G. (1975). *Letters,* vol. 2. Princeton, NJ: Princeton University Press.

Khan, M. (1974). *The Privacy of the Self.* London: Hogarth.

Lacan, J. (1977). *Ecrits* (translated by A. Sheridan). New York: Norton.

Lévi-Strauss, C. (1967). *Structural Anthropology.* New York: Doubleday.

McLean, A. (ed). (1980). *The Rosary of the Philosophers*. Edinburgh: Magnum Opus Hermetic Sourceworks No. 6.

Meissner, W. (1984). *The Borderline Spectrum*. New York: Jason Aronson.

Meltzer, D. (1978). The clinical significance of the work of Bion. In *The Kleinian Development,* Part III. Strath Tay, Perthshire: Clunie Press.

Schwartz-Salant, N. (1982). *Narcissism and Character Transformation: The Psychology of Narcissistic Character Disorders*. Toronto, Ontario: Inner City.

———— (1986). On the subtle body concept in analytical practice. *Chiron*. Wilmette, IL: Chiron Publications.

———— (1988a). Archetypal foundations of projective identification. *Journal of Analytical Psychology* 33:1.

———— (1988b). *The Borderline Personality: Vision and Healing.* Wilmette, IL: Chiron Publications.

Searles, H. (1979). Dual- and multiple-identity processes in borderline ego-functioning. In P. Hartocollis (ed.), *Borderline Personality Disorders*. New York: International Universities Press.

Williams, R. (1980). *Christian Spirituality: A Theological History From the New Testament to Luther and St. John of the Cross*. Atlanta, GA: John Knox Press (British title: *The Wound of Knowledge*.)

CHAPTER NINE

The treatment of chronic psychoses

C. T. Frey-Wehrlin, R. Bosnak, F. Langegger, Ch. Robinson

*Though said to be a report, this short paper by Dr. Frey and his
colleagues from the Zürichberg Clinic in Zürich is in fact a
thought-provoking disquisition on the subject of chronicity in
psychological illness. As such, it contains a wealth of ideas for the
workaday clinician, some of them tending to the optimistic, some
to the pessimistic. The authors propose that our concern for the
chronic patient is truly a concern for something chronic in
ourselves—'the shadow of our individuality'.*

A.S.

As it is now more than thirteen years since the Zürichberg
Clinic opened, we welcome the opportunity to report on
our experiences with psychotic patients and to follow it up
with some reflections based on these experiences.

First published in *The Journal of Analytical Psychology* 23:3, in 1978.
Published here by kind permission of the senior author and the Society of
Analytical Psychology.

To begin with, a brief description of the setting: the Zürichberg Clinic is a State-accredited, closed psychiatric clinic. It houses 35 patients in two buildings. Although in the annexe boarders are free to come and go, the main building is run as a closed nursing home, the centre of which is a closely supervised eleven-bedded ward.

The team looking after the patients consists of the following: five analytically trained physicians and seven analytical psychologists provide individual psychotherapy, usually three times a week. (All twelve work with out-patients as well.) Two art therapists introduce the patients to drawing, painting, and modelling in clay. There is also a weekly general discussion group as well as a Gestalt group, psychodrama, a group for physical education and another on music; a therapist for breathing technique is available when required. The nursing team consists of a dozen nurses (male and female). A further six people do the housework and kitchen work. The director, and the administrator who also works as a therapist, are assisted by two secretaries. Contact among the personnel is assured by regular conferences several times a week as well as by frequent personal conversations.

Patients with all kinds of psychiatric diagnoses, except severe organic illness, are represented; one-third suffer from schizophrenia, one-sixth from manic-depressive psychosis and the rest mainly from severe neuroses and addictions. More than half the patients are under 30 years old. About half are Swiss. In addition, about 20 nationalities have been represented, mainly from Europe and the United States, and psychotherapy has been conducted in ten languages. This mixture is fortuitous; admissions are in no way selected.

It would be tempting to try to convey an impression of the variety of our lives to you—the routine day, interrupted by feast days and holiday camps, the empty boredom which repeatedly afflicts the whole community, the silent or noisy despair of individuals, natural death by old age, or suicide, and the successes, sometimes after long and arduous labour, sometimes sudden and unexpected. Surely almost all modern psychiatric private nursing homes are familiar with such events, which offer nothing new. How often, for example, are spectacular successes, on closer investigation, reducible to average expectations?

In this paper we should like to focus on one aspect of our clinical work which, however peripheral, nevertheless makes constant and insistent demands on our attention. We should like to discuss the dark side of the healing process, that of the chronic and incurable. As early as 1861 Griesinger (1871) had noted in his text-book that while one-third of the inmates of psychiatric hospitals in Germany get well and one-third improve, the other third are incurable. Do these figures differ essentially from those of today?

Pschyrembel's medical dictionary defines 'chronic' as 'slow to develop, slow in its course'. But this is not the meaning the term has for us. 'A case has become chronic' means that our therapeutic efforts have been of no avail, have become ineffectual. 'Experience teaches that active treatment is of no further use.' The patient is then removed from a 'therapeutic' institution in order to make room for another who may be helped; he is transferred to a 'caretaking' institution where less effort is made because it is no longer worth it. 'Chronic' means no further development, final standstill. It means unchangeable—hopeless.

How do these patients come to us? Maybe one of our colleagues has been working with a patient for a longish time as an out-patient when the condition worsens, thus necessitating admission. Or, again, a case is admitted because treatment at another clinic has failed to bring about the desired result. The experienced clinician sometimes knows that it is a hopeless case. Nevertheless, we respond as if we did not know this and proceed to treat such cases, in our usual way, in tacit expectation that 'progress' will be made. Nor are we strangers to ambition in therapy; we like the challenge of a difficult case.

New surroundings and the therapist's enthusiasm have a stimulating effect on the patient: his condition improves. Nonetheless we know the improvement will not last, and deterioration, when it comes, is therefore not unexpected. But renewed improvement brings new hope: relapses can be 'explained', e.g. by the unfavourable effect of a visit by a relative.

But there comes a time when all this changes. The therapist leafs through the patient's records kept by the physician in charge in which the condition and behaviour of the patient are recorded. This is how the therapist experienced the patient in the last session—but, alas, the entry was made four years ago. It is now that the therapist comes to realize that, from the clinical point of view, four years of intensive work have been wasted. Furthermore, he must reckon that possibly, or even probably, nothing is going to change in the future. He is treating a chronic case.

This realization changes the situation in a fundamental way. The joint efforts of therapist and patient hitherto were based on the expectation that, sooner or later, the patient would get well. This fundamental assumption has now been demolished. The disquieting question arises whether the attitude which aimed at an ultimate recovery was ever really appropriate. This can hardly have been the case since it left out a reality—the chronic nature of the case. On the contrary, the expectation of a cure had prevented the therapist from completely accepting his patient; he had put him under pressure of becoming a success, and the patient could not live up to this expectation.

Paradoxically, it is at this point that, sometimes, a ray of hope appears which, every now and then, may be fulfilled. Now liberated from the pressure to succeed, the patient finds he can breathe freely in the new atmosphere, and thus may still find his own way to recovery (Rupp, 1974).

If we remind ourselves of the original meaning of the word *therapeia*—'tending'—psychotherapy continues even when there is no success in sight. Thus 'to accompany' takes the place of the 'urge to heal'—a more modest approach. 'The great departs; the small approaches' is the essence of the sign *P'i*, Standstill (Stagnation) in the *I Ching*. This finds expression in the method of the analysis. It remains analysis in the strict sense, inasmuch as the unconscious continues to lead; the patient reports phantasies, dreams, hallucinations. But the interpretations become more modest. They are limited to integrating the unconscious products into the framework of the patient's by now restricted existence (and thus, perhaps, opening it up a little). Often the interpretations are limited to what Fierz, with reference to Klaesi, once called 'valuing'—that is, the value of the unconscious products is recognized (personal communication).

An example may serve to illustrate that this, too, may be meaningful. A patient had been in the Clinic for ten years. He was completely absorbed in observing his stomach and in the scrupulous observance of a self-prescribed diet. At times he was bedridden; then again there were times when he felt more free and could even do regular errands for the Clinic. One day he decided to exchange our Clinic for a dietetic nursing home. Once there, he telephoned occasionally, complaining of loneliness and asking for visits. Then one day, completely without warning, he committed suicide. Would it not be reasonable to assume that the familiar surroundings of our Clinic and regular talks with his therapist could have prevented this?

We should like to raise the question of how the therapist can stand having spent years doing 'futile' work.

To begin with it should be noted that 'futile' has been put in quotation marks. Certainly the work of the analyst does not serve to re-establish the patient's 'capacity to work and play'. But caring for the sick and for invalids is practised everywhere, be it as Christian charity or as some form of social ethos or other. Such an ethos may motivate us for part of the way, but in itself it is not adequate. It is possible to sustain a great effort for any length of time only if one does it for oneself. This observation is not as pessimistic as it may sound, since it refers not so much to the ego as to the self. For even though the ego may enjoy the patient's transference—that is, the feeling of being loved and of power— this, too, becomes tedious in time, all due respect to our narcissistic needs notwithstanding.

We believe that our response to the chronic patient has deeper roots. Let us remember the therapist's astonishment when he noticed that the clinical picture of his patient had not changed during four years. Apparently he did not have the impression of doing meaningless work, he did not feel that his work had been wasted although, objectively, this was the real state of affairs. What then gave him the feeling of doing something worthwhile? What is our concern for the chronic patient if it is not the concern for our own chronic illness? It is that which is most distinctly our own, that from which we suffer; although it may have been touched upon during our own analysis, yet it has remained untransformed. It is sick, unproductive, evil and infantile—it is the shadow of our individuality.

This shadow can be realized very little, if at all. Nevertheless, it continues to live and wants to be accepted. Therapy in the spirit of Jung's analytical psychology does not mean, even with chronic patients, 'objective treatment'; rather, it means engagement and encounter which corresponds symbolically to the alchemical process in as much as both partners are involved. Indeed, the chronic defies transformation but not recognition, and such recognition may become both profound and differentiated. In this way reflection and awareness are brought about.

But why does chronic illness defy transformation? We know that Chronos, the father of Zeus, knew how to prevent all further development by devouring his children. Only Zeus could be rescued by his mother and taken to a safe place until he could outwit his father and defeat him 'with guile and strength' (Kerenyi, 1951, p. 29). Ever since, Chronos, whose reign corresponds to the Golden Age, has lived on the outermost edge of the earth, on the Isles of the Blessed.

The myth reveals that aspect of the resistance which prevents any change in the chronic. He remains where the 'honey flows', in paradise where life knows no hardship. Expulsion from paradise is resisted with any and every means; thus a violent attempt to eject him from paradise, to push him into life, may provoke an attempt at suicide. If, however, a genuine rebellion on the part of Zeus takes place—or, to put it analytically, if the arousing affect of the therapist is derived from a syntonic countertransference (Fordham, 1957, p. 142f.), then an unblocking of the chronic condition may yet occur, effecting a transformation to a greater or lesser extent. Even an experienced therapist needs more than just 'guile and strength' for the timing and doing of such actions—he also needs luck. In the final analysis the therapy of chronic patients consists of waiting for this moment—even if it never comes.

Working with chronic patients suggests, inevitably, the comparison with Sisyphus. Again and again Sisyphus rolls his boulder to the summit of the mountain where it slips out of his hands and disappears into the abyss. Sisyphus follows it into the depths. According to Albert Camus,

> It is just during his descent, in the interval that Sisyphus interests me. ... I see this man descending with measured tread, approaching the agony of which he cannot see the end. This hour is like a sigh of relief: it will return as surely as his torment. It is the hour of his consciousness. Each time when he leaves the heights and gradually descends into the caverns of

the gods he transcends his fate. He is stronger than his boulder. [Camus, 1942, p. 155]

The awareness which emerges from our efforts on behalf of the chronic patient includes, in addition to subjective, also objective knowledge. The increasing differentiation of the analysis reveals psychic micro-structures which do not necessarily become accessible during routine, especially ambulatory, analysis. What we see here is psychology in the broadest sense which extends far beyond the individual patient. It seems to have been this aspect that interested Jung above all else during his clinical years. His patient Babette was for him 'a pleasant old creature because she had such lovely delusions and said such interesting things' (Jung, 1963, p. 128). But he added that he had 'seen other cases in which this kind of attentive entering into the personality of the patient produced a lasting therapeutic effect.' Meier describes a similar case (Meier, 1975, pp. 130ff.), and Fierz reports the same of Binswanger, who carefully explored cases described in his studies of schizophrenia for months but without any therapeutic intention or hope (Binswanger, 1957). While these investigations were being conducted, a significant improvement was registered in each case.

There is something else which must not be overlooked. It is well known that a chronic schizophrenic can experience, albeit seldom, a spontaneous remission even after many years. Should this happen, it will make a difference to the patient, who has to re-enter life, whether the duration of his illness—possibly many years of his life—figures as a great void or whether it was filled in by a stable human relationship and regular meaningful discussions. This, we believe, must be the aim on which to concentrate in our work with chronic patients. For it is by no means certain that severe schizophrenia can be cured by psychotherapy. Jung was also sceptical in this regard (*CW* 3). Therefore we do not see our job as technical manipulation but as an empathetic accompanying of the patient. This is far removed from resignation: it is confidence in the regulatory powers of the unconscious, which far surpass our conscious potentialities.

It appears that we have arrived once again at hope. It is always there as long as life goes on. But we are not concerned only with hope; we are also concerned with the knowledge that it may not be fulfilled. Hope lives for the future. We believe that work with chronics is to be done in the present, for the sake of the here-and-now person who faces us as well as for ourselves.

REFERENCES

Binswanger, L. (1957). *Schizophrenie*. Pfullingen: Neske.

Camus, A. (1942). *Le Mythe de Sisyphe*. Paris: Gallimard.

Fordham, M. (1957). Notes on the transference. In *Technique in Jungian Analysis*. Library of Analytical Psychology, Vol. 2. [Reprinted 1989 with corrections and new introduction by J. Hubback.] London: Karnac Books.

Griesinger, W. (1871). *Die Pathologie und Therapie der psychischen Krankheiten*. Braunschweig: Wreden.

Jung, C. G. (1963). *Memories, Dreams, Reflections*. London: Collins and Routledge & Kegan Paul.

Kerenyi, K. (1951). *Die Mythologie der Griechen*. Zurich: Rheinverlag (Harmondsworth, Middlesex: Pelican Books, 1958).

Meier, C. A. (1975). Einige Konsequenzen der neueren Psychologie. In *Experiment und Symbol*. Olten: Walter.

Rupp, P. H. (1974). *La disperazione dell'analista*. Venice-Padova: Marsilio.

CHAPTER TEN

The energy of warring and combining opposites: problems for the psychotic patient and the therapist in achieving the symbolic situation

Joseph Redfearn

As Editor, I should like to pick out the ideas in Redfearn's paper that have strongly influenced me since I first heard it in 1977.

1. *Psychosis involves a distortion in the relation to the Other who tends to get used as a dumping ground.*
2. *The self always contains a body-self. But in psychosis, particularly, the physical pole of the psyche–soma spectrum is activated (or suppressed). This needs to be taken into account in therapy.*
3. *When considering who or what might function as a transforming container for psychotic process, one should not be too idealistic; many improvised solutions can do this.*
4. *At the level of the primal relationship, simple and straightforward affect is translated into something far more primitive and explosive.*

First published in *The Journal of Analytical Psychology* 23:3, in 1978. Published here by kind permission of the author and the Society of Analytical Psychology.

5. 'Affective psychoses represent premature attempts to attain whole-person feelings.' This preserves a prospective or teleological function for psychosis.
6. There is something that can be called 'pseudo-health'. This is based on an unrelated projection of bad stuff rather than achieved via 'suffering and transformation'. Though noticeable in psychotics, this can also be seen in non-psychotic persons.

It is worth adding that there is still no residential centre in Britain of the kind wished for by Redfearn.

A.S.

I want to discuss some of the problems the therapist may have in coping with conflicting opposites in his 'psychotic' patients and in the psychotic parts of his 'normal' patients and of himself. Of course, the psychotic patient may often impute evil motives or intentions to the therapist when an impasse or frustration arises, but it is not always as simple as that. The patient may actually need to unload pain or evil into, or onto, the therapist. For the patient this may be a matter of survival or at least of bodily health.

The level at which psychic and psycho-physical interactions of this type take place I am calling the level of the primal relationship. It is in many ways similar to that which exists between the mother and her baby. At this level we are sensitive to emotional atmosphere, even to a quite detailed and specific degree. So-called narcissistic needs *are* bodily needs. The need to *unload* badness and later to *project* badness is a physical as well as a psychic necessity.

Using the terminology of Erich Neumann (1954), we are dealing with the uroboric stage of psychic development and the early part of the great mother stage when we have a life-giving all-powerful world or great mother, and a world-destroying and annihilating great mother.

Many of us are familiar with the untreated psychotic patient who apparently *has* to act out violently, even murderously, in order to obtain relief for himself. By the same token we as therapists may need to distance ourselves or at least share with other helpers the bad or destructive projections and the physical effects of these bad feelings 'put into us' by our psychotic patients. And so the problem becomes a wider social one.

At the level of the uroboros we are probably dealing with undifferentiated psychic energy and an undifferentiated cosmos. Later, we are dealing with the differentiation of opposing drives and with the corresponding opposing emotions and images, and still we are up against forces of the most powerful and elemental kind, in both creative and destructive relationships with each other. We must not forget that there is a disintegrative process in nature and in the human psyche which is itself the opposite of the creative synthesis of opposites which we associate with the symbolic process. Ignoring the death-dealing, implacable, maiming aspects of nature and of ourselves is a perilous and suicidal attitude. In dealing with psychotics we need to explore these levels in ourselves, in our patients, and in society.

This primal psychic level has much to do with the archetypal aspects of union and separation, and with the immense creative and potentially destructive energies involved. Union has to do with love, merging, linking, feeding, the *coniunctio oppositorum,* and creation. In a less positive form it has to do with hallucinations, delusions and ideas of reference.

Separation in its positive aspects has to do with differentiation, with the avoidance of distress, pain, and over-excitation. We avoid the pain of conflicting feelings by separating. We discontinue unions which are unbearable—too depressing, too much of a strain, bad for the health, poisoning or debilitating or depleting or injuring us, or which are simply too confusing and chaotic. We avoid being painfully penetrated, or invaded, or swallowed up, or taken over, or annihilated—treated as a non-person. But the psychotic person in his need to survive does all these things to us, and he has to, or else suffer these things himself. For brevity we use some such term as splitting *defences* in the patient. They are experienced as extremely *offensive* if they are at all effective.

The healing of splitting defences is always painful to patient and analyst. It requires, in order of priority, survival, recognition, concern, and even love on the part of the therapist. Fortunately the patient often teaches the therapist how to provide these things in time.

The containing and holding aspects
of the mother–therapist and later of the ego

If we take the alchemical image of opposing psychic forces or substances coming into contact inside a container, with the absorption or creation of energy, we can use this image as a model with which to understand the phenomena of psychosis.

First of all, let us consider the symbolic process, the process involved in therapy and in individuation. A personal conflict or life crisis will result in the activation of conflicting unconscious tendencies—opposing archetypal activities. In the working-out of such conflicts, the healthy person will be able to use some containing element in order that the energy produced will be harnessed and used creatively rather than being wasted, or producing destruction, explosion, or disintegration. In other words he will, in the course of maturation, have learned how to sustain and resolve conflicts within himself. The capacity to sustain and resolve conflicts is usually regarded as an important aspect of the ego. In the early months of life the mother and the environment subserve this holding function, and the maturing ego introjects the mother's particular ways of holding and containing, of restraining, delaying, and delimiting conflicting instinctual patterns. The symbolic attitude is normally dependent upon the introjection of the mother's holding capacity. It may have to be learned from the therapist, of course, *by example*.

If the holding capacity of the ego is not adequate to enable the conflict to be sustained and result in the emergence of a life-enhancing symbol or in creative activity, various makeshift vessel-like functions may be used. A parent or parent-substitute, a friend or analyst, the analytical situation, conventions, rules, moral principles, rituals, a persona function, dramatization, turning the conflict into a play activity, or the framework or structure of aesthetic activity, all these are in universal use for providing the structure, the limits and the inhibitions within which the ethical conflict can be resolved. All these are therefore versions of the alchemical vessel, or are parts or fragments or miniature versions of it. They could be called ego-aids or ego-substitutes in this context.

This 'alchemical vessel' in the mature person corresponds with a sense of personal identity based on the body image. In other words, the vessel has basically a human form. At this basic level the vessel, the body of the great mother, and the body-self of the individual are not differentiable (cf. Neumann, 1955).

As I have said, this containing function, although innate, is normally experienced and differentiated through the experience of the baby of its mother's affirmative, recognizing attitude towards himself as a person (Newton & Redfearn, 1977).

The mother–vessel–self archetype is at first coterminous with the cosmos and is at first relatively unbounded and undifferentiated. The containing and limiting of excitation is done by the actual mother. Later the mother—her insides, so to speak—are experienced archetypally as paradise, a treasure house, or as hell, depending essentially on whether she is experienced as giving herself or taking herself away from the baby.

Later still, the mother acquires more human dimensions, and the containing function is located in the individual's own personal bodily self. In the joys and sorrows of the personal relationship between mother and infant there still goes on the sharing of treasures and the pangs of hurt in the give-and-take of feeding, playing, and communication.

Going back to the idea of the alchemical vessel's being an analogue of the body-ego, we must understand that the 'vessel' of the strong mature individual can contain and transform large amounts of energy produced by the meeting of opposites. On the other hand, for example, the 'vessel' of the weak, schizoid individual can contain and harness little energy. He is easily over-excited. Energy easily reaches the level where it is experienced destructively. It soon assumes omnipotent dimensions, and it tends readily to be experienced either as an attribute of the 'ego', or to be projected and thus be alienated from the ego. The situation in either case involves an absence of real responsibility in relation to the energy or forces concerned.

Thus for the borderline person the approaching 'Other' has often to be pushed away or else experienced as part of oneself or completely under one's control. If incorporated, the 'Other' may become bad and have to be extruded. All these phenomena are consciously experienced in the body-ego of the stronger person. The body-ego of the strong person can 'contain' large amounts of love and energy, whereas the body-ego of the weak person can 'contain' little before spilling over in premature ejaculation, metaphorical or literal, or in acting-out or in anger (see Lowen, 1966). On the other hand, we hear of holy men capable of actually taking into themselves not only the problems but even the bodily diseases of friends or others, of suffering them and of getting over them. Whether these stories are strictly factual or not, they illustrate my concept of strong vessels.

Now, as the heirs of Wilhelm Reich assert, the amount of containable energy depends on the absence of neurotic 'armouring' and the aliveness of the body. I myself am not equating aliveness with absence of suffering or even of disease.

For example, the bodily pseudo-health of many eccentrics, ascetics, schizophrenic and hypomanic persons may be achieved at the expense of relatedness rather than through suffering and transformation. And this can apply to the 'narcissistic' person who is well within the range of the normal.

This hypothesis, namely that there is apparent health based on projection of the bad, and another kind based on acceptance and transformation, is at present just a suggestion for medical and bio-energetic research, rather than a statement of undoubted fact.

According to my hypothesis, it is not the ego that is doing the unloading or projecting but an archetypal function of the body-self. Later it has to do with the narcissistic self-image, or egotism, not, I suggest, with the ego.

In the case of patients functioning at this level, an affirmative primal feeling in therapist or attendant is very sensitively picked up and reacted to. However, this affirmative primal attitude may have to be patiently worked towards during many months of therapy and is not necessarily the 'instinctive' response of the born therapist. One's 'instinctive' response tends to be similar to or the opposite of that which the real mother originally had, or developed, towards the patient. One may have to learn from the patient over the course of time how to be able to take an affirmative or recognizing attitude towards his 'evil' or 'destructive' impulses, particularly when these involve *actual* loss and sacrifice from the therapist.

At this schizoid level of mental life, both approaching, getting closer to the patient, and separating or distancing, have to be handled with great sensitivity. For the schizoid person, the excitement which we all feel on increasing closeness tends to be experienced as invasive, destructive, or deleterious. Conversely, the withdrawal of the wanted person brings about extremely negative and destructive images or impulses, which are often projected. Thus the withdrawing loved mother or beloved person becomes a loathsome witch, a murderess, someone who ought to be got rid of. The other person has to be omnipotently controlled or becomes the object of intense energetic feelings or impulses. Thus 'I want to be closer to you' becomes 'you have sexual designs on me', or 'we are going to be married.' 'I hate you for refusing to be close to me' becomes 'you are going to murder me'; and 'I hate you for leaving me after such a short visit' can become 'you are Satan', at the level of the primal relationship. Not only is natural and correct distancing important, but so is unforced timing. At the primal level of caring, the mother is able to take her timing from the baby and his natural functions. Forcing her own time on her baby constitutes a gross disturbance, particularly at the autonomic level, and may result in a precocious ego–self relationship, a false, compliant ego-like structure rather than one truly related to the self and the unconscious, autonomically based bodily functions.

At this level the symbol does not exist, the metaphor is the experiential reality, because the excitement of the conflicting opposites cannot be contained and transformed. There is no 'as if', no sense of humour, no tolerance of ambivalence, and so all these functions have to be carried by the therapist.

'Primal scene excitement' in its most basic archetypal form belongs to this sphere of experience. In its most archaic form the engulfing interacting parent-creatures are represented in imaginal monsters or in very primitive muscular and autonomic patterns. These experiences are prehuman and prepersonal and antedate the emergence of the human self-image. This is why as the persona and the shadow are analysed, the primal scene or the *coniunctio oppositorum,* and the link between the 'I' and one's body, may assume bizarre and monstrous forms on the one hand, or sublime or god-like forms on the other.

Both the persona and the shadow are partial body-selves, at least to the extent that they remain as unadaptive and stereotyped patterns relatively alienated from the ego. I prefer to use the terms 'persona-function' and 'shadow-function' to describe the healthy, ego-available forms of these bits of the self.

The uncontainable opposites may of course originate in the environment, in the form of a psychotic or seriously disturbed parent, incessantly warring parents, or insupportable double-bind situations. I am reminded of a patient who in her psychotic state complained of not existing in her body and of a feeling of being situated outside her body. When I met her mother with her lying self-deceptions, I felt precisely the same feelings as my patient complained of, and I knew exactly why the patient felt as she did. R. D. Laing (1961) in England and Harold Searles (1965) in the United States have convincingly described massive introjections of psychotic parents and psychotogenic situations, and so there is no need for me to elaborate on these. Jung was possibly the first to emphasize how parents in a sense force themselves, their world, and particularly their unconscious complexes on their children.

At the schizoid level, bodily impulses and affective discharges are experienced as cosmic events. Later in life, unintegrated patterns of affective discharge, when they are alien to the ego, are experienced in the same way, i.e. as alien forces. Patients describe their unintegrated discharges as mighty winds or as elemental forces, and so on. Jung gives an excellent example in his dream of his own struggle against a strong wind with his shadow going before him (Jung, 1963). He observes that the shadow is thrown by the tiny light of consciousness. Newton and I described how in a borderline patient her pregenital bodily impulses and her infantile rage were at first experienced in this way, i.e. as uncontrollable elemental forces, and how through the affirmative primal relationship with the analyst these parts of the self were gradually contained by and functionally related to the now more friendly ego (Newton & Redfearn, 1977).

'Containment by the ego' should not be confused with the concept of mastery and control, which is a manic or obsessional defence, as illusory as mastering the wind or controlling the lightning. Premature and stereotyped posturing in relation to these archetypal forces are rife in collective psychology and certainly should not be added to by the analytical psychologist. All 'techniques' constitute illusions of this sort. Premature reductive interpretations as well as naive introjections and idealizations on the part of the therapist may both be damaging, because both increase splitting defences. If there is a split between the bodily and the spiritual, we should not make matters worse with one-sided interpretations.

So much for the pre-personal level of psychic functioning. An analyst who is not aware of this level of functioning in himself could not be expected to cope with patients in whom things were wrong at this level. A mother who was not functioning well at this level, not being a person, could not help her child become a person with a personal sense of identity.

Manic and depressive parts of the self

Whereas the schizoid or paranoid person splits and projects the bad in order to survive, we might say that the depressive person takes in the bad in order to preserve the loved Other, and the manic person denies his feelings of badness and dependence upon the loved Other. The depressive person tends to take the Other into himself whole, denying the bad parts and denying his anger for fear of loss and fear of damaging the Other. So one can say that affective psychoses represent premature attempts to attain whole-person feelings. They are premature because the goodness or badness is not fully accepted before being transformed. Manic denial is short-cut transformation, depressive introjection is defensive incorporation of the bad. Using an oral metaphor, there is as yet no chewing and taking in only the good while spitting out the bad.

By about the age of eight months, as all parents know from experience, the baby is able to relate to his mother as a person, to distinguish between her and others, to differentiate her from himself, and even to care for her in a loving way. We think that his love for her causes him to feel sad or ill, rather than to hate her, when she seems to be cross with him. Paranoid and splitting mechanisms are replaced by depressive ones in which aggression is contained by the child because of the value to him of the loving primal experiences he has had with her. The normal infant can begin to delay or inhibit his impulses. He remembers his mother in her differing aspects, coming and going, giving and withholding, loving him and being angry with him, and so on.

The good and bad great mother now has a much more human form, the infant is more outside the mother, more of an individual person, provided that his mother has affirmed him as such and continues to do so. We are now entering Neumann's patriarchal stage, the beginning of Margaret Mahler's stage of individuation and separation from the mother and from the symbiotic capsule containing mother and child in the dual unity of the primal relationship (Mahler, 1969).

Both depression and mania, it seems to me, involve premature and unsuccessful attempts to swallow the loved Other whole, with opposite but equally ineffective ways of dealing with bad or unacceptable feelings.

As far as treatment is concerned, I suppose one's main pre-occupation in treating depressive patients is to protect them from their own self-destructiveness and help them dare feel angry with the loved Other. One's main pre-occupation with manic patients, on the other hand, is often to assert and maintain one's own identity and point of view, because one feels constantly in danger of being swallowed up and taken over by them. The depressive patient feels devoured by the self, the manic patient feels he has devoured the self, as Jung so well understood (CW 7). The self includes the archetypes in projection, including the mother and often the combined parents. I well remember the excited and omnipotent state I was in when I first felt I had devoured my analyst, and he coped by relying non-analytically on my good feelings and on the established relationship between us. Where this does not exist, therapy of manic conditions is not possible in my experience. The patient usually terminates the relationship as he feels perfectly well.

It would be hardly conceivable to me to deal analytically with depressed patients without using notions about anger, bad feelings, swallowing and incorporation, feelings of being over-whelmed, and so on. It would be hardly possible for me to relate to the manic parts of my patients or myself without using similar, I hope well-digested, concepts of denial of dependence, control, triumph, and contempt.

I hope I have managed to give some indication of how I am always trying to relate the so-called symptomatology of the patient with his behaviour, his body-self, at the level where we can understand these so-called defence mechanisms in terms of unconscious phantasies and, fundamentally, to archetypal pro-cesses and the self, which includes the actual functioning of the digestive system, let us remember. To become caught up in the patient's fantasies without relating them to his actual behaviour or to things happening to him is to become swallowed up in him and in his psychosis, which is abandoning him in a very real sense.

Countertransference towards psychotic patients

The infectiousness of manic patients is of course well known; one tends to be swallowed up by them in the sense of being taken over by their mood and viewpoint, until the snapping point is reached where one can no longer go along with them and one has to take over, to contain *them,* in other words. For example, they may be spending all the family's money or refusing to pay one's fees. This snapping point in several patients in my case was a real 'gut' reaction. I found that to go along with them in their world was an increasingly gut-twisting, gut-tightening exercise until I rescued my guts by asserting myself and my own viewpoint. I am quite sure my intestines were actually involved in the way these words indicate. Incidentally, one of my manic patients expressed herself very pertinently one day just before she had to be hospitalized by telling me that her fondest wish at that moment was to rip out my guts, and it felt as if she were doing just that at the time.

Of course the therapist who cannot lose himself in—i.e. allow himself to be swallowed up by—his patient is no good either, although he may be good for certain moods and conditions. Although one must be prepared to struggle to maintain one's identity and values rather than be overwhelmed by the patient, one must also be prepared at all times to have one's values and identity shattered in some sense by new evidence, new circumstances, new aspects of the patient.

Countertransference feelings, or the awareness for the archetypal atmosphere at any moment, are the best guide to the psychopathological level and nature of the situation between patient and therapist being constellated. Although relatedness at a primitive level is a *sine qua non* of therapy, I myself find that when a patient has got into me to such an extent that he or she is having striking telephathies or clairvoyant dreams about me, or seems to be exerting a disturbing influence over me of this kind, it is time to summon consciously suitable resources to counteract this state of affairs. I have always found that a simple effort of awareness and will has been sufficient to effect the necessary distance or separation. Feelings of being 'got into' or 'got at' or 'swallowed' are for the experienced therapist an infallible guide to the patient's unconscious wishes and phantasies, and can give valuable information about where the patient wishes to enter you and about the amount of sadism involved in the entry or penetration. It is not the words of the personal question or remark that is the guide in this matter, but the way in which it is asked and the amount of discomfort caused in the therapist.

The countertransference feelings which I have experienced most frequently with psychotic patients are perhaps worth listing. I have often felt dismay and sadness when a patient seems to be slipping away from where one can be with him; indignation when a patient is everything good and I am all bad, and often a feeling of being robbed in such cases; I experience cold horror at schizoid callousness, for example at a description of so-called love-making when schizoid defences are prominent; I have often felt completely overwhelmed by the flood of unconscious material from patients in danger of psychosis and have found that it is often wise to say so; I have sometimes been frightened when a patient is splitting off his fear and making me feel his fear for him; tightening and twisting of the guts is a commonplace, particularly in potentially violent group situations, or when it is becoming imperative to 'cut off' from the patient for his sake or one's own; I sometimes experience numbness or weakness in the arms when a strong impulse to strike the patient is being inhibited; murderous feelings when a witch anima is being constellated. I have listed negative feelings, but the primally deprived patient often elicits impulses of primal love in the therapist—impulses to hold, stroke, caress, feed, and so on, which are more embarrassing to enumerate than the negative ones.

Now the energy with which the psychotic defence, e.g. splitting or projection, is invested is the amount of energy which has to be held and harnessed if therapy is to take place. This is the energy of the warring and combining opposites to which I have referred. It is a moving experience when a patient's holding and balancing ego replaces the patient endeavours of the therapist, and when the alienated, dreadful forces of unintegrated instinct become accepted as part of the inner world of a responsible human being. Sometimes, for example in children, this can happen quite quickly in therapy. In other cases it is a matter of months or years of patient work against the gradient of one's own instinctive nature.

The symbolic attitude requires giving full value to the unconscious and to the psyche, including visionary and numinous experience and so-called phantasy. Expressions such as 'acting-out' seem to be expressions with a bias in danger of under-valuation of the psyche. What the patient with the symbolic attitude achieves is a synthesis of acting-out and not-acting-out— a new attitude towards the impulse and the emerging symbol. We as therapists try to achieve a similar attitude towards the patient and his visions. Just as a mother who is too realistic or too autistic can kill or distort the vital magical omnipotence in her baby and can destroy all the joy of living, so the therapist who is too realistic or too autistic can prevent the therapeutic process from taking off at all. Yet he must always be true to himself and sincere in his transactions, particularly with the psychotic patient, so that if the therapist has not coped with the primal forces in himself he cannot have the necessary empathy and integrity to cope with them in his patient. This applies to the persona of course, but with psychotic patients it applies to the shadow and the anima and splitting and differentiation between good and evil at the deepest levels of the psyche, where psyche and body image and bodily activity are no longer distinguishable.

The organization of therapeutic environments

Psychotic patients demand that the relationship with the therapist be right, or got right *at the primal level*. Neurotic patients have it right anyway, more or less.

The frustrating thing about treating psychotic patients is the difficulty of providing enough treatment at this level. It is obviously not enough merely to see patients, even daily, if the rest of the time they are in a psychotogenic environment. This is why the Agnew project, places like Chestnut Lodge, and the Philadelphia Association in England are so valuable and important. We need an analogous institution for London Jungian analysts.

We in London have no residential centre in which we can look after our patients in analysis at times when they need such an environment. We have a few friendly hospitals, particularly where our members work, which go some way to providing this facility, but none where the whole staff are involved in this kind of approach to psychosis. The classical medical training and approach and the classical psychoanalytical approach are both highly schizoid, and the emphasis on the nineteenth-century scientific approach and the selection of doctors in key posts for academic brilliance exaggerate splitting between feelings and behaviour, feeling and thinking, patient and therapist, rather than healing these splits and humanizing the therapist and through him the patient. However, the younger generation of doctors do not seem as badly affected in this way as our own, and we can probably look forward to a greater understanding by the medical profession of the matters I have discussed in this paper.

Summary

The psychotic patient may not merely *project* his shadow onto the therapist. He may sometimes need to *act out* or in some way *unload* bad parts of the self onto the therapist or onto the environment in order to maintain his experience of integrity or his bodily health. These phenomena belong to the primal level of relationship analogous to that between mother and baby, when the mother is the vessel containing and meeting the interplay of opposing forces in the child. This holding and containing function of the therapist, as with that of the mother, is, hopefully, introjected by the successfully treated patient. It constitutes an important aspect of ego functioning and is necessary for the symbolic process. It is closely related to a personal sense of identity based on the body image.

The necessary affirmative holding attitude on the part of the therapist is not usually the natural or instinctive reaction to the patient. It may have to be worked towards by both patient and therapist over a long period. At this level, getting closer to the patient and withdrawing from him require great sensitivity. The timing of events may have to be taken from the patient and not imposed upon him. The withdrawing loved person so easily becomes the evil one; the treasures of her insides so easily become poisonous, persecuting, or loathsome creatures or objects. The insides of the archetypal mother, the insides of the therapist and the phenomena of the world are experienced in some sense as one. Archetypal activity is unintegrated and is experienced as ego-alien cosmic forces.

In the affective psychoses the opposites are partially but not fully assimilated and transformed in the symbolic process. The depressive person identifies with the bad in order to preserve the good aspects of the Other, whereas the manic person denies and projects feelings of badness or dependence onto the Other (often, of course, the therapist).

As therapy proceeds, the good/evil Great Mother projections assume more human form, and the energy of the conflicting opposites is held and harnessed by the patient in the symbolic process.

REFERENCES

Jung, C. G. (1963). *Memories, Dreams, Reflections.* London: Collins and Routledge & Kegan Paul.

Laing, R. D. (1961). *The Self and Others.* London: Tavistock.

Lowen, A. (1966). *Love and Orgasm.* London: Staples Press.

Mahler, M. S. (1969). *On Human Symbiosis and the Vicissitudes of Individuation.* London: Hogarth.

Neumann, E. (1954). *The Origins and History of Consciousness.* London: Routledge & Kegan Paul. [Reprinted 1989, London: Maresfield Library.]

––––––– (1955). *The Great Mother.* London: Routledge & Kegan Paul.

Newton, K., & Redfearn, J. W. T. (1977). The real mother, ego-self relations and personal identity. *Journal of Analytical Psychology* 22: 4.

Searles, H. (1965). *Collected Papers on Schizophrenia.* London: Hogarth. [Reprinted 1986, London: Maresfield Library.]

CHAPTER ELEVEN

Schreber's delusional transference: a disorder of the self

Alan Edwards

Edwards puts forward what can be described as a 'post-Jungian' viewpoint concerning the case of Schreber. To Jung's idea of an anima inflation, he adds the possibility that there may have been a 'disorder of the deintegrative–reintegrative processes' of the self (without ruling out some inborn defect). Professor Fleschig, Schreber's doctor, functioned as a paternal self-object, felt to be hostile and dangerous. Schreber identified himself with a maternal self-object, hence his gradual 'unmanning'.

From the prospective or teleological point of view, Schreber could be seen as trying, via the agency of the self, to 'heal the pathological splits ... between the maternal and paternal self-objects'.

A.S.

First published in *The Journal of Analytical Psychology* 23:3, in 1978. Published here by kind permission of the author and the Society of Analytical Psychology.

Introduction

It was in 1907 that Jung published 'The psychology of dementia praecox' (*CW* 3), and for him, and also for analytical psychology, the study of disorders of the self has always been of major interest. Now, with the presentation by Fordham of his clinical work and theoretical views on autism (1976), it seems possible to begin to extend his approach and insight into other clinical areas, and to look again at the schizophrenias, borderline states, narcissistic personality disorders, and homosexuality.

Just as in molecular biology, research focuses on the complexities of the nucleus of the cell, the D.N.A., and the R.N.A. messenger processes, so in our field it is the pathology of the original self, and of the deintegrative–reintegrative archetypal processes, the fixations of, and regression to, the early internalized self-object relationships and the interference with the development of identity, which are of concern. With these ideas in mind, I thought it might be of interest to look again at some features of the paranoid psychosis and psychotic transference towards his physician described by Daniel Paul Schreber (1955) in his *Memoirs of My Nervous Illness*. Originally published in German in 1903, it was translated into English by Macalpine and Hunter in 1955.

Clinical account

Schreber was an eminent judge who, before his illness, had been given positions of increasing responsibility. Though married, he was childless, and this had been for him a matter of some concern. His young wife was diabetic and had had a series of six still-births. His first psychotic breakdown was at the age of 42, from which he recovered after six months. When he was 51 there was a recurrence, and, as before, he was treated by Professor Fleschig of the Psychiatric Clinic of the University of Leipzig. After seven months he was moved to a mental hospital, the Sonnenstein, where he remained for a further nine years. During this time Professor Fleschig continued to remain at the centre of his persecutory delusions and hallucinations, using, Schreber thought, supernatural and hypnotic powers over him in a ruthless way. In his account, however, he insisted that he was not just airing grievances, and that religious truths had been revealed to him which he wished to make common knowledge; that he had been transformed into a woman and made pregnant by divine rays in order that 'a new race of men might be created'.

It was Jung who introduced Schreber's book to Freud, who then later published his classical paper, 'Psychoanalytical notes upon an autobiographical account of a case of paranoia (*dementia paranoides*)' (1911c). The argument presented by Freud was that the main aetiological factor in this paranoid illness was the negative oedipal conflict, with the defences against the acknowledgement of the unconscious homosexual love for the father. He also postulated fixation at the narcissistic stage of libidinal development. Jung felt dissatisfied by Freud's analysis and in *Symbols of Transformation* (*CW* 5) gave his own views on Schreber's condition.

At the outset, while in bed one morning, Schreber had a feeling, 'which thinking about it later when fully awake, struck me as highly peculiar. It was the idea that it really must be rather pleasant to be a woman succumbing to intercourse.' This idea developed further during the psychosis, and he became convinced that he was being 'unmanned' by divine rays in order to be impregnated by God, and the world thus renewed. 'The male genitals retracted into the body, and the internal sexual organs were transformed into the corresponding female sexual organs.' He asked for a scientific approach to be made towards the facts that he was presenting and thought that his body should be dissected after his death.

In his exalted and persecutory state he felt that his experiences were akin to those of an immaculate conception, and in his delusions he was both the virgin mother and suffering child hero, a world saviour and redeemer. In the divine 'miracle' which furthered these processes he felt he was not only emasculated, but also suffered splitting and smashing of bones in his head, ribs and spine, pathological changes in his internal organs, and had his body distorted in many strange ways, being given several heads at one time.

God for Schreber could be divided into two Zoroastrian gods, Ormuzd, a higher god of love and wisdom, and Ahriman, a lower god of evil, death and destruction, and also into anterior and posterior realms. The anterior realms had maternal qualities and could be healing and give states of bliss and sleep, while the posterior realms were severe and paternal, and could be persecutory. God, he thought, wished him to develop 'voluptuousness' in order that he might imagine himself as 'man and woman in one person, having intercourse with myself'. Schreber complained of God's lack of continuous contact, when he felt that God was withdrawing from him, which was the reason that when he was alone with an empty mind, he felt compelled to make loud bellowing noises.

Fleschig was believed to have contact with God and, at other times, to be God, 'Godfleschig', and to be in conspiracy with the anterior realm of God to the harm of the whole Schreber family. He could seem like a woman, on occasion a charwoman, or he was able to be swallowed. He had visions once that Fleschig had shot himself; he saw his funeral, and also the destruction of the whole world. 'About that time I had Professor Fleschig's soul and most probably his whole soul temporarily in my body. It was a fairly bulky ball or bundle which I can perhaps best compare with a corresponding volume of wadding or cobweb which had been thrown into my belly by way of a miracle, presumably to perish there. In view of its size it would in my case probably have been impossible to retain this soul in my belly, to digest it, so to speak; indeed when it attempted to free itself I let it go voluntarily, being moved by a mind of sympathy, and so it escaped through my mouth into the open again.'

Discussion

Jung said that 'a successful life makes a man forget his dependence on the unconscious' (CW 3). If the separation from the mother has not been made, 'the mother imago represents the unconscious, and turns into a Lamia'. The demands of the unconscious act like 'the bite of a poisonous snake'. According to the myths it is the woman who secretly enslaves a man, so that he can no longer free himself from her, and becomes a child again.' 'This demon-woman of mythology is in truth the sister–wife–mother, the woman in the man who unexpectedly turns up during the second half of life and tries to effect a forcible change of personality. It consists in a partial feminization of the man, and a corresponding masculination of the woman.' In the second half of life 'the assimilation of contra-sexual tendencies then becomes a task that must be fulfilled in order to keep the libido in a state of progression'.

Since the original contributions by Freud and Jung, numerous papers have been written by psychoanalysts about various aspects of Schreber's psychosis. Additional historical information has been gathered about his family, his sister, and his wife, and additional hospital case records were found, and the publications of his physician father have been further assessed. Schreber's father was an acknowledged expert, in his day, on methods of child-rearing, believing that from the beginning the strictest discipline was necessary. Within the first year, 'the art of renouncing' had to be taught, with the child being allowed to watch his mother or nurse eat food, and then when he reached for it, the morsel was taken away. In later years he believed it was important for children to sit upright, with shoulders back, and to this end he had designed various pieces of apparatus and straps.

Over the years analytical interest has shifted from the conflicts of the oedipal phase, the unconscious homosexual love for the father, as the basis for the paranoid projections, to those of the pre-oedipal phase, the intense ambivalent feelings towards the mother, and the fears of being devoured and disintegrated. R. B. White, in an excellent paper (1961), demonstrated most clearly the pre-oedipal conflicts and defences in relation to the infantile destructive impulses towards the mother, the failure to integrate them and their projection into Fleschig and God. Looking at the links now between homosexuality and paranoid illness, most analysts would see them as presenting differing defensive systems in relation to similar nuclear pre-oedipal conflicts.

For analytical psychology Schreber's psychosis is primarily approached as a disorder of the self. Here it is of value to refer to Fordham's (1976) concepts of the primal self, contributing to developing psychic structures by the process of deintegration, which he sees as a psychic as well as a physiological process. 'Deintegrates carry within them the attributes of wholeness and treat the external object as part of that wholeness', and, further, 'all the structures developed, including the perception of real objects and so of the "external" world, conform at first to the absolute criteria of the self, i.e. it is made up of self objects' (pp. 88–93). Fordham also observes the need to make a differentiation between the self and the self-object, and their representations.

In schizophrenia we are presented with a defect in the self and a failure in the deintegrative–reintegrative processes, with a fixation and regression to an early oral primitive level of self-object relationships, with splitting, merging and a lack of differentiation and clear boundaries. Psychotic identifications are based on these self-objects, which play compensatory and defensive roles. This schizophrenic defect, with the associated lack of clear definition from the human and non-human environment, means a considerable degree of psychobiological vulnerability and difficulty in adaptation.

Schreber's delusional and hallucinatory experience was vast, complex and disconnected, but one is able to begin a clarification when one understands it in terms of primitive self-object relations. Schreber's predominant identification was with an idealized maternal self-object, a merger of divine and mythological great mother figure, and that of the divine child, with the helpless infant in himself, compelled to 'bellow' when the parent withdraws.

As Fordham said, the deintegrates carry within themselves the attributes of wholeness, and that certainly applies to the paternal self-object projected on to Fleschig. He is both divine and human, male and yet female, noble and yet also containing powerful, ruthless, omnipotent, sadistic impulses, parts of Schreber's infantile shadow. The representations of the self-object seem to fuse both part object and whole object images and reveal deep splits and persisting 'enmity' between these primitive organizers of the psyche.

All the important self-object representations show the evidence of archetypal situations, and from the material preserved one gets, in addition, the feeling of the constant unconscious

activity of the self behind the psychotic transference attempting
to heal the pathological splits, particularly between the maternal
and paternal self-objects. God was trying to transform him not
only into a woman, but also into a man and woman in one person,
'having an intercourse with myself'.

The attempts of the self to bring about a creative renewal
within the psyche of Schreber, a new synthesis of the self-object,
and a firmer and more differentiated structure, are unsuccessful,
and one is reminded of Jung's suggestion that in schizophrenia it
might be that 'the destructive process is a kind of mistaken
biological defence reaction'. The possibility of psychosomatic
processes analogous to those seen in auto-immune disease, when
the body suddenly may not recognize a tissue as homologous,
treats it as foreign antigen, and forms immune antibodies, which
seek to destroy it, has been further taken up both by Stein in
discussing psychosomatic illness (1967), and Fordham in relation
to autism (1976, p. 90). If such a process were happening here,
and parts of the self were being treated as non-self, it would seem
to be in relation to the paternal self-object projected on to Fleschig
in the regressive reconstruction of the early stressful relationship
to the father who had intruded into the nursing situation so
forcefully, and had done so much to usurp the mother's role.

It was Jung also who supported the idea that biochemical
changes might play an aetiological part in schizophrenic disorders of the self; 'up to a certain point psychology is indispensable in explaining the nature and causes of the initial emotions
which give rise to the metabolic alterations. These emotions seem
to be accompanied by chemical changes that cause specific
temporary, or chronic disturbances or lesions' (CW 3, p. 272).

Certainly there was a factor in this illness which was
irreversible. There may have been an inborn defect of the self, or
as a result of the infantile stresses there may have developed a
disorder of the deintegrative–reintegrative processes with pathological splitting occurring between the archetypal self-objects.
Though well compensated for over many years, with increasing
masculine responsibility in the second half of life, and the
disappointments of having failed to become a father himself, the
acute regression took place in an attempt to reconstitute the early
situation and the self-object relationships. One can see only too

clearly the complexities and difficulties that would exist for the physician, or analyst, caught in a delusional transference of this kind, and how the maintaining of a self-object relationship merger of this intensity might well be an impossible task.

REFERENCES

Fordham, M. (1976). *The Self and Autism*. Library of Analytical Psychology, Vol. 3. London: Karnac Books.

Freud, S. (1911c). Psycho-analytic notes on an autobiographical account of a case of paranoia (*dementia paranoides*). *Standard Edition* 12. London: Hogarth.

Schreber, D. P. (1955). *Memoirs of My Nervous Illness* (translated by G. Macalpine & R. A. Hunter). London: Wm. Dawson.

Stein, L. (1967). Introducing not-self. *Journal of Analytical Psychology* 12:2.

White, R. B. (1961). The mother conflict in Schreber's psychosis. *International Journal of Psycho-Analysis* 42.

CHAPTER TWELVE

Masochism: the shadow side of the archetypal need to venerate and worship

Rosemary Gordon

Non-Jungian clinicians may well feel at home with Gordon's description of her actual clinical work with patients, because it is close to and exemplifies general psychoanalytic method and practice.

However, her vision is rooted in analytical psychology, and this has led her to explore the possible origin, meaning and function of the psychopathological syndrome of masochism in some of her patients. As with Freud, Klein and some other analysts, this search has led Gordon back to the thesis that there exists an original death drive—also interpreted by Erich Neumann, for example, as a 'wish for a weak ego to dissolve in the self', or by the Kleinian analyst Betty Joseph's suggestion that masochism may be based on the infant's belief that the price to be paid for the love of the parents is the surrender of personal separateness and individuality. But, unlike most psychoanalysts,

First published in *The Journal of Analytical Psychology* 32: 3, in 1987. Published here by kind permission of the author and the Society of Analytical Psychology.

her Jungian understanding leads her to link the death drive to themes like 'death and rebirth' and the symbolic meanings of death.

Guided by the material from her patients, by a review of the rituals and body postures in the various religions, and by themes discernible in literary works such as D. H. Lawrence's short story, 'The Woman Who Rode Away', she proposes that there is a universal, archetypal drive in humans to surrender and to worship something beyond personal being, and that masochism is the negative, the shadow side of this archetypal drive. She argues that such a pathological or perverted form can be said to exist if the need for pain is self-chosen and is an end in itself, instead of just an inescapable part of a larger goal or task.

Gordon also discusses the clinical implications and consequences in analytic work, while pathological masochism predominates, in terms of transference, countertransference, the negative therapeutic reaction, and the ineffectiveness of interpretation.

A.S.

Introduction

This paper is essentially speculative. The reactions, behaviour, and phantasies of several patients have led me to reflect whether there might be a connection between masochism on the one hand and, on the other, the belief in, worship of, and surrender to, a deity, albeit in its perverted, its shadow form.

Five cases of masochism

A man whom I will call Richard had been in analysis with me for 18 months. He was in his early fifties, a lecturer in a theological college, and married, with three grown-up children: two sons and a daughter. He was of average height, sported some middle-age spread, and always wore dark and very conventional suits. He complained of finding it very difficult to be alone, to find satisfaction in his profession, and to have the right sort of relationship with both his junior and his senior colleagues.

The main theme in many sessions was his preoccupation with death, his fear of death, his anger with death. And closely related to this battle with death was his anxious concern about the existence of God. Indeed, he felt angry and resentful that God did not seem to deign to prove to him that He exists. He did not give him the sign, the evidence for which he craved. For in spite of a life ruled by his belief in God, he was a man of the age of scientific and concrete proof, a man dependent on belief because unable to give himself over to faith. As time went on, his belief became more and more threadbare, and the existence of God seemed to him more and more unlikely and unconvincing. And then phantasies of being beaten, phantasies that excited him sexually, began to possess him. As these phantasies grew in intensity, he found himself driven to act them out with women he picked up here and there and who were willing to do as bidden. He was intensely disturbed and guilty and very angry with analysis, with me, his analyst, and with God, in the way that Sartre had expressed it when he cried out, through one of his characters: *Il n' existe pas, le Salaud* [He doesn' t exist, the bastard].

I then remembered a number of patients who had described to me masturbation phantasies in which religious rituals had taken on a markedly masochistic quality. One woman had described lying on an altar and being solemnly whipped. Another woman saw herself also on an altar in a convent being held fast, hands and feet, by four nuns, while a fifth nun, the mother superior, whipped her, and this had to happen in full view of all the sisters. A third woman patient dreamed of being beaten somewhere in a dark church and woke up to find that she was having an orgasm. And there was the male patient, Patrick, whom I described in *Dying and Creating* (Gordon, 1978). He had told me soon after he had started analysis with me that he was much involved with Artemis, the Greek goddess. For the worship of Artemis involved an annual event in which the most beautiful, most intelligent, most courageous and most perfect youth was chosen to be her sacrificial victim by being beaten to death. Patrick was a schoolmaster. The masochistic experience of this rite governed his masturbation phantasies—that is to say, he then experienced himself as this perfect youth–victim, while the sadistic role of the sacrificer tended to be enacted in his relationship to one of the boys in his class to whom he was attracted, and whose qualities he admired and idealized.

Thesis

These experiences and reflections led me to the hypothesis, expressed in the title of this paper, that masochism is closely related to man's need, probably an archetypal need, to venerate and to worship some object, some existence that transcends one's personal being; but that masochism, that impulse to want to expose oneself to pain and to suffering, is the inferior, the shadow-side, of the need to worship and to venerate. Masochism, though not often seen in these very stark, extreme and perverse forms in which they showed themselves in the patients I have just described, is nevertheless a frequent and pervasive factor in clinical work, affecting the process and the outcome of analysis. I have, therefore, thought it worthwhile to explore it in this paper.

Literature on masochism

The phenomenon of masochism seems to figure very little in Jungian literature. In fact, there is not a single reference to it in the *Index* to Jung's *Collected Works*.

It is true Jung had thought and written a good deal about sacrifice, pain and suffering and cruelty. For instance in his paper, 'Transformation symbolism in the Mass', he makes the point that '. . . for the neophyte it would be a real sin if he shrank from the torture of initiation. The torture inflicted on him is *not* a punishment but the indispensable means of leading him towards his destiny' (*CW* 11, para. 410). But in the case of punishment, initiation and sacrifice, pain is not self-chosen, nor is it the primary objective, as it is in the case of masochism. Rather, it is an imposed and inescapable part of the larger task or goal.

However, in the writings of one or two followers of Jung I have found it mentioned and discussed more directly. For instance Erich Neumann, in his *Origins and History of Consciousness* (1954), relates it to his concept of 'uroboric incest' in which a weak ego dissolves in the self, and this unconscious identity with the stronger solvent, the uroboric mother, brings pleasure, which must be called masochistic in the later perverted form. The other valuable contribution has been made by Mary Williams in her two-part article, 'The fear of death', published in the *Journal of Analytical Psychology* (1958, 1962). She writes:

> I will now make the assumption that there are two main ways of avoiding the fear of death. In the sadistic method the individual forms a counter-phobic identification with death as the destroyer. The victim is then the mortal who must die in fear and pain while the destroyer experiences the ecstasy of immortality. ... The masochistic method derives from the sadistic method and must be understood in terms of the latter, for masochism is a counter-phobic reaction to unconscious sadism. The sadist identifies with the invulnerable destroyer and projects his mortality on to his victim. The masochist identifies with the mortal victim and projects the invulnerable destroyer; thus the destroyer is sought as the saviour who will rescue him from his mortality. [1958, p. 160]

Thus, like Neumann, Mary Williams talks of the ultimate aim of masochism as 'death in ecstasy', or 'the ecstasy of immortality'.

Searching out Freud's thinking about masochism, I found that he distinguishes primary masochism from secondary masochism. And while he regards secondary masochism as a reversal, a turning upon oneself of the sadistic impulses and feelings experienced towards another, primary masochism is the direct expression of Thanatos, the death drive, when its object is still one's own self; it is not yet the consequence of aggression, which in defence of one's ego ideal has been directed outwards.

Freud was never at ease with his concept of a death drive, which had in fact first been put forward and developed by Sabina Spielrein as Jung acknowledged in *Symbols of Transformation* (*CW* 5, para. 504), where he described the several forms taken in mythology by 'the Terrible Mother who devours and destroys, and thus symbolizes death itself'.

However, in Melanie Klein's theories the death drive has taken on a primary and crucial role, manifesting itself in and through the ego's struggle to preserve itself. In *Envy and Gratitude* (1957) she writes:

The threat of annihilation by the death instinct within is, in my view—which differs from Freud's on this point—the primordial anxiety and it is the ego which, in the service of the life instinct, possibly even called into operation by the life instinct, deflects to some extent that threat outwards.

Thus pioneers like Freud, Klein and some of the analytical psychologists, in their search for the roots of masochism, are led back to the thesis of Thanatos, that is, to the existence of an original death drive or death wish. But Freud and Klein do not, or so it seems, accept, or at least they pay no attention to, concepts such as 'the transformation of impulses' or to the theme of 'death and rebirth' or to the 'symbolic meaning of death', or to man's possible basic need to search for something or somebody that transcends his personal being. And yet, in order to understand the masochistic impulse and the masochistic experience, we must consider and explore further these ideas. For masochism is, after all, evinced not only in the pursuit of physical pain, but also in such psychological states as longing for surrender, for dependence on others, for helplessness, for self-abnegation or for immersion and unity in and with an 'other'. It is also interesting that while some regard masochism as a means of symbolic self-annihilation, others understand it as a way of resisting the experience of the annihilation of self. Instead, pain is used as proof that there is some sort of identity and some presence of ego-consciousness. Masochism is then understood as a sort of pinching oneself to know one is awake—which is how Betty Joseph has interpreted it in her paper, 'Addiction to near-death' (1982).

However, to me one of the most meaningful contributions by a psychoanalyst to an understanding of masochism has been made by Masud Khan in his paper, 'From masochism to psychic pain' (1979). He argues there that the human individual needs his—or her—psychic pain to be witnessed silently and unobtrusively by the 'other', and that it is this need which has 'led to the creation of the omnipresence of God in human lives'. It is the increasing disappearance of God as the witnessing other, from man's privacy with himself, so he believes, that 'the experience of psychic pain has changed from tolerated and accepted suffering to its pathological substitute, and thus the need has rapidly increased for psychotherapeutic interventions to alleviate these pathological masochistic states'.

Masochism in religious experience

Khan's thesis meets quite naturally my reflections about masochism in religious rites and rituals and in ascetic and mystical practices. The presence in the religions of frustration and denial of physical and emotional needs, and indeed the actual infliction of pain on oneself—or on others—is almost ubiquitous and universal. Circumcision, subincision, flagellation, fasting, abstinence from sexual, social and other appetitive needs—be they physical or emotional—and sacrifice of self, or else of what is loved and valued, all these are well documented, well known and in fact quite familiar. The various physical postures also express and communicate humility, surrender and abandonment—postures such as the folding of arms, the clasping or joining of hands, bowing, kneeling and prostration, all these convey non-resistance, submission, yielding, obedience and renunciation.

The introspective reflections and experiences that Marion Milner has recorded under her pseudonym, Joanna Field, in her book *An Experiment in Leisure,* published in 1939, also lead in a very similar direction. She writes:

> All this would explain why certain symbols had so often forced their way into my thinking; it suggested that they might in essence be concerned with the creative spirit of man, with man's capacity to find expression for and so lay hold upon the truth of his experience; they might be a history of man's struggle with the angel of God to force his name from him. ...
> And although it had led me to discover that one wants among other things pain, suffering, inferiority, it had also led me on to the growing belief that this need to suffer was not in its essence perverse. ...
> Perhaps Groddeck was right in believing that the desire to suffer is as innate as the desire to hurt and is in its origin an essential part of the process of physical creation.

There is indeed a 'very thin' line between the sincere desire to surrender one's personal, egotistical and presumed mortal and transitory needs, desires and wishes to something or somebody beyond oneself and a perverted masochism, where the experience of pain has become an end in itself. Such perversion, so it seems to me, parallels to some extent Arnold Hauser's (1965) description of mannerism, or the mannered style in art which he has defined as the perversion and almost caricaturing of a given style by concentrating on some inessential details, and making them the central feature of one's own work. Thus when pain, suffering and self-abasement have become the primary objective rather than only a preparation for an experience of surrender and union with what is believed and felt to be the holy, the eternal, the transcendent, then we are indeed dealing with a perversion, with pathological masochism. It seems to me that it is the realization of this distinction which led the Buddha in his search for enlightenment to abandon the rigorous asceticism he had been taught and had practised and to counsel instead what he described as 'The Middle Way'—that is, the reining in, but not the total rejection and destruction, of one's personal needs.

I must once more return to the theme of sacrifice which has such a prominent place in the religions. Here I have found Elie Humbert's paper, 'Le prix du symbole' [The price of the symbol] (1980) to be quite seminal. He points out what is obvious, yet rarely noted or remembered, that etymologically 'to sacrifice' denotes 'to make sacred'. And he discusses and analyses in that paper the fact that in order to find or to create a symbolic order and so give meaning to life, to one's personal life as well as to one's natural and social life, so as to save oneself from chaos, man is willing to forgo the satisfaction of his impulses and daily needs such as hunger, cold, rivalry, sex, love and so on (p. 252).

A very powerful example of this impulse to escape from a sense of comfortable meaninglessness through a quest for the unknown is described in the short story entitled 'The woman who rode away' by D. H. Lawrence. I read this story a long time ago but re-read it recently. Married to an American self-made, now rich, silver-mine owner living in Mexico, the woman—he never gives her a name—uses a few days absence of her husband in order to ride away from home, drawn by a 'vulgar excitement' to encounter somewhere, somehow, signs of the Indian people she has heard described as 'ancient, wild and mysterious savages'. Indeed, she meets men who without using force constrain her to follow them up to their mountain village. She loses all self-will and all self-direction. There is no struggle in her against this, though she is also given strange potions that ensure further her loss of sense of self. She is treated like a precious object. She is fed, housed, massaged and clothed—in blue, 'the colour of the dead', she is told; but she is kept in isolation, apart from the other people, except for the daily visits of one of the priests and of the only interpreter. 'They were gentle with her and very considerate ... they watched over her and cared for her like women.' She is really left in no doubt about her fate. And indeed at the very moment of the winter solstice, after a day of much ritual dance and ceremony, when 'she felt little sensation, though she knew all that was happening', the oldest man, the priest, 'struck home, accomplished the sacrifice and achieved the power' (Lawrence, 1943).

In this short story Lawrence portrays the almost orgiastic abnegation of consciousness and the willing, near-ecstatic acceptance of sacrifice of self.

How can we understand this drive to sacrifice our physical needs and appetites, and indeed our actual body? I believe that such denials and abnegations of self have as their aim the suppression of what is felt to be but a temporary, a transitory part of ourselves; it aims to liberate us from the domination of our body over our mind or psyche. We all know that the body will indeed return to dust quite shortly after death. And we all know, we have all observed, the unreliability of this body when, for instance, it begins to let us down in the course of the ageing process. Is asceticism not perhaps a rehearsal of death, an attempt to experience already in this life what we think death, being dead, may be like, so as to rob it of its capacity to surprise us or to find us unprepared? It was wisdom—or more likely it was rational foresight—that made the king of Kapilavastu, Suddho-dana, try to prevent Gautama, his son, from ever seeing illness, old age and death. He knew that knowledge of this would draw his son away from his palace and into the forest in search of enlightenment.

Masochism in clinical work

To come now to the more daily, the more run-of-the-mill, experience in our analytic work. Although masochism is frequently the expression, albeit the perverted expression, of man's need to worship, venerate and to search for the transcendental, yet, as might be expected, its goal is usually more earth-bound and less lofty. Nevertheless, it is most often unconsciously in the service of securing love and admission to the admirable, the idealized. As Betty Joseph has suggested in the paper (1982) I mentioned earlier, the masochist, building on his childhood experience or misunderstanding of how to gain or how to maintain the parents' love, believes that the price to be paid for this love is the surrender of his personal separateness and individuality.

It is worthwhile to remember here that Freud himself wrote that there are three forms of masochism: erotogenic masochism, moral masochism and feminine masochism.

Clearly, the five patients I described at the beginning of this paper showed primarily the erotogenic form of masochism. In the case of the patients I want to describe next, we have a much more complicated picture. They all show features that we quite often encounter in our work, features that reveal the interaction of a number of complex and different psychological mechanisms.

I shall first describe in some detail a patient I will name Bob. He had been in analysis for many years. He was a designer and very anxious to become a good and inventive designer. He longed to reach and to use his own creative resources. Longing to achieve this had been one of his main reasons for coming into analysis.

He was the elder of two boys. His father, an engineer, a quiet and somewhat withdrawn man, had been away fighting in the Second World War when Bob was between eight and twelve years old, the very years when he most needed the presence, encouragement and inspired companionship of a man.

His mother had been a professional ballet dancer who, after the birth of her two sons and then the absence of her husband, became a teacher of dance and drama. She was—as she came to appear from Bob's description of her—a very lively person, somewhat self-centred, devoted to her work and profession, with easy access to her feelings and her creativity, but not really interested in, or talented for, making a home, enriching such home, or giving much time and attention to her children. She had a close woman friend with whom she collaborated in her professional work.

Bob was a tall, quiet, shy, timid, diffident, insecure and passive person, who looked ten to fifteen years younger than his age.

He had great difficulty in asserting himself, either in his work, in relationship to colleagues and bosses, or in his personal relationship with friends, partners or acquaintances.

He seemed very cut off from his affects and impulses; and his feelings in the transference were subdued. Only when he could tell me of some new failure or of some new mishap, some new loss of prestige, achievement or argument did a flash of triumph, of masochistic triumph and satisfaction, enliven his facial and verbal expression.

But the analysis jogged along quietly. Yet he had many interesting dreams, and some of them were filled with strong emotions. There were several about a birth-giving: either he himself or some domestic animal, such as a cat, for example, was bearing a baby. But even this potentially forward-looking theme tended to be vitiated in some way or other: there was not enough food for the new baby; or instead of milk the baby was offered shit; or he, the mother, the birth-giver, was rejected and socially excluded and shunned; or else the baby was damaged or disposed of as rubbish. There was in these dreams so much hurt and pain, but he would tell them in his quiet, gentle and bland manner, as if they had been dreamed by someone else.

Strangely enough, my own feelings for him in my counter-transference remained consistently patient, affectionate and maternally caring. Why, I often wondered, did I not—at least sometimes—react with impatience, anger and/or irritation, as indeed his father had shown him and expressed to him when he returned from war service and did not, as Bob remembered, seem to be particularly pleased with the way his eldest son had developed. It may well be that his father experienced Bob as part of his own shadow, as a caricature of himself, representing his own lack of a positive and secure confidence in his masculinity.

I did begin to suspect that perhaps there was no lively and potentially creative centre to be found in Bob. When both of us came close to a loss of hope—and yet there were the dreams!—he decided that he would like to try his hand at some art therapy. The results were truly surprising. Bob brought his painting to his analytic sessions. They were a revelation! The paintings were quite remarkably lively, colourful and full of imaginative forms—of persons, of creatures like animals, of objects—expressing joy and fun as well as fear, anger, violence and even horror. They showed a capacity to be playful—playful in Winnicott's sense of 'play'—that he had until now been unable to draw on and use and enjoy consciously. But at first, as with his dreams, Bob displayed and discussed them with me without much affect, enthusiasm or even involvement.

But now my own reactions to him changed: I became more fierce and challenging. I felt anger, as if on behalf of these pictures, *his* pictures, at what seemed to me to be his dismissal of them and his churlish and almost sadistic refusal to acknowledge as his own the paintings before us. And, as I began to express some of these reactions, it seemed as if a father—a more potent and potentially more enabling father than he had experienced in his own personal history—had become activated, inside each one of us and between us. At first Bob reacted with sullen, sulky and hurt withdrawal into more silence. But then, slowly, he rose to my challenge: he became overtly more resentful, sometimes abusive and finally openly and honestly hostile and aggressive. This then seemed slowly to enable him to protect and to defend what he had made and created and to relate to it as coming from him and belonging to him. This then enabled him to stand by and to protect that part of himself from where his pictures had drawn their existence and their aliveness.

It seemed to me that he was now beginning to extricate himself from the envy and from the sense of total and hopeless impotence in relation to his lively and artistic mother; emerge also from the delusion that all creativity is feminine and belongs to the woman, the mother, who castrates males and leaves them with only one way of associating with the forces of creation; that of being her vassal, her slave, or, at best, of being her flirty and admiring eunuch.

However, before Bob had achieved this extrication, and while he was in the midst of this battle in and through the transference to both the mother–analyst–me and the father–analyst–me, he had a rather bad car accident. It had not been altogether his fault, but had he been more alert and attentive, he might have been able to avoid it—at least that is how he himself explained it to me.

It took many months to understand the many meanings of this accident and to work through—in the relative safety of the consulting room—the emotional upheaval and the emotional experience of it. What emerged is that the accident was indeed a murderous attack on the much admired and much envied mother. It was also a murderous attack on the father, whom he thought of either as absent and unavailable, or, if present, as inadequate and impotent because he had not succeeded in taming and containing the mother. He had also been unable to guide Bob into true and enjoyable manhood. But, in as much as Bob, when in a somewhat less hopeless and less depressed state, was identifying with the enviable mother, or when in a more depressed state with the inadequate father, the accident was also a suicide, a killing of him who had been swamped and taken over by one or by both parents. This suicide was then an expression of the despair that he would never be able to shed the incorporated and introjected 'others'; that he would never manage to overthrow their domination inside him; despair that he could ever become his own self.

But we worked and worked through the emotional experience and the symbolic meaning of the accident; it then took on the quality, not only of murder and suicide, but also of parturition, of birth and sacrifice; and sacrifice is, of course, the essential and always present constituent of all *rites de passage*.

Bob's case seemed to show up the temptation to idealize, then to project and then to incorporate the person carrying the idealized bit. But inevitably she (in Bob's case the mother) remained experienced as a somewhat alien presence inside him, and hence an obstruction, an obstacle in the way of discovering his own true self and his own creative, powers. The fact that his creative, idealized mother had remained like a foreign body inside him provoked envy, a murderous envy. The sadistic attack on the internalized mother, who was still a part of him, thus ended in the masochistic attack on his own body. This was of course a very dramatic example of a sado-masochistic acting out. It also shows the power of envy and how the search for one's true self, in cases where there has been much internalization, can produce the simultaneous enactment of both sadism and masochism.

I want to give one other example of masochism, but in its less dramatic and therefore more often encountered form.

Leslie, a man in his late thirties, had several nice things happen to him, which had raised his hopes that he might eventually have more time to do that by which he felt most fulfilled: painting and writing poetry. However, two nights later he dreamed what he described as an absolutely horrible dream' which left him in a desperately bleak mood. He told me the dream only in the next session:

I have to go somewhere, to my office I think. I am at a bus stop. But I have to wait a terribly long time. I turn round for a moment; and just then the bus I have been waiting for rushes by—without me. And then I see that though I wear a shirt I have no trousers on, which is most embarrassing. Then I am back in my flat; I am now properly dressed. And now I realize that where I want to go is actually nearby; I do not need to take a bus at all to get there.

As we talked about the dream I became aware that the 'happy ending' did not make him happy at all. The grim mood persisted; he seemed to cling to the first, the negative, the unhappy part which, I felt, was the masochistic part, a tendency in him which he and I were aware of and had become quite familiar with. This bleak mood continued into and through the next session. This impelled me to end it by asking him: 'What do you need all this pain for?' I kept to myself the possible answer: 'To attack you' (the analyst) and 'to attack myself' (the patient). When he came to the following session he felt and looked much more cheerful. He had suddenly remembered that his mother used to damp down any joy at achievement. And he remembered the day when he had won the first prize as the best actor in his school and indeed in the county. But his mother, instead of congratulating him—at least he did not remember that she did—warned him, 'You know such a talent might suddenly disappear.' 'She always spoiled a good experience,' he added. 'Am I now doing this to myself? After all, only my father was allowed to be "great".' Fortunately for this patient the unconscious identifications were more accessible to consciousness, were in fact actually more felt and experienced than had been the case with Bob. In Leslie's case the self-attack seems to have emanated from an internalized mother, and he probably colluded with her in an attempt to placate her, to obey her and to please her in guaranteeing that father alone was the only great and powerful one. But he did also resent it and felt anger and envy about it.

Discussion

I mentioned earlier that almost inevitably masochism has clinical consequences. It is often one of the root causes of the negative therapeutic reaction, for it tempts the patient to cling to his hurt, suffering and unhappiness and to the memories of all the saddest events and circumstances of his past. And when interpretation touches on painful areas, this does not easily evoke in him compensatory drives, memories and attitudes that could then challenge him to do battle with the causes underlying the pain. Rather, he will most likely grasp the pain, hold fast to it and relax into its pleasurable effects. Also, unless it is painful, such patients often maintain, they have not been given an interpretation at all.

Naturally the analyst's countertransference is very strong and difficult. I find that either I am drawn into the masochistic mood, in which case I may begin to share the patient's despair, see no way out for him and commiserate and collude with his hardship and his general bad luck; or I may get very bored and perhaps even sleepy. Or else I begin to feel very irritated and feel arising in me a certain sadistic reaction to the patient. Then I am likely to experience anxiety and guilt, though on the whole I try to protect the patient from my sadism. Yet sometimes such sadistic reactions may have a function. I felt just such irritation with Leslie, and I admit it was out of that irritable and sadistic reaction that I had asked him why he needed his pain. In his case it bore fruit, for he did then come to dredge up the memory of his mother who 'always spoiled a good experience'.

It must be clear from what I have said so far and from the patients I have described that masochism has usually multiple causations; it is rarely a single event, or even a single trauma that can explain or be held responsible for it.

However, in all these patients there was an element, a desire to reach through love, surrender and submission something or somebody beyond themselves, idealized maybe, but nevertheless experienced as being beyond and superior to themselves. It is true, in the cases of Patrick, Bob and Leslie the apparent cause was the relationship to the real and earthly persons of the mother and/or the father; in Patrick and Bob's case the latter was too absent, but he was too overwhelmingly present in Leslie's case. In the case of Patrick his 'virgin' mother, so seductive and so plausible to the neighbours, with her Janus-like double-facedness, must have seemed mysterious to her little boy, so that she came to appear to him as goddess and witch. As for Bob, he longed so much to reach that fascinating creative spring, that muse to which only women, it seemed to him, could have any access, while Leslie's masochism appeared to be rooted in the fact that his mother, and so many others, all rendered willingly and selflessly homage and devotion to his famous father, so that refusal to join them or even any signs of competition with him was experienced by him as rebellion if not blasphemy.

If my hypothesis is valid, if behind the masochistic phenomenon lies an archetypal need to worship something transcendental and sublime, what effect could this knowledge have on our clinical work and on our reflections about the wider world?

I believe that our transference reactions to our masochistic patients may well be affected if we become aware that there might be a link between masochism on the one hand, and the shadow side of the need to worship and to venerate on the other. For instance, it may stir us to ask: what is the patient seeking out as a, for him valid, object of veneration? How can we help him to recognize there his own unfulfilled potential? Has he been tempted to idealize it and then to project it?—in which case he may come to feel intense envy and murderous rage towards the recipient of his projection, because it may have left him feeling empty and destitute. On the other hand, he may have projected onto the worshipped personage—be it human or divine—not idealized characteristics, but shadow characteristics like envy, rage, fanaticism, murderousness and so on; in other words, feelings and impulses which had remained unconscious and thus unacknowledged as belonging to himself. In that case veneration and worshipfulness may have fastened on to an evil, sadistic, diabolic and pseudo-heroic figure. The gang leader, the terrorist, the demagogue, the self-styled freedom fighter, any of them may satisfy his impulses to surrender, to follow and to abandon the sense of personal responsibility, while justifying at the same time the experience and the enactment of what consciousness and conscience has forbidden and condemned.

The need to venerate, if it is indeed an archetypal need, intrinsic to us, men and women, cannot be squashed or eradicated easily or quickly. Nor should it be. For it is the origin not only of much that is evil but also of much that is great and good and beautiful, and what man has made and achieved.

By scrutinizing the object worshipped, the analyst may be able to help throw light on what in a person—or in a group of persons—has remained in the dark, in unconsciousness; and so he may discover what is there to be struggled with, to be developed further, to be confronted, to be transformed. Such an examination could then help assess the health or the sickness, the positive or the negative potential in the worshipful attitude. It is also important to assess whether this need to venerate and worship dominates over all other needs; and, furthermore, whether the search for pain, for submission and subjection of the self is the primary or even the only purpose and goal. Such an overview may assist one to recognize to what extent one is dealing with a more or less natural, or with a masochistic, disposition.

There are undoubtedly very many more themes to discuss in relation to masochism. I have, for instance, left aside the problem of masochism and the feminine and the masculine principle. I have also left out masochism and the trickster; and indeed many other themes that may be relevant to masochism. But each of them needs, I believe, a whole paper to itself to do it some justice. However, there is one sentence in Jung's paper on 'The psychology of the trickster figure' which prophetically touches, I think, though in a personalized form, on what I have set out to suggest here, namely that there is a link between masochism and the search for meaning, for spirit. It seems appropriate that I end this paper by quoting Jung. He writes:

The unpredictable behaviour of Trickster, his pointless orgies of destruction and his self-appointed sufferings, together with the gradual development into a saviour and his simultaneous humanisation ... these are just the transformations of the meaningless into the meaningful and reveal the trickster's compensatory relation to the saint. [CW 9i]

REFERENCES

Gordon, R. (1978). *Dying and Creating*. Library of Analytical Psychology, Vol. 4. London: Karnac Books.

Hauser, A. (1965). *Mannerism*. London: Routledge & Kegan Paul.

Humbert, E. (1980). Le prix du symbole. *Cahiers de psychologie Jungienne* 25.

Joseph, E. (1982). Addiction to near-death. *International Journal of Psycho-Analysis* 63:4.

Khan, M. (1979). From masochism to psychic pain. In *Alienation in Perversion*. London: Hogarth Press. [Reprinted 1989, London: Karnac Books.]

Klein, M. (1957). *Envy and Gratitude*. London: Tavistock Publications.

Lawrence, D. H. (1943). The woman who rode away. In *Full Score*. London: The Reprint Society.

Milner, M. (1939). *An Experiment in Leisure*. London: Chatto & Windus.

Neumann, E. (1954). *Origins and History of Consciousness*. London: Routledge & Kegan Paul. [Reprinted 1989, London: Maresfield Library.]

Williams, M. (1958). The fear of death (Part 1). *Journal of Analytical Psychology* 3:2.

———— (1962). The fear of death (Part 2). *Journal of Analytical Psychology* 7:1.

CHAPTER THIRTEEN

The psychopathology
of fetishism and transvestism

Anthony Storr

This early work of Storr's has stood the test of time remarkably well. Indeed, its concerns are as relevant now as they were over 30 years ago. For instance, Storr's intention of showing that the teleological viewpoint can add something to the conventional psychoanalytic one, and his criticisms of Freud's interpretation of the Medusa mythologem, are directly relevant to the project of a book such as this.

Then there is Storr's use of a phrase like 'subjective masculinity' (to depict what it is that some perverts and fetishists lack). This is anticipatory of the approach of Robert Stoller, who argued that gender identity, looked at from a psychoanalytic standpoint, is an internal matter, not a behavioural one.

The third theme that I would like to highlight concerns the way Storr conceptualizes the interplay of masculine and feminine, male and female factors in psychopathology. On the

First published in *The Journal of Analytical Psychology* 2:2, in 1957. Published here by kind permission of the author and the Society of Analytical Psychology.

personal–historical level he is referring to the relationship with the parents, as individuals and as a couple. On a more impersonal, archetypal level, he is touching on something of great complexity and importance: the struggle to wrest phallic power from the Great Mother and the unforeseen problems for the individual when that is attempted by means of identification.

Finally, Storr's reflections on what Western societies demand of men and how that affects their gendered self-conception show that, in this area at least, not a lot has changed since 1957.

A.S.

Introduction

The subject of the sexual perversions and anomalies, with the possible exception of homosexuality, has hitherto been regarded as a field in which the concepts of Freudian psychoanalysis are especially applicable. Analysts of other schools have made few contributions to the study of these conditions; and psychiatrists who are more interested in classification than in treatment have been content to relegate these cases to the diagnostic scrap-heap of psychopathic personality.

Since I believe that the theoretical concepts of analytical psychology can further our understanding of these conditions, I have attempted to put down in this paper various tentative conclusions from my own experience with patients. Most of the paper is concerned with the perversions of fetishism and transvestism; but there are also some remarks on sadism, masochism and male homosexuality.

The psychoanalytic explanation of the perversions of fetishism and transvestism can be found in the papers of Freud, Fenichel and Gillespie. Can analytical psychology add anything to the psychoanalytic point of view?

One of the most valuable insights which Jung has given us is that symptoms, however bizarre or unpleasant they may seem, have a positive value for the development of the personality. If this concept is applied to the study of the sexual perversions, it can, I believe, be demonstrated that these disorders represent a striving towards normality rather than a flight away from it. Moreover, we can also detect in the perversions evidence of the compensatory function of the unconscious, which is such an important concept in analytical psychology and comparatively neglected by psychoanalysis.

Psychoanalysis is principally concerned with tracing the genesis of symptoms, analytical psychology with their prospective implications. I hope to show that the teleological point of view can add something to the reductive.

Space forbids an exhaustive survey of the psychoanalytic literature on fetishism and transvestism; but, although later writers lay greater stress on the sadistic impulses of the pervert, Freud's original contention that these disorders are closely linked with castration anxiety remains unchallenged.

Freud pictures a small boy, who, through the experience of infantile masturbation, has already learned to value his penis highly; but who lives in fear of losing it on the ground that his parents disapprove of his sexual activity. His fear is enormously increased if he happens to see the female genitals. They *are* beings who have had their penises removed, and so it is all the more likely to happen to him. He must never experience this shock again; and so he phantasies that women possess penises after all, and the fetish represents the female penis.

Gillespie (1956), in his recent paper on 'The general theory of sexual perversion' says of this:

> Ever since the analysis of Little Hans Freud stressed the fateful conjunction for a little boy of an external castration threat for masturbation with the observation of female genitals, leading the boy to the conclusion that castration really may happen to him. Now few will be disposed to deny that such experiences may have an important crystallizing effect and may give conscious form and expression to the fear; but as a full explanation for such a dominating and far-reaching anxiety Freud's theory seems to depend too much on accidental and external factors, too little on endopsychic ones. [p. 4]

My own experience in the treatment of perverts leads me to agree with this statement emphatically. Perversions are the outward and visible signs of a far-reaching disturbance in endopsychic structure; and external factors, such as the experience of seeing the female genitals, are usually only important in so far as they reflect the endopsychic situation.

Impotence and castration

One of the striking features of the behaviour of persons suffering from sexual deviations of the type under discussion is that they can only feel themselves to be potent, or fully potent, under certain specified conditions. The fetishist needs his fetish, the transvestite his cross-dressing, before he can experience the subjective feeling of full masculine potency: and they are partially or completely impotent unless these special conditions are present.

It follows from this that such people, consciously or unconsciously, feel themselves to be less masculine than their fellows. It is my contention that the essential background to these disorders is not so much the fear of castration as the feeling of being castrated; and it is found that this feeling of being lacking in masculinity extends far beyond the specific difficulty in performing the sexual act.

In reviewing the histories of patients with any form of perversion one often finds that they have been unable to compete with other boys at school; can seldom defend themselves if attacked, and seldom attack others; are poor performers at games; rarely attain any position of authority in their early years; and often fail to live up to their intellectual promise. They thus, whether consciously or not, feel inadequate in many respects compared with other men; and this is expressed metaphorically as castration, or the condition of not possessing the most characteristically male attribute, namely, the penis.

It is clear that these patients usually have a great deal of repressed aggression, a characteristic which is fully recognized by psychoanalytic writers. In many cases of fetishism the sadistic element is obvious. Perverse phantasies often contain the aggressive elements, which are not allowed to emerge in real life in relation to women. The compensatory function of the unconscious is particularly obvious here. The phantasies contain just those elements which are lacking in conscious behaviour; and the milder and less effective these patients are in their day-to-day behaviour in relation to others, the more violent their sexual phantasies are likely to be.

However, the point I wish to make here is that these patients are not so much frightened of castration as convinced that they are castrated. Two clinical examples may serve to illustrate this point.

(1)   A homosexual patient of 40 came to see me because he was greatly troubled with the sado-masochistic perversion of tying himself up. During the course of treatment he dreamed that he had no genitals; and that he was about to leave his room to look for them. But his way was barred by another man who stood in the doorway with a sword in his hand.

The patient was actually in love with the other man who appears in the dream and attributed to him all the masculine virtues. He felt himself to be worth very little in comparison with this man whom he so much admired, and projected on to him all the masculine qualities which he himself had failed to develop. The contrast between the patient's own feeling about himself as castrated and his feeling about the other man as possessing masculine strength in the shape of a sword is clearly demonstrated. The dream also illustrates how the fact of his projection on the other man bars the way to his own development. So long as he continues to feel that he has nothing and the other man has everything, he cannot get any further.

(2)   The second example comes from a man of 28 who also was homosexual. He remembered having the following dream in childhood, probably before the age of nine: 'I was in a bathroom, surrounded by a whole group of large men. I go round from one to the other cutting off their penises and collecting them in a basin.'

There again is the contrast between the smallness of the patient and the largeness of the men. But in this instance the patient is not content to remain passive, he takes active steps to possess himself of the phallic power of the animal.

The subjective feeling of being inadequate as a man, i.e. castrated, may be present even if the patient can perform the sexual act with apparently full satisfaction. A further case illustrates this point.

(3)   A man of 28 consulted me with the single symptom of having a compulsive interest in circumcised penises. He felt he had to look at medical books, read anything he could about the operation of circumcision, and tended to speculate about the penises of other men.

This patient was perfectly potent with women, and had had several affairs: he was engaged to be married, and had never had the slightest sexual difficulty. Nor had he any particular homosexual inclination, at any rate at the conscious level. He himself was not circumcised in childhood, and had believed from early years that men who had had the operation were stronger, tougher, and more masculine than himself. When he was about seven years old he had retired behind some bushes in the garden to pass water in company with his brother and another little boy. They naturally enough compared penises, as small boys commonly do. (In later life these same small boys compare bank balances, cars, jobs, and other trappings of masculine achievement—but the underlying idea is the same.) On this occasion, the visiting child said to my patient that he did not like his (the patient's) penis as much as his brother's; the brother had been circumcised, whereas my patient had not. Later on, the compulsive interest in circumcision developed. He even went so far as to have the operation performed on himself in adult life, hoping in this way to establish himself on an equal footing with other men. But this attempt to treat concretely and literally a condition which was psychological and symbolic was, naturally enough, a failure; in spite of being himself circumcised, his compulsive interest in circumcision remained exactly the same.

I have already stressed the fact that this patient was, at a conscious level, sexually normal and fully potent with women. Before his heterosexual life had become established, he had masturbated while looking at pictures of the circumcised penis: but by the time I saw him, this tendency had disappeared, and the symptom was of comparatively little importance to him. It is obvious that some psychoanalysts would at once say that this man was unconsciously a homosexual; and this may be true in the wide sense in which Freudian analysts use the term; but there was remarkably little evidence of it in the sense of his being attracted by men or boys. The most obvious fact about him was his sense of inferiority compared with other men and his intense competitiveness, which was largely unconscious.

The relevance of this case to the main theme of this paper may not be immediately obvious: but I want to make the point that I do not believe it is possible to understand the sexual perversions from one point of view only. In the cases I have seen, the psychopathology has been as much a matter of a struggle for power as of sexual guilt and repression. The basic, archetypal theme is the feeling of castration or masculine inadequacy on the part of the patient; the symptom represents an attempt to transfer masculine power from a person who is thought to possess it to the patient who is thought to be lacking in it.

It is a convention of our Western civilization that men are expected to achieve something, to make some mark in the world; and, however potent a man may be sexually, he still may feel inadequate if he has not achieved whatever he may be capable of in the way of worldly success. This particular patient had passed through school and university in a safe and comfortable fashion, and had arrived in a safe and comfortable job in a well-established firm of stockbrokers, where he was paid a good salary and had remarkably little to do. It would have been possible to take the view that this was all he was good for had it not been for his symptom, which drew attention to the fact that he felt inferior to other men, and therefore could be assumed to have potentialities within himself which were not finding expression in the external world. This view was confirmed by his revealing that he had in the past had phantasies of achieving great things, but, owing to his too comfortable existence in the present, had not made any great effort to put his phantasies into effect. He was, in fact, of exceptionally high intelligence; but he had never been able to make adequate use of his gifts as he did not believe in them. This could in part be attributed to the fact that his father had never shown any particular regard for him; and he had at an early age come to feel that, in the eyes of men, at any rate, he was of very little account. No such conviction existed in the case of women, with whom he was very successful: and this I attribute to the fact that his early relationship with his mother was more or less satisfactory.

Homosexual fetishism

In this case the circumcised penis was treated like a fetish. It is not generally recognized that homosexual fetishes exist. Fetishism is usually described only in heterosexual terms. Nevertheless, Walker and Strauss (1948) describe two cases in their book on *Sexual Disorders in the Male*: and they make the interesting remark, with which I fully agree, that: 'It is exceedingly likely that many cases of homosexuality could be interpreted as "phallus-fetishism"' (p. 184).

If I am right in thinking that the characteristic feature of patients suffering from perversions is their subjective feeling of being castrated, or lacking in masculine potency, then one would on theoretical grounds expect that part of their drive towards self-realization would be concerned with finding their own masculinity which they feel to be lacking. If people feel themselves to be lacking in some quality which is nevertheless present in themselves but unconscious to them, they are attracted by persons who display this very quality. I believe this to be true of heterosexual attraction also; but it is especially obvious in many cases of homosexuality. The refined, delicate type of homosexual is usually most strongly attracted by a tough, aggressive, muscular male, often of a lower social class than his own. Marcel Proust (1941, Vol. 7) who, from personal experience, knew a great deal about homosexuality, describes homosexuals as 'lovers from whom is always precluded the possibility of that love the hope of which gives them the strength to endure so many risks and so much loneliness, since they fall in love with precisely that type of man who has nothing feminine about him, who is not an invert and consequently cannot love them in return; with the result that their desire would be for ever insatiable did not their money procure for them real men, and their imagination end by making them take for real men the inverts to whom they had prostituted themselves' (p. 21).

It is often a tragic fate for homosexuals to be so attracted by the people with whom they are least likely to be able to make a relationship. This type of homosexual is really being driven to seek through projection what he feels to be lacking in himself. He attributes to his beloved object all the qualities of tough maleness which are unconscious in himself; and it is only when he has been able to withdraw this projection and realize his own maleness that the attraction ceases to exercise compulsive power over him.

In the same way, a man who has completed his masculine development and who is faced with the problem of the anima may learn to withdraw this projection from women and achieve a new integration. The compulsive element of falling in love will then disappear and will be replaced by an increased conscious capacity for relationship.

I have quoted a case where the penis itself was treated as a fetish. Here is another example in which hair, a very common fetish object, had the same meaning for the patient.

(4)   A dark-haired young man consulted me on account of homosexual feelings. One of the chief features which attracted him in other men was fair hair. It seemed to him that fair-haired men possessed all the qualities of masculine self-assurance and potency which he felt to be lacking in himself; and he had often had the phantasy of dyeing his own hair a lighter colour in the hope of emulating them. This case seems to me to be exactly parallel to the man who was attracted by circumcised penises. Both patients are attracted by a single aspect of another person which seems to them to epitomize and represent their idea of masculinity. Both choose characteristics of other people which are the opposite of those which they themselves possess and both try to emulate the people they are attracted by, in one case by having an operation, in the other by the phantasy of dyeing the hair.

(5)   Another homosexual admitted that from his earliest years he had had a compulsive interest in corduroy trousers. He remembered being sexually excited by the sight of a man wearing these garments when he was aged about 5. Later on,

he made a collection of corduroy trousers. When he put them on he felt an access of sexual feeling, and either used to masturbate, or would repair to a public lavatory to find a young man with whom he could have sexual relations. He was an excessively immature, mother-fixed boy who had always been brought up to be smartly dressed: corduroy trousers would have been thought vulgar by his mother, and, although it is commonly believed that corduroy trousers are effeminate, in this particular instance they had the significance of garments which were worn by men who were more masculine than himself.

In these cases, the fetish represents a means whereby the patient can identify himself with someone more masculine. These are special instances of what has been called 'apprentice love', and are analogous to the normal adolescent attractions towards older men which are felt by most developing boys. These attractions have a positive, educative value: a fact which was well recognized by the Greeks, for they serve to evoke in the adolescent qualities of masculinity which might otherwise remain unconscious and therefore only potential. In the same way, homosexual fetishes have a positive value for the development of the personality; a fact which is not clearly brought out in other psychopathological studies. It is most important in treatment that the fetish should be accepted and given value by the therapist; for it is only when the patient can accept it himself that his development can proceed to a point where he no longer needs it. All these cases illustrate the compensatory function of the unconscious, a theory put forward by Jung: what is consciously lacking in the patient—in these instances, certain aspects of masculinity—is to be found in the unconscious; and what is unconscious in the patient is to be found in projection upon other people or part-aspects of people. In the homosexual cases so far discussed, the fetish object clearly represents the penis. Most authorities, with the exception of Strauss and Walker, do not recognize the existence of homosexual fetishism: they confine their description of cases to those in which the fetish by which the patient is attracted is clearly something associated with the female, such as feminine undergarments or jewellery.

Heterosexual fetishism

The psychopathology of the heterosexual type of fetishism is disputed. Hadfield (1950), for example, says: 'In all cases of fetishism we have analysed, the fetishistic object proved to be a breast substitute: for the breast is the first loved object of the infant, even before the mother herself becomes so' (p. 376). Freud and Fenichel, on the other hand, are quite categorical in their view that the fetish represents a feminine (maternal) penis. My own view is that the fetish is a magical object which has both a phallic and a maternal significance. If I am right in thinking that the fetishist feels himself to be castrated, then one can say that he has identified himself with a woman. The phallus is, as it were, given up in order to preserve this identification. But sexual activity is impossible without the phallus, and so the problem is raised for the fetishist of how he can preserve his feminine identification and at the same time engage in phallic activity. This is rendered possible if the woman shows evidence of being phallic; which explains the necessity of the fetish being present before the patient can be active sexually. The identification with the phallic woman is carried a step further in the case of the transvestist.

The double significance of the fetish is brought out by the following case.

(6)   A young man was sent to me on account of a total failure to keep a job or succeed in any examination. He had previously been diagnosed as schizophrenic, and although he was not frankly psychotic, he certainly showed many symptoms of a hebephrenic type.

The fetishism which he presented was as follows. He was compulsively attracted towards boys who were crippled and especially those who wore supporting irons on their legs. He himself wished to wear irons, and got an erection when he put on a home-made substitute. He used to read anything he could get hold of about homes and hospitals for cripples, and knew a good deal about poliomyelitis and its results. If he had the good luck to see a cripple in the streets he would follow him for miles.

The apparent origin of this symptom was extremely interesting. When the patient first went to school, one of his schoolfellows was a crippled boy who wore an iron on his leg. This boy was brought to school every day by his mother in a car, and was given a good deal of special attention as he was unable to walk. My patient was very envious of this; for his relationship with his own mother was a bad one, and he dearly wished to have for himself the extra love and attention which the crippled boy received. The leg-iron became for him something which had a double significance. On the one hand, it represented masculine potency, exactly as in the cases previously quoted: on the other, it had the significance of a gift from the mother which gave support and added strength. He longed to be passive and helpless in order to get maternal affection: at the same time, he wanted to be masculine and active, a wish that found expression in a passionate interest in football. When he identified himself with the crippled boy by putting on his homemade leg-iron he was obtaining maternal affection in phantasy; and he was then able to feel more secure and more sure of himself as a man, with the result that he could experience his own sexuality.

It seems to me probable that this case throws some light on the opposing views held by psychopathologists. I have already mentioned that some authorities claim that the fetish has a phallic significance; others that it represents the breast. In some cases at any rate it probably represents both at once. All these patients are men who are uncertain of their masculine powers. It might be postulated that for a male child to develop normally two things are needed: first, a mother who will give him the affection and security which every child needs; second, a father with whom he can later identify. Either or both of these necessities may be absent: and it may be that, in cases of fetishism, the fetish represents whichever of these two requirements has been most conspicuously absent.

It is quite clear that in some cases of heterosexual fetishism the maternal, or breast, element is the most conspicuous.

(7) A man came to an out-patient department with the complaint that he had a compulsive attraction towards feminine jewellery, especially bangles. He had had a vicious

and neglectful mother, and as a small child frequently went to bed feeling miserably unhappy. But he found that if he took one of his mother's bangles to bed with him he felt more at peace; and he stole one from her dressing-table which he kept for some years. The maternally comforting and supporting aspect of the fetish is clearly shown in this case. He wished his girl friends to wear bangles because he felt so uncertain of himself as a man that he wished every woman to display some evidence of being a mother as well as a potential mistress.

In the fifth book of the *Odyssey* (Homer, 1935), the tale is told of how Odysseus made a raft and set sail from Calypso's isle: and of how Poseidon saw him, and raised up a tempest which all but overwhelmed him. But Ino, the daughter of Cadmus, came to his rescue, and told him to discard the clothes which Calypso had given him and to take her veil instead:

> Here, take this veil imperishable, and wind it about thy breast; so is there no fear that thou suffer aught or perish. But when thou hast laid hold of the mainland with thy hands, loose it from off thee, and cast it into the wine-dark deep far from the land, and thyself turn away. [*Odyssey*, Bk. V, l. 340]

When Odysseus finally reaches land safely, he does as he is told, and returns the veil to the water. He has received the feminine support that he needed in his extremity; but, once the danger is over, he must not keep it any longer, but must once again rely on himself.

Some fetishes have the significance of Ino's veil. They seem to represent a magical protective device which safeguards the man against the dangers of being overwhelmed by the unconscious; a safeguard that is particularly needed in the potentially dangerous situation of sexual intercourse. It seems that whenever a man is faced with any dangerous situation requiring him to exhibit the sum of his masculine strength, he likes to have a feminine symbol to support and strengthen him further. When the mediaeval knight sought to prove himself in a tournament, he often carried a token of his lady's favour, such as her glove, into battle with him: an outward and visible sign that she loved him; and no doubt he felt all the more confident because of it. In the last war, fighter pilots used to take stockings or brassières with them which their girl friends had given to them. It might be argued that this is merely an example of adolescent boasting; but it is only those who are uncertain of themselves who need to boast.

The phallic mother

It is clear, then, that the fetish has a double significance, both masculine and feminine. The image of the phallic woman, which is found in these conditions, is of great interest. Masculine symbols are constantly found in association with mother goddesses, especially with terrifying figures such as Hecate, whose symbols are the key, the whip, the dagger, and the torch. Witches ride on phallic broomsticks, and the various mother goddesses are frequently pictured as having phallic attributes. The phallic woman is an archetypal figure found in various representations all over the world. The existence of this figure is a living expression of the psychological truth that everything has origin from the mother, who is therefore symbolically both masculine and feminine.

Fetishists and transvestites are persons whose ego development is incomplete. They are not established as males with a separate existence and a consciousness of their own masculine potency. The power still belongs to the phallic mother, and their problem is to wrest the phallic power away from the mother and gain possession of it. The fetish is a magical device whereby this is attempted, and hence has a positive significance.

In transvestism, the patient assumes female dress not because he wishes to be a woman, but because he wishes to obtain the phallic power which is still felt to belong to the woman.

(8)   A man of 28 complained that he had the compulsion to dress in his wife's clothes about twice a week. He then masturbated. He was having normal sexual relations with his wife at the same time, but she was not particularly active sexually. He therefore felt rather reluctant to approach her sexually as often as he would have liked. When he put on her clothes, he described his sensations as those of 'support and

comfort'; he especially dwelt on the tactile sensations aroused by wearing stockings, which he described as 'comforting'. The maternal element in this is obvious. At the same time, he felt enormously self-confident in female clothes, and experienced an access of male potency. By identifying himself with a woman, he became, paradoxically, more of a man.

In this particular case, the archetypal theme was thrown into prominence by the personal background. The patient's father was a weak man, a nonentity with whom he could not identify in such a way as to evoke his own latent masculinity. The mother was a strong character who had always dominated the home and who 'wore the trousers'. She was thus particularly fitted to receive the projection of the great mother with the phallic attributes: and this projection was later transferred to the patient's wife.

One way of overcoming the great mother is to identify with her: this is the method adopted by transvestites. Another is by having intercourse with her. Neumann (1954), in *The Origins and History of Consciousness,* says: 'Jung's second conclusion, the significance of which has not yet been generally accepted in psychology, demonstrates that the hero's 'incest' is a regeneration incest. Victory over the mother, frequently taking the form of actual entry into her, i.e. incest, brings about a rebirth. The incest produces a transformation of personality which alone makes the hero of mankind' (p. 154).

Some primitive tribes require the adolescent to have intercourse with the mother. By thus reducing her to a human level, by putting her on a par with other women, the boy overcomes her power over him and attains masculine independence.

(9)   An epileptic male patient of high intelligence was both a sadist and a fetishist. He wanted to tie up women and beat them: he also wanted to wear mackintoshes. He was an extremely immature individual who had always felt inadequate compared with other men.

His earliest recollection of mackintoshes was that his mother had given him one when he was about six. He was extremely pleased with it, and he put it on in front of a mirror with nothing on underneath. He then experienced an erection

and sexual excitement. He occasionally repeated this procedure in adult life, obtaining a feminine mackintosh, putting it
on, and masturbating: but for the most part he wanted women
to wear mackintoshes and then to have intercourse with them.

The mackintosh in the first instance, therefore, had the
significance of a gift from the mother which resulted in his
'becoming sexual': a transfer of phallic power from her to him.
Why should he later want to renounce this and, as it were, give
it back to the woman again? Since his problem was to overcome
the mother, it seems probable that what he wanted to do was to
act out the archetypal theme of overcoming the mother by
having intercourse with her: and this situation could not be
complete unless the woman showed evidence of being a phallic
woman by wearing a mackintosh.

This interpretation is borne out by his sadistic wishes. His
phantasies were all concerned with proving himself to be
stronger and more powerful than the woman, which he could
only do by overcoming her.

The archetypal theme of overcoming the terrible mother and
thereby gaining possession of her phallic power is well illustrated
by the story of Perseus.

Perseus was the son of Danae and Zeus. His ultimate destiny
was to overcome the father, firstly in the shape of Polydectes, a
king who desired to marry Danae: and secondly in the person of
Acrisius, his maternal grandfather, who had originally persecuted his mother by shutting her up in a tower. But before
Perseus could deal with the paternal side and reign as king, he
had to deal with the maternal side in the shape of the Gorgon.
Pallas Athene appears to him in a dream and tells him about
Medusa. Perseus then goes to the court of Polydectes, who is
pressing his unwelcome attentions upon Danae. Polydectes
laughs at Perseus, because the latter has no gift to bring him,
unlike the other young men who are attending the court. 'Thou
sayest that thy father is one of the gods. Where is thy godlike gift,
O Perseus?'

We see here that Perseus compares unfavourably with the
other young men. They have all got something which he has
not—and it may be recalled that at the beginning of this paper I
suggested that in the cases I have described the basic condition

was one of the patient feeling himself to be lacking something which other men possess.

When Polydectes taunts him, Perseus accepts the challenge and says: 'The gift of the gods shall be thine. The gods helping me, thou shalt have the head of Medusa.' He has determined upon the fight with the dragon, but realizes that he cannot undertake it unaided. Athene appears again, this time accompanied by Hermes. Perseus receives from them, or from the nymphs to whom they direct him, the following articles: first, a sword with which to cut off the Gorgon's head; second, a wallet into which to put it when he has cut it off; third, a shield in which he may see Medusa reflected, and so avoid being turned to stone by facing her directly; fourth, a pair of winged sandals, to carry him swiftly and safely over the seas; and fifth, a helmet which renders him invisible.

As Neumann (1954) points out, the hero's path can only be trodden 'to its triumphal conclusion with the help of the divine father, whose agent here is Hermes', and with the help of Athene, whom Neumann takes as representing a new, feminine, spiritual principle (p. 216). I have already pointed out in my clinical examples that the child needs to receive affection from both parents, a male and a female contribution, if he is to overcome the fear of the mother and attain his full masculine stature. Perseus is given both a weapon which he can use actively, at one level corresponding to the phallus; and also magical means of protecting himself, the shield and the helmet, which are comparable to Ino's veil and represent maternal support and protection. It is by means of the positive relationship with the parents that the danger of remaining too long under their domination is overcome. It is obvious that all the gifts which Perseus receives from Hermes and Athene can be interpreted at various levels: they are true symbols, and represent masculinity and spirituality, the intellect and the power of consciousness as well as the instinctive basis of masculine development.

Perseus sets off, overcomes the Graeae, who are related to the Gorgons, and eventually cuts off Medusa's head and puts it in his wallet. Medusa's head is of great interest psychologically. Freud wrote a paper on it in 1922, in which he attributes the phallic attributes of Medusa to the fear of castration. He says:

The hair upon Medusa's Head is frequently represented in works of art in the form of snakes, and these once again are derived from the castration complex. It is a remarkable fact that, however frightening they may be in themselves, they nevertheless serve actually as a mitigation of the horror, for they replace the penis, the absence of which is the cause of the horror. This is a confirmation of the technical rule according to which a multiplication of penis symbols signifies castration.

The sight of the Medusa's head makes the spectator stiff with terror, turns him to stone. Observe that we have here once again the same origin from the castration complex and the same transformation of affect! For becoming stiff means an erection. Thus in the original situation it offers consolation to the spectator: he is still in possession of a penis, and the stiffening reassures him, of the fact. [p. 105]

I cannot agree with this view. The Gorgon's head is hardly to be interpreted as a reassuring object, in spite of the multiplicity of snakes; on the contrary, it is described as extremely terrifying. Being turned to stone, and thus completely immobilized, is surely not parallel to having an erection, a condition which is usually the precursor of an increase in masculine activity. The theme is surely that of being 'petrified' in the face of an overwhelmingly powerful figure which possesses both male and female characteristics: in other words, the great mother in her most destructive aspect.

It is the task of the hero to free himself from the influence of the great mother by overcoming her, and thus gaining possession of her phallic power, which he still lacks. Perseus puts the Gorgon's head in his wallet—presumably the sack or wallet which every man carries about with him, and which is still known by its Latin name of scrotum.

He is then able to free Andromeda from the sea-monster, a theme that I cannot elaborate here. He then uses the head to dispose of Polydectes and his court, whom he turns to stone by displaying it. But before he uses the head in this way, he has to return the sword, the shield, and the winged shoes to Athene and Hermes: an exact parallel to the returning of Ino's veil to the sea by Odysseus directly the immediate danger is over.

Perseus's final accomplishment is also interesting. He returns to find Acrisius, the maternal grandfather, who was responsible for the trouble in the beginning by shutting up Danae in a tower. Here Perseus takes part in a competition with the other young men in throwing the discus. But before he takes part, he takes off his helmet and cuirass and stands naked before the assembled crowd. In fact, he has reached a stage of masculine development in which he can afford to reveal himself fully, just as he is: for he has overcome the mother, and can now compete effectively with other men. Of course, he throws the discus much further than anyone else: and, equally inevitably, a gust of wind catches the discus, it strikes Acrisius, and kills him. Perseus can now ascend the throne and reign happily with Andromeda.

Summary

I have tried to show in this paper that fetishists and transvestites are persons who, because of a certain type of immaturity, feel themselves to be inadequate as men: that their symptoms are an effort to remedy this situation, by an attempt to transfer masculinity from other person to themselves, whether this person be male or female: and that this attempt is paralleled in the mythological theme of the hero's struggle with the bisexual dragon: and I have also attempted to show that the opposing views of other psychopathologists can be reconciled if this interpretation is accepted.

REFERENCES

Fenichel, O. (1945). *The Psycho-Analytic Theory of Neurosis*. New York: Norton.
———— (1953). *The Collected Papers of Otto Fenichel,* First Series. New York: Norton.
Freud, S. (1922). Medusa's head. *Standard Edition* 18. London: Hogarth.
———— (1927). Fetishism. *Standard Edition* 21. London: Hogarth.
Gillespie, W. (1956). The general theory of sexual perversion. *International Journal of Psycho-Analysis* 37:1.

Hadfield, J. A. (1950). *Psychology and Mental Health*. London: Allen & Unwin.

Homer (1935). *The Odyssey of Homer* (translated by Butcher & Lang). London: Macmillan.

Neumann, E. (1954). *The Origins and History of Consciousness* (translated by R. Hull). London: Routledge & Kegan Paul; New York: Pantheon. [Reprinted 1989, London: Maresfield Library.]

Proust, M. (1941). *Remembrance of Things Past* 7. London: Chatto & Windus.

Walker, K., & Strauss, E. (1948). *Sexual Disorders in the Male*. London: Hamish Hamilton.

CHAPTER FOURTEEN

The androgyne:
some inconclusive reflections
on sexual perversions

Michael Fordham

Fordham observes that Jungian analysts have neglected the perversions. He also suggests that Jungian interest in imagination and phantasy can go on in an excessively disembodied way. For these reasons, Fordham's approach to perversion makes use of terms and concepts of his own and those of psychoanalytic writers (Freud, Klein, Bion and Meltzer).

This enables Fordham to point out parallels between Bion's theory of beta elements, alpha elements, and alpha function and Jung's idea of the archetype, with its instinctual and spiritual poles. The androgyne, itself an archetypal image, acts as an organizer for polymorphous and physical sexual activities. In his use of the image of the androgyne, Fordham is emphasizing the part played in internal life by images of which the individual may not be aware.

First published in *the Journal of Analytical Psychology* 33:3, in 1988. Published here by kind permission of the author and the Society of Analytical Psychology.

Fordham makes a further suggestion about why it is that perverse mental process leads or does not lead to actual perversion: could this have something to do with psychological type? He concludes that, though interesting, this is not sufficient as an explanation.

A.S.

I have chosen to write on the subject of sexual perversions partly because there is virtually no literature on the subject from Jungian analysts. Besides that, I am encouraged to make the attempt because the late Kenneth Lambert, for whom this paper was originally written and delivered at a memorial meeting in Cambridge, was one of the few Jungians who contributed to a small volume on paedophilia. His article reached a high standard, so I can be said to be following his lead and thus pay some tribute to him. Like myself, he had been influenced not only by Jung but also by the English school of psychoanalysis and especially by Klein, Bion and Meltzer, though I am not sure that he assimilated much of Meltzer's essay *Sexual States of Mind* (1973). In addition, we both paid particular attention to childhood and infancy. A glance at the chapter headings of his book, *Analysis, Repair and Individuation* (Lambert, 1981), reveals one more aspect of our common ground: our interest in the interaction between analyst and patient: 'Resistance and counter-resistance', 'Reconstruction', 'Transference and countertransference', 'Dreams and dreaming'. He was concerned with the practice of analytical psychology set within the concept of the self as the transcendent function. The self stands behind the process of individuation, dependent not only on the ego but also on a dynamic concept of the organism integrating and deintegrating. These studies by Kenneth Lambert greatly furthered the work of what has come to be called the London school of analytical psychology based on the Society of Analytical Psychology.

Though Jung's later writings pay little attention to infancy and childhood, both Kenneth Lambert and myself have done so and understood the importance of infantile sexuality in the genesis of perversions. Jung gave little indication that he thought

either subject important. In saying this I do not wish to assert
that Jung paid no attention to the perversions; indeed, one of his
seminal cases in 'The psychology of the unconscious' (*CW* 7),
where he develops his theory of the collective unconscious and its
archetypes, is a homosexual. That man had exalted religious
dreams, and Jung understood them in relation to initiation. He
cited primitive rituals in which the adolescent member of a tribe
is submitted to homosexual intercourse so as to bind him into the
male community life.

A *definition*

I do not think that this kind of homosexuality, encompassed
within a ritual, can be classed as a perversion since the initiate
then goes on into marriage, where he presumably performs his
sexual function well enough. Such a reflection demands a
definition of perversion, but it is not so easy except for extreme
forms, especially those that are sadistic, masochistic or otherwise
shocking. Indeed, we seem not to have gone much further than
the notion, initiated by Freud, that any sexual activity that
prevents genital heterosexual intercourse, or replaces it, must be
counted a perversion. That could be somewhat bettered by adding
that, in perverse sexual activities, infantile sexual phantasies
and practices are exploited and become a more or less persistent
dominant feature in an individual's sexual life.

It is now well known that, although Jung paid scant attention
to perversion, he did not think that human beings could be
regarded simply as male or female. Even though their bodies
proclaimed radical differences, he maintained that they each nur-
tured within their psyche male and female elements, which he
termed the anima in the case of a male and the animus in the case
of a female. I have not been able to find anything about gender
identity in Jung's writings, but I think it justifiable to say that he
assumed such a conception. That is to say, he assumed that the
mental and emotional life of the sexes should be in line with the
physical configurations of each and that the possession or absence
of a penis, breasts and the internal organs making child-bearing
possible should be sufficiently recognized for these organs to

function in a healthy and productive fashion. It is by making that assumption that I can regard his relative absence of interest in the perversions comprehensible.

The anima and animus, and the archetypes, are conceived to be innate; they are not conceived as only physically sexual structures but are shaped by personal genetic and cultural experience.

The forms in which these archetypes function facilitate the relations between men and women by positive projective identifications that mitigate the essential mystery of the opposite sex (if negative they can lead to disagreeable illusions and consequent quarrels). Each archetype commonly expresses itself as moods and phantasies in the male or firmly held opinions in the female. The tendency of the animus to become forceful and rigid has given it a bad name. So I must add that, if functioning well, the animus facilitates a woman's organized mental life. Thinking of the functioning of the archetypes in this way helps us to recognize some of the roots of the process of identification with the opposite sex in both men and women, and how, if excessive, it can lead to lesbianism and homosexuality, as Freud so brilliantly demonstrated in his essay on Leonardo (1910c), and also used in a positive sense to understand the root of Schreber's delusion. But we must remember that the animus and anima are archetypes, and so their functioning does not conform to directed thinking, but to primary process thinking and to emotional actions and reflections.

I will now hypothesize that it is the dynamic energy in animus or anima identifications which may result in a man experiencing himself as a woman or a woman as a man. This state can lead to the perverse use of physical organs by making them simulate the normal form of intercourse. That effort may not be enough, however, and the delusion of being a man or a woman can lead to the demand that surgeons construct the desired organs by plastic surgery.

You will not expect me to believe that perversion is merely a matter of homosexuality or lesbianism. The term refers to a positive galaxy of behaviours: sadism, masochism, voyeurism, transvestism, masturbation, paedophilia and so on in their many forms, and it is not absent by any means from heterosexual activities. As an example of what this means, a male married man with five children could not become potent unless he imagined his wife was a prostitute and he became angry with her because she never had an orgasm. Besides this, he enacted other perverse voyeuristic activities in private, and because these were all acted upon I would class them as perversions. I say this because I am not inclined to think of phantasies as perversions proper.

The next of Jung's propositions that I wish to consider relates to the forms in which archetypes can express themselves. He compares them to the spectrum in which the colours are arranged in a sequence from red to violet (cf. *CW* 8, para. 384). We know that at each end there are infra-red and ultra-violet waves, which are not perceptible. By this analogy he seeks to express the idea that while there are a large number of forms in which the archetypes can express themselves and of which we can become conscious at either end, there are the absolute unconscious entities called instinct and spirit. I do not need to take into account the extremes and will confine myself to considering how at one end physical actions predominate and at the other phantasy and mental life—either being possible with relation to any possible archetypal configuration. I like Jung's analogy because it depicts the relation of archetypes to each other, merging into each other yet having a definite position. It also infers their relation to the whole in the light from which the colours are derived.

With this formulation in mind I read with much interest Bion's (1962) ideas about alpha and beta elements because he postulated that, by means of alpha function, beta elements can be transformed into alpha elements—the prototype of dream, phantasy and myth. Jungians had not developed such a detailed hypothesis, though there were indications that the study of myths and other ethnological material facilitated the transformation.

To some, Bion's way of putting it is difficult because he is trying to develop 'Alice in Wonderland mathematics'. If, however, his formula is translated to mean that an infant has a basic archetypal system which functions first at the infra-red end of the spectrum, and we consider alpha function in terms of maternal reverie (internal to the infant as well as operated by the mother), or when an infant seems to be in a similar state, looking as though he is having thoughts or phantasies when this is unlikely, or when he is in a mindless state, then we might say that he is having proto-thoughts or proto-phantasies, to coin two phrases which may be enlightening.

Another feature of Jung's work was that not only did he analyse myths and religious matter but also used them to start forming a geography of the psyche, which some of his followers have developed, a particular example being in *Creation Myths* by von Franz (1972).

An archetypal figure which has relevance to the subject under consideration is the androgyne. In his study of the transference, in which Jung uses an alchemical text as a paradigm of the transference, he found that the symbol for the end of the alchemical process was an image of a hermaphrodite, the androgyne. In a contradictory statement, he asserts: 'I have never come across the hermaphrodite as a personification of the goal [as the alchemists do] but more a symbol of the initial state, expressing an identity [of the ego] with anima or animus' (*CW* 16, para. 533). He considers the sexualism of the alchemical material to be due to the undeveloped state of the alchemical mind which '. . . knew nothing about the psychological problem of projection and the unconscious'. These quotations occur in the middle of discussion of the uniting symbol as it appears in individuation through transference analysis.

I must interpolate that I doubt Jung's explanation. It may, however, be that his statement is condensed. My own experience suggests that the androgyne can remain primitive when knowledge of projection is available not only intellectually but also in emotional experience.

Elsewhere Jung refers to the androgyne (e.g. in the *Mysterium Coniunctionis, CW* 14) in a historical perspective. It appears as Adam in the anthropos doctrines of the Gnostics in Paracelsus. In alchemy it has a number of forms: Rebis and Mercurius, among others. In Christianity itself Jung mentions a doctrine of the bisexual nature of Christ, while I have been impressed by the reports of St. John of the Cross, who records that in the initial stages of the mystical life God satiates and intoxicates the mystic with his breast of love. As a rough statement we can regard these images as projections or introjections, according to whether the experiences are internal or external.

You will perceive by now that a Jungian has a special interest in imagination and phantasy but is orientated in a way that these can become disembodied. Partly because of that I have found the work of Melanie Klein particularly helpful with her interest in unconscious phantasy which can be equated with archetypes. I have also been influenced by Bion and Meltzer.

I will now consider two cases that interested me because of the contrast they present. One man is predominantly homosexual, the other is heterosexual in practice and cannot understand why he ever had a serious homosexual relationship.

Case 1

The first case concerned a man in his middle thirties, whom I will call James. He had a male lover, and the couple were stable, which made their relationship 'respectable'. They had lived together for several years, and it was, on the whole, mutually satisfactory. The arrangement, that each was allowed freedom to make sexual experiments with other men, sounded somewhat forced, but it worked fairly well, though it could cause pain when the desires of one of them were left unsatisfied by the 'experiments'. They were, however, basically loyal to each other. James was overtly the more sensitive of the two, the smaller and the more feminine in the sense that he wanted to talk about and discuss difficulties in their relationship, whereas his lover, who was presented as the more masculine, a man of few words, preferred to ignore them or brush them off.

Sexual activities had not so far featured much as problems in his analysis. They seemed to be based mainly on part object relationships, by which I mean they were activities to produce comfort when skin contacts were important, whilst genital, anal or oral acts produced excitement. The pair made periodic excursions to 'gay' clubs, where they hoped to encounter other gay men with possible novel practices that produced new forms of excitement, though these excursions were usually disappointing. Apart from that, James visited lavatories where he knew gay men congregated, but again the encounters were disappointing because his hopes or phantasies were not realized. In these activities it was more apparent that he was attempting to find self-satisfaction.

In these excursions especially, he functioned on a part-object basis. He explored the uses to which his hands and penis could produce excitement in the orifices of his own body or in that of his temporary partner. The emphasis was on over-excitement rather than on pleasure. In his relationship to his permanent partner, James was, as I have said, the more feminine, so although much of their relationship was on a part-object basis, he, James, acted as a container and aimed to work at the relationship so as to foster it. His partner, who was bigger than he was and had a close relationship with his father, had scant use for James's feeling approaches; when painful subjects arose he tended to cut off altogether. At work, though, they could develop a useful and productive combination.

At no time did James explore his life with the aim of curing himself of his homosexual practices through his analytical endeavours, but he mentioned that several times he had enjoyed sexual intercourse with women and that it is much pleasanter to penetrate the vagina than the rectum. On each occasion the friendship with the female terminated after making love. Why that was so remains uncertain, though I explored, without success, the possibilities that the woman was degraded by submitting to him or he was afraid of being absorbed into her. He was attracted to women none the less, if they were intelligent, lively and pretty. He practised one other perversion, apart from genital masturbation: he found great satisfaction in anal activities, passing big stools and letting them squeeze down his legs. As an alternative, he would go into a wood and defecate there or find a place where there was as much liquid mud as possible, undress and roll about in it. He also liked his bed to be dirty as well as the room in wich he worked.

You may or may not be surprised to hear that this man was a highly intelligent and competent executive: moreover, he had a capacity to develop and generate new and original ideas in his work, though he had not reached the status and recognition he longed for. It is, I think, relevant to add here that in his transference he learned to differentiate his female and masculine characteristics, and with it came the realization that his maternal and paternal behaviour made for the successful operations that he deployed in his work, so that one can say that, in a mental and emotional sense, his work was sexual.

A prominent feature of this man's analysis had been his interest in gaining insight mostly of a mental kind; in this there is an almost complete absence of phantasy. His strong ethical and moral standards are important. They inhibited his sexual development and hence the recognition that sexually he had become his mother's penis, which was far from his consciousness. His bisexual homcsexuality could be understood on that basis and also the nature of his transference.

I will now turn to a particular aspect of the patient's transference. He struck me as working particularly hard at his treatment. He regularly brought some problem that had arisen between interviews and made discoveries that were beneficial. But from time to time I began to find his work boring and tended to feel drowsy, and on more than one occasion actually went to sleep. It was a state of affairs that is unusual, indeed rare, as I have always had difficulty in understanding how to get bored. He noticed it, but was tolerant; he understood how dull his talk might be, and I got the impression that he himself was also inclined to think so. He surmised that I must have heard what he said over and over again from other patients. He also brought in my age as an excuse for me; that was partly true. There is a danger here that the collusive element in the transference could take over, and the analysis will then be in danger of breaking down or becoming sterile. After some time I located what it was that made me 'bored'. I thought he was conducting his analysis on the basis of a conception of how an analysis should proceed. I do not mean to say that his good work was not productive, nor that my interventions were not useful to him, but there was the trend that I will attempt to define which needed analysis and further understanding.

It was apparent from the rather brief references to his parents that his mother was the dominant partner in her marriage and that his father was in important respects unsatifying to her. Taking that in relation with his transference to me, I concluded that there was an unconscious collusion with his mother to fulfil herself in a way that his father could not. I could point out that in his development he had been scholastically precocious, but when his mother died during his adolescence he fell into a depression, which so decimated his achievements that he was no longer able to follow his scholastic pursuits, and that interfered with his later achievements.

This is a good place to comment on the initiatory element in homosexual practices. My patient felt a loyalty to the male group to which he belonged. He held that this was general among homosexuals—it was disloyal to engage in heterosexual activities or to become heterosexual. Comparing this with the primitive rituals to which Jung refers, one has to conclude that the ritual element had been interrupted or not completed. Perhaps that ritual element is being expressed in his analysis and possibly may be completed—I put that as a hope because in my analyses of homosexuals I have seldom found they become heterosexual. Whatever other benefits they get from their struggles with themselves, and they can be considerable, the change to heterosexuality does not take place.

Case 2

Henry, my second case, is 37 years old. He has been married twice and has one child by each marriage. His first wife was his girlfriend at school, whom he married when he was 22. Their sexual relations were unsatisfactory in that, to his chagrin, he was frequently impotent.

Before this his sexual development has not been seriously deviant. As a boy he had explored genital differences with a girl and been initiated into masturbation by a male friend; so his failure with his wife was humiliating and had led to strained relations between them. He links his sexual inadequacy with women to a growth disorder from which he suffered. He did not grow properly at first; he was small and skinny, characteristics that made him much teased and sometimes bullied at school. In his humiliation he started a sequence of sexual phantasies during adolescence which he enhanced by taking drugs like cannabis and LSD, though he used them in an experimental way and was not addicted. The main period of experimentation took place when he developed a number of phobias with persecutory colouring. He felt his job was killing him, so he left it and went off with a brilliant and unstable friend, John, whom he found inspiring. With and through him, he discovered art, literature and politics and played rock-and-roll music in John's band.

During his analysis he retailed a sequence of memories. John had a girlfriend, whom he subsequently married. She was exceptionally beautiful, slim below and with large generous breasts—the type Henry especially admired and who usually excited him sexually. He, John and this woman engaged in various sexual exploits, including stripping.

One day the three of them went by car to the country. The woman was told by John to strip, which she did, and Henry was also instructed to strip. John told the woman to sit on Henry's knee, which she also did. To his surprise and consternation Henry found he had no erection. John then carried the woman off into the car and had intercourse with her. From behind Henry noticed the woman's legs as they negotiated the objects in the car. He was asked to kiss her face while John was occupied below, but he did not enjoy doing this and he desisted.

It was after that episode that he went to a hotel and performed intensive anal masturbation in which he then and afterwards felt himself to be a woman being copulated with by the devil's enormous penis.

At this period he felt very desperate, but finding he could 'chat up women' he started making relationships with them, though he was liable to be impotent and sometimes afraid of his impulse to attack their breasts, especially when they were very large. His self-esteem was restored by a passive woman, with whom he made love for hours on end—even 'all day'.

I will not expand further on this man's rich and polymorphous sexuality, except to say that it was while he was working on the feminine part of himself and his quite strong and sometimes frightening homosexual phantasies that he became puzzled as to why, in his adult life, he had never behaved sexually with one of his male friends with whom he had had close and intimate relationships. He was convinced all the same that by nature he was androgynous—a better word to use, I think, than bisexual.

If we consider these two cases together, they have in common homosexual and heterosexual trends; the one is acted on, the other expresses itself in autoerotic acts (especially anal masturbation) and dramatic phantasies. In the first there were no anxieties about impotence or sexual inadequacy, in the other it was a matter of great importance, for if he was not potent his self-esteem was shattered; but I never heard of the first patient being impotent, his penis was a reliable organ.

It is quite evident that each dealt with his infantile sexuality in different ways. James's sex life operated at the infra-red end of Jung's spectrum, that of the other, say, in the middle of the spectrum. If we use Bion's formulation, we can say that in relation to sexuality the alpha function had not operated much to produce alpha elements, the precursors of phantasy. In his case we can infer that the failure of the alpha function was due to his being an extension of his mother. This kind of extension is complicated and can be observed in mother–infant observation when a mother will project her animus into her son so that he becomes forced by her potency to ever greater achievement. If that persists and the child is gifted, then we have the groundwork for his developing into a female–male androgyne. I am of the opinion that James had developed along that line. I would cite in favour of this hypothesis that his mother was much the more powerful of his parents and that he has not yet mentioned any period of mourning over her death; she is part of him and in that sense is not dead.

To continue with this construction, we have to account for his mental achievements. That must be due to innate intelligence, but even so there must have been a capacity to convert beta elements into thoughts. I would speculate that this was established in relation to the breast. Bion (1962) has a good formulation here: a no breast is a bad breast within the infant if it struggles to extrude it either by evacuating it as excrement or transforming it into a thought, which for my patient became food for the mother's animus and later pressured him into mental achievement.

In contrast, and it is the contrast I wish to highlight, my second patient was positively flamboyant: he had developed a rich, varied sexual life, and he turned readily to women for personal consolation and sexual satisfaction. They usually responded, though the woman that he fell passionately in love with, and who was sexually dramatic, eventually rejected him. He soon fell into the arms of another one.

This was quite the contrary with James, who did not lack male sexual partners but, in other respects, could not have been less like my second patient. I never heard him refer to any part of a woman's body except her vagina. Pre-genital relationships did not take place with women; he was sturdy and boyish. He gave no evidence of appreciating a woman's physical beauty, nor did he phantasize about what she might be like in her mysterious insides.

One might profitably consider these two cases with respect to type theory: the first patient being a sensation type with thinking and feeling as secondary functions; the second an intuitive and also with thinking and feeling as secondary functions. Though these ideas do something to facilitate description, they do not focus enough on the psychopathology of the two cases. Why had the initiatory process in James stopped at so-called initiatory practices, and why had the other's polymorphous sexuality burgeoned in acts as well as phantasy, growing into a very real appreciation of women? The former was not lacking in homosexual phantasy, while the latter had embarked on heterosexual activity which did not, however, develop. We can speak of each as androgynous with a different emphasis.

We are, I think, getting to know more about how it is possible for these variations to develop, partly through transference analysis, partly through constructions about the patient's infancy and childhood, and more recently through studies on mother–infant observation. A recent construction by Masud Khan (1979) is derived from observations on transitional objects. He considers that there is, in the case of perversions, a 'collated internal object' which is placed in the space between mother and infant whose content is a mixture of male and female objects. This collated object seeks a real partner, but according to Khan it can never be actualized and so leads to disillusionment. It is this which leads to the sense of alienation sometimes found among the perverse. I cannot say that my cases showed the characteristics Khan requires; indeed, the sense of alienation and precarious identity applied to the heterosexual patient at one time more than to the other, and that has now largely been repaired.

I have isolated a form of transference exhibited by the homosexual which indicated that he was conducting his analysis on a deeply unconscious premise which I was supposed to hold, and it may be assumed that I did so with great fixity of purpose, almost driving me to become unconscious in a very concrete way. One of the characteristics of the collated internal object is that it contains the mother's dissociated unconscious. We are back to Jung, according to whom the act of a mother was the major factor in determining most childhood disorders. Like so many early insights, it became prematurely generalized, but that does not make the perception less significant—it can be thought about and developed and modified if necessary. Jung's view was one-sided and failed to take into account the part played by an infant or child in introjecting the mother's masculine unconscious or animus. For example, to do so the child must have developed far enough to experience his mother as a woman with a penis (without testicles, be it noted) which can be continued in beta elements, sexual acts or translated into mental life and achievement. That is a possibility which would be fostered by a strong mother with firmly held moral principles and a weak father, the picture of his parents that he gave. Such a construction is, I think, plausible.

Kenneth Lambert worked on constructions which had been sadly neglected by analytical psychologists. I think that they can give a valuable perspective on a patient's conflicts and make it easier to sort out what is infantile and perverse in an adult and what is polymorphous and valuable in an adult. They assist in distinguishing what Jung distinguished as the androgyne; that is, a symbol for the initial state on the one hand and of the goal on the other.

Summary

After a brief introduction on the relevance of the animus and the anima, Jung's model of the spectrum to indicate the range of possible archetypal experience is related to Bion's postulate of beta and alpha elements.

Two cases are then described. Both are bisexual, but one is a practising homosexual while the other channels his homosexuality into very intense masturbatory phantasies. The possible origins of the differences are then discussed in the light of Jung's and Bion's conceptions and also the 'collated internal object' as defined by Masud Khan.

REFERENCES

Bion, W. R. (1962). *Learning from Experience*. London: Heinemann. [Reprinted 1984, London: Maresfield Library.]

Freud, S. (1910c). Leonardo da Vinci and a memory of his childhood. *Standard Edition* 11. London: Hogarth.

—6 Khan, M. (1979). *Alienation in Perversions*. London: Hogarth. [Reprinted 1989, London: Maresfield Library.]

Lambert, K. (1976). The scope and dimensions of paedophilia. In W. Kraemer (ed.), *The Forbidden Love*. London: Sheldon Press.

———— (1981). *Analysis, Repair and Individuation*. Library of Analytical Psychology, Vol. 5. London: Karnac Books.

—6 Meltzer, D. (1973). *Sexual States of Mind*. Strath Tay, Perthshire: Clunie Press.

von Franz, M.-L. (1972). *Creation Myths*. Zürich: Spring Publications.

CHAPTER FIFTEEN

The archetypes in marriage

Mary Williams

This paper, which has not been published before, has enjoyed a vogue amongst trainees at the Society of Analytical Psychology, probably because of the way in which Williams makes use of animus/anima theory to enlarge the more recent clinical concept of unconscious collusion within a couple. She shows how the parental images, themselves a blend of the personal and the typical, influence partner choice and also the on-going vicissitudes of marriage. Finally, her summary of Jung's idea of there being a container and a contained in marriage leads on to further discussion of the impact in marriage of projected parental imagery, containing, as it does, infantile wishes and desires.

Thus, classical Jungian theory is intertwined with a more developmental approach.

A.S.

First presented as a lecture to the Analytical Psychology Club, London, in 1971. Published here for the first time by kind permission of the author.

In this chapter I discuss anima and animus figures and their spell-binding power in marriage. I also give an account of clinical research in which I took part at the Tavistock Clinic under the aegis of Henry Dicks, in which he looked anew at the phenomena unfolding before our eyes. Only those working hypotheses developed and tried out over the years that confirm and elaborate Jung's findings are discussed.

First of all, I would like to discuss the meaning of terms I use. The concept 'archetype' is understood as a *psychosomatic entity,* an understanding Jung moved towards in his later work and which has been developed by Fordham, Stein and others. This enables us to grasp something of the experiences of infancy which may occur again in marriage in which continuous body intimacy is the vehicle of psychic experiences of the union of complementary opposites. In infancy the mother and baby join on the nutritive level through the mouth orifice finding the nipple, and in adulthood the man and woman join on the genital level by the vaginal orifice finding the penis. These complementary images are innate potentials waiting to be activated. These are part images of the anima and animus which as archetypal images spring from the feminine and masculine elements in men and women, respectively. When experienced in projection, the ordinary man and woman are perceived as possessing a fascinating power. The first carriers of the images are the parents, whose special characteristics may modify the typical image to a greater or lesser extent, depending on the degree of ego development achieved. To be able to see a person as a complicated whole human being is an achievement of maturity, rarely reached, says Jung, for this ability rests on the degree of self-realization achieved.

A less familiar concept I use is that of *collusion.* This is an unconscious transaction by which one partner 'carries' certain contents for the other as if by agreement. Its function in marriage is to preserve those illusions that have influenced the choice of partner. R. D. Laing, in his book, *The Self and Others* (1961), describes collusion as follows:

> The one person does not wish merely to have the other as a hook on which to hang his projection. He strives to find in the other, or to induce the other person to become, the very embodiment of

that other whose co-operation is required as 'complement' of the particular identity he feels impelled to sustain (p. 101).

'Successful' collusion occurs when the partners support mutually projected roles based on shared ideal images. The non-ideal, even horrible, will be discounted, denied or otherwise defended against in order to preserve the feeling of security obtained from the ideal images. In the simplest kind of successful marriage, the partners may even call each other 'Mum' and 'Dad', like the children do, and become 'Darby and Joan' characters in their old age. The shadow side of such marriages is located in the neighbours' goings-on and in the sensational press. As no personal development takes place within these marriages, however, the death of one of them is a disaster that is quickly followed either by the decline of the other or by another marriage. What, then, is the criterion of a successful marriage in a more mature sense? I would say that it depends on a sufficient degree of ego development before the 'fatal compulsion', as Jung calls falling in love, to weather disappointments and to work through them towards a more real value judgement of the partner's strengths and weaknesses in relation to those of the self. Only then is a partnership built on mutual co-operation possible.

It will be noted that the idea of *unconscious choice* of partner appears in Laing's definition. I am reserving his choice by *complement* to refer to heterosexual choices based on an image of the opposite-sex parent. The choice by *contrast* is an addition from Dicks (1967) which involves much psychopathology that I do not deal with in this chapter. The notion of unconscious choice is as old as Plato, at least. He had the idea that man and woman were once one, that they got separated and spent their lives trying to find the other half again. Jung's discoveries in this respect were more scientific. In the course of his word-association experiments in the first decade of this century, he found that there was a high correlation between responses of mothers and daughters and fathers and sons. Following up on the marriage partners of each, he found the choice was most often of someone with characteristics of the opposite-sex parent as revealed in the tests. Thus, identification with the parent of the same sex led to the choice of a partner resembling the other parent. He did not pursue those marriages that revealed other characteristics.

When people fall in love, the fascinating parental image is transferred to the love object with a similar intensity and blind affect as was experienced by the young child towards the parent. The other one is sensed as a completion or complement, owing to the projection of the ideal images. The two yearn to become one flesh.

The state of fusion brings about the reverse feelings to that of the union of complementary opposites. It seems as if they are familiar to each other, even identical. 'We felt we'd known each other all our lives', 'We seemed to have everything in common', are expressions often heard. Jung wrote of this state in 1925 in an article entitled 'Marriage as a psychological relationship': 'The greater the area of unconsciousness, the less is marriage a matter of free choice, as is shown subjectively in the fatal compulsion one feels so acutely when one is in love'—the state of 'primitive identity' of the loved one with the self, each presupposing in the other a psychological structure similar to that of the ideal image. Normally sexual intercourse strengthens this feeling of unity and identity, 'not without good reason, since the return to that condition of unconscious oneness is like a return to childhood' (CW 17, paras. 324–325).

In the same article, Jung talks about collusion, though he does not call it that, but the phenomenon of *the container and the contained*. The illustration he gives, however, is of partners who carry certain contents for each other. The woman contains the emotional life of the man, and he contains her spiritual life, by which Jung explains he means her complexities and potentialities. The man being over-complex and therefore apt to dissociation seeks for unity through what he sees as the woman's simplicity, but he disturbs the very thing he needs by seeking it in her. Conversely, her need for him to give her simple answers increases his dissociation. I have had a few such cases. They drive each other crazy and need an intermediary to interpret each to the other.

Dicks has another hypothesis that covers similar ground. 'Subjects may persecute in their spouses tendencies which originally caused attraction, the partners being unconsciously perceived as a symbol of "lost" because repressed aspects of the subject's personality.' I would add, following Jung, that it may not only be repressed parts but those not yet developed. In passing, I would like to point to the attraction between opposite psychological types which seem to me to fall into this category. If they cannot take on trust what they cannot understand, a dreadful enmity may ensue.

Absence or attenuation of sexual intercourse are the most usual presenting symptoms in couples seeking help, but there are crisis points that threaten the twosome and precipitate referral. They include pregnancy, discovery of a lover or other secret life, a disturbed child, a disturbing adolescent, a problem relative, and various forms of loss and separation from familial figures.

Jung noted that neuroses that flower on marriage contain a 'counter-argument' against the spouse for not being like the ideal parental figure.

Dicks arrived at a similar conclusion. His first hypothesis runs:

> Tensions and misunderstandings between partners result from the disappointment which one, or both of them, feel and resent, when the other fails to play the rôle of spouse after the manner of a preconceived (ideal) model or figure in their fantasy world. ... The parties treat each other *as if* the other were the earlier object.

He goes on to say,

> Regression occurs in the means used to coerce or persuade the parent image with the old, childish resources of revenge or of gaining favour. Forbidding and rejecting qualitites are attributed and evoked each by the other. ... The bad object is shuttled to and fro ... the essence of *collusion*.

The traditional cultural stereotypes play an enormous rôle even in sophisticated people, as they correspond pretty closely to the archetypal forms. They not only influence the individual's ego ideal but may be used in attacks on the partner. For instance, a common type of marriage seen at my clinic is between an apparently weak, often semi-impotent man and an aggressive, demanding woman from whom he progressively withdraws. She attacks her husband for not being a man, but she was attracted to him in the first place because he seemed kind and gentle and would look after her. She really feared that the challenge of male potency would expose her own inadequacies as a woman. He was attracted to her because of her spontaneity and apparent warmth and was appalled to find an insatiable demon. Afraid of her devouring nature, intercourse becomes out of the question—which suits them both admirably. A main variation of this theme is of the complaining victim wife of a tyrannical husband.

I was interested to find descriptions in Jung's *Two Essays* (*CW* 7) regarding animus/anima problems in marriage which could be comments on these marriages. They follow a comment on the value of initiation rites.

> Just as the father acts as a protection against the dangers of the external world and thus serves his son as a model persona, so the mother protects him against the dangers that threaten from darkness of the psyche. In the puberty rites, therefore, the initiate receives instruction about these things of 'the other side', so that he is put in a position to dispense with his mother's protection. The modern civilized man has to forgo this primitive but nonetheless admirable system of education. The consequence is that the anima, in the form of the mother imago, is transferred to the wife, and the man, as soon as he marries, becomes childish, sentimental, dependent and subservient, or else, truculent, tyrannical, hyper-sensitive, always thinking about the prestige of his superior masculinity. The last is of course merely the reverse of the first. The safeguard against the unconscious, which is what his mother meant to him, is not replaced by anything in the modern man's education. Unconsciously, therefore, his ideal of marriage is so arranged that his wife has to take over the magical rôle of the mother. Under the cloak of the ideally exclusive marriage he is really seeking his mother's protection, and thus he plays into the hands of his wife's possessive instincts. His fear of the dark incalculable power of the unconscious gives his wife an illegitimate authority over him, and forges such a dangerously close union that the marriage is permanently on the brink of explosion from internal tension—or else, out of protest, he flies to the other extreme, with the same results. [paras. 309–311]

> Take for example, the 'spotless' man of honour and public benefactor, whose tantrums and explosive moodiness terrify his wife and children. What is the anima doing here? ... Wife and children become estranged; a vacuum will form round him. At first he will bewail the hard-heartedness of his family, and will

behave if possible even more vilely than before. That will make the estrangement absolute. . . . Then follow remorse, reconciliation, repression, and in next to no time, a new explosion. Clearly the anima is trying to force a separation. [paras. 305–306]

Personally, I have not found this happening unless the woman's animus is involved, so we will see what Jung has to say here. Later, when describing the animus, he writes:

The men who are particularly suited to [animus] projections are either walking replicas of God Himself, who know all about everything, or else they are misunderstood word-addicts with a vast and windy vocabulary at their command. . . . The animus is (also) a jealous lover. He is an adept at putting, in place of the real man, an opinion about him . . . if the woman does not stir his sentimental side, and competence is expected of her rather than appealing helplessness and stupidity, then her animus opinions irritate the man to death. Men can be pretty venomous here, for . . . the animus always plays up to the anima—and vice versa, of course—so that further discussion becomes pointless. [paras. 328–333]

It is, perhaps, not strange that a pair of lovers, trapped by the mutually projected ideal images and encapsulated from the real world, remain relatively immune from interference from the shadow sides of these images. This immunity may even weather quite lengthy periods of cohabitation, for the familial figures which carry it are as yet excluded from the magic circle. Their inclusion in marriage—as the marriage certificate makes plain, if not the actual ceremony, which may exclude them—sometimes has immediate and dramatic results. A pall descends as the partners notice the black side of the image. They cry, often in unison, 'You are not the man/woman I married!' or, as a New Yorker cartoon put it: 'I'm beginning to think you never were the man I married!' True, but they are not yet seeing each other but the reverse side of the image.

Another factor has entered—that of the *incest taboo*. Jung describes incest as an expression of the libido which serves to hold the family together. It could be defined as *'kinship libido'*. It seems that while the feeling between couples is of that cosy familiar kind of intimacy, it is still incest, but good. The anti-libidinal forces—those that split the family apart—bring in the feeling of taboo with its unclean and dangerous connotations, and attraction turns to disgust.

When negative aspects of the images gain the upper hand, these may be as collusively adhered to as were the real ones. One can fall in hate as well as fall in love. It is a fearsome experience to observe a chronic sample in which the therapist is ignored while two people, each feeling the victim of the other, accuse each other of similar crimes. It appears that the libido has gone into a fight for survival based on the mutual need for self-justification. In one couple the death of a child had brought this need to a head, and the imputation of blame had made it impossible to mourn the death together. Albee's play, *Who's Afraid of Virginia Woolf?* describes this situation well. In it, the child they never had is the shared object of fantasy and mutual recrimination. This gives us a hint as to what the trouble is about. The injured and resentful child in each partner is fighting against acknowledging dependence on untrustworthy parental figures. They cannot trust each other with their loving selves, for this would make them vulnerable to real hurt. What we see is essentially a game, however deadly, in which the characters are pawns in the hands of the mutually hated and feared parental images. Its illusory yet powerful quality gives the observer an eerie impression. Such marriages are usually as immune from intervention, as is the idealizing couple.

The way in which images are shared is another aspect of collusion, for which I am indebted to Teruel's (1966) research. He saw couples together for diagnosis and remained relatively passive in order to allow the interaction to develop. He noticed that the first object (or objects) significant to both which was brought into the interview represented the disturbing factor in the marriage. This might be the mother or father of one of them, for instance. He called this the *phenomenon of the emergence of the dominant internal object* (p. 232). References to the characteristics of this object were taken to be statements about the nature of the shared internal object, e.g. that it was disgusting, violent, inadequate, dead, etc. He proceeded to show how one partner might contain the disturbing object for both of them, in which case that one would be carrying a '*double charge*' and might even be clinically ill. In other cases, the object would be thrown from one to the other as described by Dicks and, of course, to the therapist in the transference.

Case material

The first case study shows the influence of parental deaths and broken illusions, the second a drama of rivalry presented through an asthmatic child; in the third, I follow the vicissitudes of a shared image of an envious old witch through the treatment of a couple.

Case study 1:   Mr and Mrs C

Parental and other ghosts are potent sources of marital disturbances where mourning is incomplete. Mr and Mrs C were a young couple plunged into a mourning situation from the start of an already guilt-laden relationship. When seen, they had been married only six months after a year of partial cohabitation, during which a child was born.

She was a perky girl who dramatized herself, he a depressed-looking young man. Almost at once, Mrs C brought her dead father into the interview. He had died suddenly when she was three months pregnant. When she realized she was pregnant, she had wanted John to meet her father, but he put it off until it was too late. 'I hold that against him', she said. Mr C sighed. 'We could be happy, but whenever anything goes wrong, she brings this up.' She retorted, 'I'll never forget. I felt robbed, and that you'd robbed Daddy too. ... Then the whole pregnancy was awful. ... People made me feel a tramp. ... I loathed the child inside me.' A string of recriminations followed, proving how the husband was responsible for her shame and degradation and how disloyal he's been. He'd even suggested the child might not be his, and once she had found him with another woman.

Mr C took it all—he blamed himself for not thinking of marriage and for hurting her by this attitude. He insisted, however, that he had never wanted her to abort, though he admitted that the pregnancy was not real to him even when she was big. Then Mrs C admitted that she had tried her best to get rid of the baby, but her feelings changed after her father died, and she went into a panic when she bled. She just had to have the baby then. She said it amazed her that she hadn't thought of marriage either, not for months after the baby was born. She returned to the attack. 'Marriage made no difference. ... John was as inconsiderate as ever.'

Mr C showed some resentment for the first time. 'No', he said, 'marriage made no difference. She still refused to meet my people or to entertain my friends.' Mrs C used this remark to prove how inconsiderate he was and added, 'I like men who are kind and understanding.' Bitterly, he murmured, 'Like your father.' Mrs C started to extol her father. 'I know I'm very jealous of people who have such a man. ... I could always rely on him in trouble. ... Mother never wanted to know ... how could she marry again so soon! ... She has even taken this man into the house which Daddy built. ... It's so disloyal.'

It was becoming clear that Mrs C was off-loading the image of the 'inconsiderate' father who had left her in the lurch as well as her own feelings of guilt and disloyalty to him, but as yet there was no evidence as to why Mr C so readily accepted the burden. I therefore asked him about his parents. He said his father drank, and his mother told him constantly what an awful life she had with him because of this. Until she died a year ago of cirrhosis of the liver, he had been blind to the fact that *she* was the real alcoholic. He had got to know his father since then and felt awful for having despised him. 'I've had to reassess all my convictions', he said, 'but I still love my mother. I can understand how my wife feels. My mother saw the baby before she died. This hurt my wife, as her father didn't even know of his existence.' Mrs C wept. 'I wanted the ashes, but it was too late—they'd been scattered. At least, I wanted his name engraved in the Remembrance Book, but John said we couldn't afford it.' She had a shock, too. When her father died, she found out that her parents had never been married. Father still had a wife alive, 'and he was so moral and so strict with all of us!' she said.

This couple were struggling with the need to preserve the image of the ideal lost parent in the face of shocking evidence to the contrary. However, it was Mrs C's father's ghost who dominated the marriage and persecuted both of them. Mrs C's success as his avenger seemed to be due to her greater need to keep intact the ideal image with which she was identified and so to project the immoral, inconsiderate and deserting one into her husband. For his part, he accepted this image as a punishment for having despised his own father in collusion with his mother. That he had presented the still idealized mother with his child before her death and had 'robbed' his wife of a chance to get her father's blessing added envy to injury, though this was a fantasy Mrs C imposed on her husband, who knew at the time that he was supposed to ask for money for an abortion—an admission neither of them could make.

Clinically, the incestuous implications were at present secondary to the more primitive theme of intense ambivalence towards the lost ones and fear of the power of the dead. An interpretation in these terms and of the need to mourn together was meaningful to them both, which suggested that in spite of the severity of the symptoms, Mr and Mrs C would be able to work through them.

Case study 2:   Mr and Mrs D

The problems of this couple illustrate the involvement of a child as the presenting symptom, so often seen in child guidance clinics. Also illustrated is the crisis point at the birth of the symptom-child in which the repetition of familial groupings facilitated the activation of the image.

Mr and Mrs D were sent by the hospital where Susan, aged 7, the younger of two girls, was being treated for asthma. It was believed that the marriage might break up, since the wife discovered that her husband had been unfaithful to her.

Mrs D started off, speaking in a rapid monotone for both of them. She gave a bright picture of the marriage—they enjoyed the same things, and so on—only the sexual side had been unsatisfactory for four or five years now. She put it down to *Susan's asthma*. They had to split up because the child had not been able to endure being left alone. They were constantly disturbed at night ... their tempers frayed ... they were tired ... Mrs D had started work again part-time a few months ago, and Susan had slept through most nights since. 'It can't be coincidence', she said, 'it helped me to go out and have people to talk to. ... I'd felt *closed in and constricted.*' She could see why her

husband had to look outside the home when Susan was so ill . . .
she's neglected him. She turned to her husband for confirmation.

Mr D answered by addressing me. 'I haven't the same feeling
as my wife. I wasn't conscious of her preoccupation with Susan.
I'm not worried about the lack of intercourse, except as it affects
my wife. I have no desire for intercourse with her.' He also
objected to being excused for his affair. 'I am responsible for what
I do. I am not a child. I don't regret the affair. It was an addition,
not a criticism of my wife.'

Mrs D had been looking hurt but was now annoyed. 'He told me
she was young, gay and attractive and thought he was God
Almighty. He wants to be *king-pin* all the time. . . . He was put
out when Susan became the pivot of my life.' Mr D retorted
blandly, 'Of course I'm king-pin to you, the children and
everybody in my business. None of you could do without me.' She
flared up. 'I've decided to accept that invitation abroad. You can
look after the children while I enjoy myself. . . . I feel I've lost my
identity. . . . I was something before I married, and now I am
nothing . . . just a drudge looking after everyone else. I want to be
looked after for a change.' Mr D looked relieved. 'I used to admire
you for your independence. By all means, go.' It seemed he also
felt closed in and constricted.

The prognosis for marital therapy did not seem favourable,
owing to the intense rivalry for the king-pin position, coupled
with Mr D's impregnability. In fact, he dropped out almost
immediately, having 'more important matters to attend to'.

None of the background figures appeared in the diagnostic
interview and were not necessary to make an assessment of the
case, but their respective family groupings were of great
significance. It was the birth of the second girl that helped to
recreate the pattern of the original families of each and to
activate the omnipotent king-pin image.

Mr D was 'an afterthought' and therefore virtually the only
child of old parents. Father was 'king-pin', and mother was
absorbed in meeting his demands. In consequence, Mr D was
brought up by his older sister and two aunts. They all doted on
him until he was a certain age, when they expected him to be a
'messenger boy', he said. He had resented bitterly doing anything
for these three women and was now again faced with three
females, all expecting something of him. It was his wife's

'independence' that had attracted him, and the first child was 'no trouble'. Mrs D was the younger of two sisters who were violently jealous of each other. Her father was also 'king-pin' and her mother 'nothing more than a slave' to him, she said. The birth of the second girl completed the likeness to their original family patterns in important particulars. When both the image and the family pattern in which it first arose correspond in both partners, the charge coming from the relevant image assumes huge proportions.

Case study 3: Mr and Mrs X

In this last case, I would like to show the vicissitudes of the presenting mother image as treatment progressed and the emergence of a second one, the split-off father figure. The case also demonstrates the phenomenon of sharing, in that the images belonging to the wife were taken over by the husband as more dramatic representatives of his inner world than those based on perceptions of his own parents. The rôle of transference is also illustrated. The treatment was completed in the comparatively short time of five months, perhaps because the images were so clear.

Mr and Mrs X, both aged 30, arrived with a protesting boy toddler, the youngest of their three children. My face must have fallen at this complication, for, before I had spoken, the wife, a fiery redhead, turned on her neat, tense husband and said, 'I told you so! We should have left him with mother.' *Her mother,* and the passing back and forth of the toddler who wanted the one who was not holding him, absorbed the rest of the interview.

Mrs X put forward, and Mr X agreed, that her mother was trying to sabotage the marriage, that she was an envious and jealous woman who aimed at preventing or breaking up all happy relationships, and that she was 'sex-obsessed'. The worst of it was that they were dependent on her to baby-sit. 'Once she moves into the house, it's a job to get her out again!' they said. It then appeared that Mrs X had tried to make her allegedly undersexed husband jealous by entertaining an old admirer, now married, and was furious because he didn't rise. At the same time, she accused him of having a 'dirty, sniggering attitude towards sex', which, from the stories about her mother, was what they both objected to in *her*. Mr X defended himself with logical argument but with desperation against her attacks. He also made an accusation: that she had tried to sabotage his studies and prevent his advancement.

Perhaps this is enough to show that *her mother* represented the shared image of the envious old witch who was out to stop them enjoying themselves, and that each tried to push it into the other one. Mrs X was more successful in this. I noticed that Mr X paled when she managed to do so, and I was hardly surprised to hear that he suffered from dyspepsia.

Progress in treatment can be assessed by following the fate of the dominant image, so I will pick out some references to it. Mrs X accused her husband of leaving her to cope with her sex-obsessed mother, which he did by falling asleep when she was present. Deducing that they both feared their own sex obsessions, Mrs X confessed that she was terrified of becoming like her mother with sexual frustration, which would, of course, be all Mr X's fault. She volunteered with a sneer that her husband was terrified of sexual activity because *his* mother had warned him that too much sex was bad for the health. This he denied—he had picked it up from boys at school. I said it sounded as if their fears of dirty sex referred to forbidden pleasures such as masturbation and to punishment for it. Mrs X turned on her husband again. 'That's just about what his love-making amounts to!' Mr X paled, and there was an uneasy silence. I remarked that talking about sex as we were doing seemed equivalent to performing in public, which was what they felt her mother did, and now it was myself who was embarrassing them. They both blushed and then laughed uncertainly.

On another occasion, when Mr X was looking ill, Mrs X attacked him for drinking sherry on an empty stomach though she had warned him he would suffer for it. Mr X rallied and accused her of being just like his mother, fussing about his health whenever he enjoyed something and then trying to prevent him doing it. Mrs X later returned to the attack by asserting that her mother had been asking her husband to visit her behind her back. Mr X was put out as he had to admit that he had once been to see her. He was then accused of liking her smutty jokes. As it happened, Mr X had recently asked to see me alone for 'sex instruction', and I had refused. Mrs X did not know this, but it was what she would suspect in the transference of their joint fantasies, which were to become progressively clearer.

More direct references to myself as the sex-obsessed mother followed. Mrs X said she had heard that this was a Freudian clinic, and Mr X said, 'Freud saw everything as sexual, didn't he?' I said I thought they were envying me my association with such an exciting father figure. Mrs X then told me about *her father*. Her parents were separated, but she had kept in touch with her father, much to her mother's fury. She reported that father had an uncanny way of phoning her when her mother was with them, and Mrs X had to fight for her right to see him. Again Mr X experienced the drama through his wife's parents, his own being seen as tolerant of each other. He did say, however, that father was 'uninterested' in his achievements—in fact, he had taken him away from school early, seeing 'no point' in further education. Fear of outdoing his father and of his envy was a new factor, which accounted for Mr X's acute status anxiety at work as well as his potency fears.

Relaxing slowly, they started to come in giggling like a couple of adolescents and played provocative games with each other and with me. After this playful phase, they were able to tell me that they were having satisfactory intercourse for the first time in their marriage.

• At the agreed last session, I enquired after her mother, who had not been mentioned for some time. They both spoke of her with tolerance, even concern. 'Poor old thing, she can't help it . . . she's not so bad really . . . she's a great help to us.' The charge had lifted from the once dreaded figure and from myself and had found its place in the attraction between them. The advent and working through of the Freud–father image in the transference coupled with a reduction of power of the envious and jealous mother image seemed responsible for this result.

Conclusion

I have outlined the views of Jung on the interaction of anima and animus figures in marriage and have shown how his original research into choice of partner was rediscovered by Dicks. The factor of collusion which preserves the illusions coming from the archetypal images about the nature of the partner is a worked-out addition useful in treatment.

Personally, I found Teruel's work on the shared image in marriage particularly useful. To see it in live culture acting on the couple and being thrown from one to the other leaves one in no doubt that it is not only shared but is a 'charged' or numinous entity which may be too 'hot' for any one person to hold for long without getting hurt. An exception to this rule is seen in Case 2, where the husband was identical with the image. This gives an impregnability that is unlikely to be dispersed by psychotherapy; indeed, the individual would see no point in coming. The transference, or 'throwing' of the image to the therapist, is illustrated in the last case reported.

Another attribute of the archetype is that it holds an energy charge which implies the presence of positive and negative poles. It is held that splitting occurs in the service of survival. We see this splitting happening in the phenomenon of falling in love on which so many marriages are based. This phenomenon has been seen as a regression to the original twosome where the hated one is not the one who is loved. 'He/she is not the person I married' is a common phrase expressing this dichotomy. But marriage itself is based on the archetypal theme of the union of complementary opposites, not in one individual as in the individuation process, but in projection onto the spouse, who is first embraced as representative of the wonderfully seductive inner image. This ideal image may survive the irritations of everyday living for some years, or its terrible counterpart may appear at once, as it did in Case 1, in which the negative aspect of the idealized father figure on his death (desertion) was promptly projected into the spouse, a guilty man who was 'forced' to carry it.

There is a social or group factor at work too. The marriage ritual reunites lovers with their family groups, as the marriage certificate, if not the ceremony, makes plain. It serves to reactivate just those 'bad' images the lovers hoped to avoid. As Mrs X remarked, once her mother comes into the house, it's a job to get rid of her. This case and others show how the specific characteristics of the image hinge on the individuals' experiences of significant persons in their lives and how this can change with treatment. Case 2 also shows the importance of family groupings in determining the flash point for the activation of an image.

REFERENCES

Dicks, H. (1967). *Marital Tensions*. London: Routledge and Kegan Paul; New York: Basic Books.

Laing, R. D. (1961). *Self and Others*. London: Tavistock.

Teruel, G. (1966). Consideration for a diagnosis in marital psychotherapy. *British Journal of Medical Psychology* 39:3.

CHAPTER SIXTEEN

The analyst
and the damaged victims
of Nazi persecution

Gustav Dreifuss

with comments by
Gianfranco Tedeschi, Jacques Mendelsohn,
Debora Kutzinski, and Mary Williams;

reply by Gustav Dreifuss

The Holocaust was an event without parallel in human history. It was perhaps the greatest collective disaster we have ever known. Dreifuss shows that the analyst of a patient who has suffered during the Holocaust has to be aware of certain clinical consequences of the patient's profound psychic injuries—such as a tendency to disclaim the capacity to make use of analysis (on account of having been damaged in the first place). What is true of the Holocaust may be relevant to any collective trauma, and the sense of guilt at having survived, well known in connection with Holocaust victims, may also be found in other situations.

What Dreifuss says about the meaninglessness of the Holocaust experience, and how this is taken up by the commentators, is also of great interest. For the question 'why was I born the person I am' is one that crops up in the analysis of nearly everyone at some time or other.

First published in *the Journal of Analytical Psychology* 14:2, in 1969. Published here by kind permission of the author and the Society of Analytical Psychology.

The theme of the relationship between Judaism and Christianity is important for at least two reasons. First, because here, as elsewhere, we can see that analytical psychology has developed Jung's ideas on 'Jewish psychology'. Second, because the figure of the Jew often crops up in the analytical material of non-Jews— these days, representing someone to envy as often as the traditional shadow personification.

A.S.

A great deal has already been written about the problem of the persecution and systematic extermination of one-third of the Jewish people, which took place during the Second World War: historians, psychiatrists, jurists, sociologists and others have worked on and written about it (von Baeyer et al., 1964; Cohn, 1967; Eitinger, 1964; Flannery, 1965; Frankl, 1964; Gilbert, 1963; Gyomroi, 1963; March, 1960; Trautmann, 1961; Venzlaff, 1967).

I want to approach the problem from the point of view of my daily analytical experience in Israel. I find myself in continual confrontation with the fact of millions murdered and of countless other victims of persecution, which induces such a feeling of awe that it does not seem possible to do other than stand silent. Yet it seems to me to be the duty of all of us, through work on the shadow and through the development of our capacity to love, to contribute to an improvement of relationships between men so as to reduce the danger of the extermination of peoples.

Since I began to work in Haifa only in 1959, my personal experience is limited to those victims of persecution who had begun psychiatric or psychological treatment immediately after the war and for various reasons needed a new therapist. Some were relatively young people, between 20 and 30, who were rescued as children and came to Israel in a children's convoy, or who were hidden with Christian families or in monasteries while their parents perished.

When I think of the many people with whom I have worked analytically for more or less lengthy periods during the last nine years in Israel, I find scarcely anyone who has not directly or indirectly suffered from the Jewish persecution. This is evident when we consider that the bulk of immigration took place after 1933 and, moreover, that every immigration resulted in the end from a fateful belongingness to the Jewish people.

Thus one sees how greatly the persecution in particular, and Jewish destiny in general, has influenced the population of Israel. Statistics (Dvorjetski, 1963) showed that 30 per cent of the working population (that means 500,000 people) were survivors of the Nazi persecution.

In contrast to the Jews who live dispersed throughout the world, the Jew in Israel is, for the first time in almost 2,000 years, a member of the majority in his country. He governs himself; has all occupations open to him. He may be a farmer, an industrial worker, or an intellectual. These facts have of course had a powerful influence on the psyche not only of those persons who have been damaged by persecution, but also on all the Jewish inhabitants of Israel. The return of the Jewish people to the land of their fathers—to the soil of their Biblical past—has had the effect of reactivating the chthonic images of the mother archetype, which may result in a development of the animal figure as well as of masculinity. This circumstance has caused a transformation in the Jewish character in an astonishingly short time and has also made a partial rehabilitation possible for many persecuted persons.

In what follows I would like to illustrate my experience with numerous cases of persecution damage by a brief reference to *one* victim of persecution.

I refer to a married man, father of a three-and-a-half-year-old son and a six-month-old daughter, who was 30 years of age at the beginning of therapy. The traumatic events of the time of the persecution which are important for us here are described in abbreviated form. Tadek, as we shall call my patient, comes from a good middle-class Jewish Polish family who lived in Warsaw. At the outbreak of the war he was eight years old. The family lived in a Jewish quarter which was later designated a ghetto.

The mother died of typhoid fever in 1942, when Tadek was 11 years old. His father was selected from among his colleagues at work, deported to Auschwitz and murdered. After the ghetto uprising Tadek was hidden by a Pole and shut up in a room. He was much afraid of being discovered, talked softly to himself and prayed to a picture of Marshal Pilsudski that he might be rescued.

In 1944 his host could not keep him any longer, so Tadek joined the Polish resistance, but was captured and shipped off in a train to Auschwitz. He succeeded in jumping out of the moving train, was found and taken to the hospital of a small Polish city in a state of exhaustion. He was able to keep the fact that he was a Jew a secret, and passed himself off as an orphan. With a temperature of 104° F (40° C) he succeeded in preventing the nurse from undressing him and thus discovering his Jewish identity.

After his recovery he was delivered to a monastery. There he succeeded in imitating the behaviour of the other pupils at prayer, and no-one suspected him. At communion he had great anxiety about biting into the wafer, for fear it would cause an outflow of blood; he had read in an anti-semitic newspaper that this happened to Jews who took communion, since they were not baptized. After the end of the war there was still another pogrom in this Polish city, but he was shortly afterwards taken out of the monastery by an aunt with whom he had been able to establish contact. Then he spent a period in various camps for displaced persons in Europe, was interned in Cyprus after the Exodus catastrophe, and in 1948 he finally arrived in Israel. He was then 17 years old.

Since his arrival he has been almost continually in dermatological, psychiatric and analytic treatment on account of psoriasis, anxieties and compulsive neurotic symptoms. He came to me in 1961 at the wish of his wife, who could not stand him any more. As she reported it, he called her a whore, hit her, never gave her credit, and was stingy. She was herself in psychotherapeutic treatment and said she wanted her husband to have treatment again, since his former (woman) analyst had died three months after he started with her. However, it soon became clear that she wanted to get rid of him and hoped that I would influence him to divorce her.

Even this summarily presented biographical material allows us to recognize what traumatic experiences Tadek had been exposed to. A childhood dream at the age of 11, in July 1942, when his mother was already dead, reads as follows: 'I am walking along a street in Warsaw with my parents. Suddenly a German comes and kills me with his rifle. My parents leave me lying on the street. They run away. I think: why have they left me alone?' And a year later, while he was being hidden by the Pole, he dreamt: 'I have died, and am waiting to be buried. The men bury me in the earth. It is dark, but I see a lighted script: "He is dead" and I think: in which family will I be born again?'

To be deserted by the parents, to be killed, death; these are the motifs of his dreams. Is it possible that the motif of rebirth gave the boy the strength to stand the difficult trials which awaited him in the ensuing years?

After a week of treatment, Tadek had already submitted pencil and crayon drawings. The picture which is important for my purpose was painted after approximately six months and was described by the patient himself in the following manner: 'Above all the cross, the symbol of eternal love. Under it the infinite, the unknown, Man. In the middle a heart, pierced through. Blood drops down and falls into a basin. The blood is above the Star of David, the Jewish symbol which is bound all around with the chain of servitude.'

The picture, which is painted in a very rational, unspontaneous and abstract style, expresses mainly the difficult feeling problem of the patient, and his suffering. The chain of servitude shows his own servitude—his lack of freedom—which portrays itself in his obsessive-compulsive neurosis and in the disturbances of his emotional life. On the basis of his own associations it shows, moreover, the servitude of the Jewish people as a whole, who were exposed to persecution and pogroms during the 2,000 years of their exile.

The Star of David at the bottom of the picture represents to a certain degree his own basis, his ground, his Jewish heritage, whereas the cross is suspended above it. The time in the monastery was traumatic for the patient as he needed to keep his Jewishness a secret, and participation in the activities of monastery life seemed to him to be a constant lie. In addition there was always the fear of being discovered to be a Jew.

Participation in the mass, religious instruction, and the activities of the youths of the monastery naturally brought Tadek into an intensive relationship to Christianity. From the point of view of religion (Christianity above, Judaism below) the picture shows the heart in the middle as the centre of life and feeling, of what is humane. But the cross as well as the Star of David are symbols of wholeness.

One can also regard the heart in the middle of the picture as a symbol of the self. In Jewish texts it is viewed as a superordinate organ, as the centre between the brain and the liver (Hurwitz, 1952, p. 145). In numerology, the word 'heart' has the number value of 32, which is the sum of the 10 original numbers and the 22 letters of the Hebrew alphabet and represents in this manner a symbol of the self. And in Tadek's picture the heart is injured! Whether this being pierced through, this being struck in one's totality is, in our case, a temporary condition or an expression of permanent damage, I do not dare to judge.

Through misfortune breaking in from without, the youth was not only robbed of his parents. He also had to fight for his life alone in the ghetto and was in continuous fear of being discovered while alone and shut up in his room. In the monastery, too, he lived in continuous fear. He had thus developed a need for warmth and security which he now sought to satisfy within his family. But his wife could not forgive herself for having married such a sick man; she is herself a weak personality who feels unloved. She does not love her husband at all; rather, she hates him and constantly expresses her aggressive feelings towards him. In short, the marriage was badly disturbed and the wife continually threatened divorce, an idea which was remote from the patient's thoughts. Symptoms of this situation were intensified tics and sexual impotence.

Through therapeutic endeavour on the part of the analyst for his wounded soul and, in the beginning, an unconditional motherly acceptance, through devotion to the unconscious, through written expression of the traumatic experiences, through participation in painting and modelling courses, a certain transformation took place in the course of the years. It also showed itself in an improvement of the relationship to his wife, for he was able to sacrifice, at least partially, his demands that she should be a good mother.

Tadek is afraid of his own aggression; for example: about a year and a half ago, he heard a documentary programme (Tevet & Clegg, 1967) on the radio in which the fate of one of the victims of Nazi persecution was portrayed. Years later this man became a murderer and has been imprisoned in Israel for some time. The implication of the radio programme was that the terrible youth of the murderer was the reason for his criminality and for the murder. Tadek got very excited during the programme and dreamed afterwards that he was being driven into the gas chambers with a lot of people. But he succeeded in working his way away from them and out of the building. At the gate he realized that his wife had remained behind and that he could not rescue her any more.

Tadek told me the dream almost without affect; of his excitement there was nothing more to be felt. It seems to me that the dream shows, among other things, his fear of being separated from his wife by some kind of outer fate, without the possibility to intervene. On the subjective level one might also speak of the danger of a loss of soul. Through his creative activity as a successful scientist, and especially in his modelling, Tadek experienced the opposite of destruction. Thus he was able, some months after this dream, to explain to his wife out of a newly won masculinity and security, and during a marital quarrel, that from now on he would stop fighting her; that peace and warmth in the family were more important than being in the right. This declaration brought about an immediate improvement of the marriage relationship.

Tadek has to develop himself further, in spite of his past experience of the persecution. He was nearly killed, was nearly murdered. That fate ordained him as a victim, even though not a complete victim, of the persecution is no reason for him not to solve his personal problems. This statement applies to those damaged by persecution in general, with the exception of certain severe cases of 'serious damage of the fundamental bio-psychology' (Winnik, 1967) or of the 'destruction of the fundamental function, namely the possibility of regeneration' (Gumbel, 1967).

After this admittedly short account of an individual fate resulting from the persecution, I want to go over now to more general Jewish-psychological problems. The personal fate of Tadek is inseparably bound together with the fate of the Jewish people, in particular with those like him who lived in a Catholic, European country which was occupied by the German army, a doubly hostile environment. Moreover, the experiences of Tadek and of all persecuted persons is a form of suffering that is meaningless. Tadek's question, which sounds at first naive, as to why he was born as a Jew in Poland and not for example in the United States, is that of a modern Job: it is asked by every victim of persecution, insofar as he is still able to do so; and we analysts most certainly have to ask the question.

The analyst in Israel is confronted on the one side with the fate of the Jewish people in the dispersion, and with the special cases of persecution damage; on the other side, he faces changes in the psychology of the Jewish people in Israel. The transformation and renewal of the Jewish character which has ensued from the last decades has happened partly because of an activation of the earthly aspects of the mother archetype. It has resulted in a strengthening of consciousness, which revealed itself especially during the renewed threat of destruction of the Jewish people in 1967.

REFERENCES

Baeyer, W. R. von, Hafner, H., & Kisker, K. (1964). *Psychiatrie der Verfolgten*. Berlin: Springer.

Cohn, N. (1967). *Warrant for Genocide*. London: Eyre & Spottiswoode.

Dvorjetski, M. (1963). Adjustment of detainees and subsequent readjustment. *Yad Vashem Studies on the European Jewish Catastrophe and Resistance* 5. Jerusalem: Yad Vashem.

Eitinger, L. (1964). *Concentration Camp Survivors in Norway and Israel*. London: Allen & Unwin.

Flannery, E. H. (1965). *The Anguish of the Jews*. New York: Macmillan.

Frankl, V. E. (1964). *Man's Search for Meaning*. London: Hodder & Stoughton.

Gilbert, G. M. (1963). The mentality of SS murderous robots. *Yad Vashem Studies on the European Jewish Catastrophe and Resistance* 5. Jerusalem: Yad Vashem.

Gumbel, E. (1967). Psychiatric disturbances of holocaust ("Shoa") survivors. *Israel Annals of Psychiatry and Related Disciplines* 5:1.

Gyomroi, E. L. (1963). The analysis of a young concentration camp victim. In *The Psychoanalytical Study of the Child* 18:484.

Hurwitz, S. (1952). *Archetypische Motive in der Chassidischen Mystik*. Zurich: Rascher.

March, H. (ed.) (1960). *Verfolgung und Angst in ihren leibseelischen Auswirkungen.* Stuttgart: Klett.

Tevet, S., & Clegg, V. (1967). *Alouette [The Lark].* Jerusalem: Israel Broadcasting Authority.

Trautmann, E. C. (1961). Psychiatrische Untersuchungen an Ueberlebenden der nationalsocialistischen Vernichtungslager. *Nervenarzt* 32.

Venzlaff, U. (1967). *Erlebnishintergrund und Dynamik seelischer Verfolgungsschäden.* Basel: Karger.

Winnik, H. Z. (1967). Psychopathic effects of Nazi persecution. *Israel Annals of Psychiatry and Related Disciplines* 5:1.

COMMENTS

Gianfranco Tedeschi (Rome)

I think that the past experiences of the anti-semitic persecutions, lived either directly or indirectly, are not so important in determining the neurosis in Jews as the process of assimilation. By this term we mean identification with cultural systems other than Jewish *Weltanschauungen.* This identification gives rise to the ego alienation of the Jew from his original archetypal constellations expressed by the Jewish culture; therefore the frequent processes of unconscious hypercompensations become sources of neurosis.

The loss and the falsification of Jewish identity is lived by many Jews as a great threat to their spiritual survival, since the need for differentiation as a Jew is a basic quality of his deep collective psyche. The Jewish people were the first in history to express in their existence, and to witness, the great religious value of the individuation process, articulating this with God's will. In the Bible, indeed, the admonishment 'Be holy because I (the Lord) am holy' is very frequent. The Hebrew term *Kadesh* [holy] means also separatedness, distinctness from. The Midrash says, 'Be different from the other peoples as I (the Lord) am different from the other gods.' The Jewish people have lived this differentiation process mainly on a level of their sociological group (the House of the sons of Israel) rather than a psychological personal dimension.

Even today many Jews try to realize their identity through the great collective themes, patterns of behaviour and values that characterized the fundamental outlines of Jewish culture. It often happens that through neurosis the Jew becomes conscious of those values, as well as of the basic culture features, and the endopsychic concomitant dispositions that help him to define himself as a member of a group (sociological individuation). Frequently this moment is very important in finding an answer to the process of assimilation.

This period can be followed by another one by which the Jew, once he has defined his cultural identity, will take a position in relation to it. Then, by the process of definition and clarification of himself *vis-à-vis* the group, he will finally achieve personal individuation. The process of assimilation is not confined to the Jews of Western civilization, but it is actual in Israel, as expressed for instance in the 'Israelism' rather frequent among the generations born in Israel.

Jacques Mendelsohn (Givatayim, Israel)

Gustav Dreifuss is right to stress the importance of being able to make sense out of a painful experience when one is working through one, if that process is to have a positive outcome. But in the case of a terrible catastrophe, such as when millions of people are murdered simply because they are Jews, any attempt to make sense of it in a general way lies quite beyond my powers.

It is different, however, when any one man who went through that hell has to struggle with the task of making his own personal sense out of it, and not one of us is spared from finding some way of living with this still-open wound. There are two different attitudes towards this—which I shall illustrate with examples— that seem to me to throw a little light on the ways in which this problem is approached; one shows how not to do it, the other opens up future possibilities, reaching beyond oneself.

I take my first example from a recent discussion in an Israeli newspaper. An orthodox Jew wrote: 'God is a great Zionist. For he allowed so many Jews to be destroyed during the Diaspora that they finally grasped that Israel is the only place to which they belong.' The cold logic of such an argument rouses in me only instinctive repulsion. God is seen fundamentally only as Fate that rules in an absolute and distant way over the lives of men, without allowing them to participate in his plans, however meaningful his intentions may be. The paradoxical result of such an attitude would be, among other things, to present men who go through such destructive plans not only as the victims but also as the blind tools of this God of Fate, not responsible in any way for their actions.

Another danger of such a point of view is that one's whole environment and what results from such a catastrophe appear thoroughly bad and hostile, and one can become fixated in such an attitude. Even if, as I have said, making sense of such happenings is not yet possible, it is at least comforting to see that the greater part of the younger, growing generation in Israel do not see blind fate as the ruling principle in life, nor do they look upon the world outside our own small country as totally hostile.

I shall illustrate this more hopeful, positive and productive attitude by quoting two remarks made by my son when he was eight years old. We were travelling round Europe with him and visited a great number of churches in all the different countries. Suddenly he came out with: 'These Christians really deserve to be pitied—they seem to be scattered all over the face of the earth.' Out of his own sense of security in having his own homeland, he clearly wished it could be as good for everyone else. He again expressed this idea of the problem of belonging together when he asked another question: 'Is the sky over Israel joined up with the sky over the rest of the world?'

This time apparently he was expressing a need to feel connected with the whole world, and was rejecting the notion of a favoured isolation. If his first comment rests on an earthbound, maternal and protective archetype then his second one seems to refer to a spiritually uniting archetype of a heavenly father. And then all men without exception would be equally the children of the same supreme father.

It stands to reason that an atmosphere such as this would in the cases Dreifuss has brought before us create a positive basis for any psychotherapeutic attempt.

Debora Kutzinski (Tel Aviv)

My contribution must of necessity be very personal: it contains the experience of one who survived five years in concentration camps and who became a practising analyst.

In every depth analysis the patient meets evil: inside himself, in others, in nature, in the world. It seems that of all evil—death, illness, natural catastrophies—the most difficult to bear is man's inhumanity to man. In analysis it is this experience which comprises the focus in the patient who has survived the holocaust. It is the central problem of his suffering, which constellates the specific task that the analyst has to face. Only in the *temenos* of a real personal relationship (and I deliberately refrain from using the terms transference and countertransference as being too technical) will the victim be able to regain a constructive attitude towards life.

But it is just at this point that the analyst may fail: he feels inadequate, has guilt feelings because of his total lack of personal experience, and he may be even overcome by the account of his patient's sufferings. The patient needs exactly the opposite: strength and firmness side by side with love and understanding; but above all he needs the unrelenting demand to accept fate and embark on the quest for its meaning.

When Dreifuss is asked by his patient why he was born a Polish Jew and not in the U.S.A. (why not even as a Nazi?) then the answer can only be: everybody has his personal destiny, his individual measure of joy and suffering. The struggle for the meaning of fate is perhaps the most important factor in the regeneration of the soul in the persecuted victim. This is why I would take issue with Dreifuss's statement: 'The experience of the persecution is a form of suffering which is meaningless.'

In order to make the analyst understand better the psychic situation of his patient during the holocaust I would like to add that from personal experience I found it extraordinary to witness how the soul itself preserved its balance in the death-camps by regressing to an almost vegetative level. No developed consciousness registered the insanity and inhumanity in which one lived. The only task was to survive each single day. The collectiveness of the situation was helpful for psychic survival, and there developed something which I would call a collective self, sustaining all of us. It is this help from the collective self which was withheld from Dreifuss's patient as he was isolated from the collective and had to deny even his identity as a Jew.

The struggle to find the meaning of her fate reveals itself in the following dream of a holocaust survivor: Longing for peace she goes with her children to Sils Maria and there has a picnic. Strangely enough the picnic takes place in the shadow of Israeli tanks standing abandoned nearby in the forest. Suddenly she notices Arabs seizing one of the tanks and then approaching, firing wildly at the unarmed group. The picnic party are completely encircled and everything is lost. The Arabs, now Nazis, start to fill trenches around them with dynamite, intending to burn them alive. The dreamer—to her astonishment unchallenged—leaves the circle and finds herself suddenly beyond the frontier in Italy. Behind her is an inferno and her children are dead.

She realizes now that hell, as in 1945, has again expelled her and that hers is to be the way of the Eternal Jew. She does not know if she can bear her fate and considers two possibilities: either to commit suicide—then she must not meet her analyst, as he would try to prevent her—or to become pregnant this very evening and to return to Sils Maria with new life in her, to be able to take her burnt children in her arms. To her question, how is one to find the way back to Sils, she is answered that one must go in a hearse and only via Merano. (In summer 1968, while the dreamer was staying in Merano, soap made from the fat of gassed Jews in Auschwitz was found there.)

Essentially the dream means: there is no peace for you anywhere. Your fate is that of the Wandering Jew, the experience of eternal tides, death and rebirth, sacrifice of the children, the voyage through the nether world (Merano) and new life.

Mary Williams (London)

Dreifuss has conveyed movingly the feeling of awe accompanying the task of analysing the victims of mass persecution, particularly, it would seem, with regard to shadow problems on account of the impersonal and therefore meaningless persecution of which he speaks. He also conveyed how such confrontation burdens the analyst with the feelings of guilt and shame of which the patient is 'innocent' and which are only evidenced in 'not me' psycho-somatic symptoms and in compulsive behaviour.

Such feelings may induce the analyst to avoid shadow interpretations altogether, so helping the patient to remain the innocent victim of circumstances, and perpetually ill; or the burden may become so heavy that it is flung back before there is enough good ego feeling to endure it. Dr Dreifuss seems to have steered between these opposites intuitively, but not without considerable suffering, perhaps because the conflicts were inevitably shared.

The main conflict in the patient seemed to me to be one of loyalties, inherent in being one of a minority group in a hostile culture, but particularly so for Tadek as his rescuers were Christians, the enemies of his people and a threat to his Jewish identity; yet there is evidence that he longed to be born again a Christian in order to be saved both physically and spiritually from the soul-destroying anti-semitic image of a Jew. Thus he prayed to the Marshal's photograph, not to his God who had deserted him as he felt his parents had. The most striking evidence is in the painting in which the central item is the 'sacred heart' of Jesus, however else it may be interpreted. It might have been taken straight from a Catholic illustration and, as he must have learnt in the monastery, this heart was pierced so that all men might be saved through the forgiveness of sins. Confession had to precede communion with the Saviour or Jesus would bleed again.

Furthermore, the Catholics taught until recent times that the Jews killed Christ, for which sin they became wanderers on the face of the earth and, curiously enough, like Christ who had 'nowhere to lay his head' were, like him, 'despised of men' and, in the final solution, ignobly executed. This myth of divine retaliation through reversal of roles makes the persecuted Jew an eternally suffering Christ figure seeking a predestined end. In human terms, however, it works against the instinct for self-preservation and becomes the perversion of masochism by which the innocent victim seeks his persecutors.

I felt the worst feature of Tadek's terrible story was that he was so constantly rescued. Survivor's guilt in his case would seem to be confused with collaborator's guilt and the shame of having to survive by such means. The maximum of survival anxiety is shown in the dream of leaving his wife behind in Auschwitz. Loyalty with its associations of regard and love threatens survival and must be abandoned.

Reflecting on the factors leading to the possibility of regeneration, I feel we would have to know more about the early relationships and genetic constitution of individuals before the effects of the hostile environment impinged. Were Tadek's 'good enough' in Winnicott's terms? Perhaps his capacity to accept help, to dare to remember, to use his imagination, and therefore to trust, suggest that they may have been.

REPLY

by Gustav Dreifuss

I do not think that a distinction between the problems of assimilation and anti-semitic persecution is desirable with regard to the neurosis of the Jews, as Tedeschi makes it. Persecution and anti-semitism in our time seem to me to be a proof that assimilation is an illusion. We only have to recall the powerful movement of assimilation in pre-Nazi Germany and the horrible disappointment in which it ended. It seems to me that whenever the level of consciousness is lowered, as happens in the psychology of the masses, anti-semitism can erupt like a volcano.

Although the psychology of Jews living in Israel may in the course of years develop differently from that of those living elsewhere, there is still a strong connection between the Jewish people inside Israel and outside it. This showed itself especially at the time of the renewed threat to the Jews in Israel in the summer of 1967. Then, in the widest circles, among assimilated Jews and even among Christians, something was touched, perhaps unconsciously. Because of this sudden apparent danger, memories of Auschwitz were revived and a basic experience broke through and showed itself in, among other ways, an almost incredible readiness to help. It could indeed be said that Israel, or Jerusalem, as a *symbol,* is, in spite of assimilation, still alive in the Jewish and Christian soul throughout the world.

I do agree with Tedeschi that a Jew may find in the individuation process a new and living relationship to his

Jewishness, but it should also bring him to the awareness that by *his* individuation he does not solve the potentially dangerous anti-semitism of his host-nation. New anti-semitic outbreaks have lately shown that this danger is real in Poland, France and America (New York).

I would not call the problem of the Israeli Jew a process of assimilation, but rather one connected with the general problem of our time, a spiritual or religious crisis like that in the Christian world. Mendelsohn's remarks on the linking of the fact of the millions of dead with the foundations of the state of Israel or the coming home of the Jews to their original home are very much to the point. In addition, I would remark that it is really difficult or almost impossible to unite the genocide of the Jews with the dominant image of God.

Because of these difficulties I try to understand the catastrophe as a punishment for sins, in the same way as the friends of Job attempted to do. Or I go back to the archetypal image of death or destruction coming before rebirth (for instance Gog and Magog), by proving with Biblical quotations that there will be a great destruction before the coming of the Messiah. The deeper reason why people choose such a meaning may lie in the fact that they are somehow unable to accept the darkness, the antimony of the self, the collective shadow. I do agree with Mendelsohn's interpretations of the remarks of his eight-year-old son. They illustrate what I had only hinted at: the influence of a new Jewish reality on the psyche of the Jew living in Israel.

In the discussion that took place directly after my lecture, I did not answer the contribution of Mrs. Kutzinski. I want to clarify two points:

(1)   The persecution of the Jews as a collective phenomenon resulting in the death of millions seems to me meaningless, just as killing in wars, for instance, is senseless. But I do agree that the main question for the persecuted victim who survived is his struggle to find a meaning in his *personal* fate. However, owing to the severe injury I mentioned in my paper, most of the victims I met in practice or otherwise are not capable of undertaking this quest for meaning.

(2)   With regard to the dream of a persecution victim related with the interpretation that the personal experience of the

holocaust brings back to the dreamer the meaning of the way of individuation, I can only say that being on the way with all its implications is an experience over and beyond the Jewish fate. In other words, the archetype of the 'wandering Jew' is in every soul; the Christian must withdraw this projection from the Jew and the Jew must be aware so as not to be the bearer of this projection and identify with it. In my opinion another important feature of the dream is the atmosphere of dread and despair, due to the traumatic experience of the holocaust and the fear of war with the Arabs. I would not be astonished if the dreamer herself were not also a victim with an irreparable injury. ...

Mary Williams' comments bring so many new and interesting points that I feel unable to discuss them adequately in the small space at my disposal. My contribution will therefore of necessity be incomplete.

There is indeed a danger that the persecution victim's analyst may avoid shadow interpretations. I hinted at this problem by saying that Tadek had to develop further, in spite of his past experience of the persecution. But according to psychiatric evaluation, Tadek is a victim with an incurable injury. This has to be borne in mind when his case material is studied, and this could only be done in fragments in this paper.

With regard to the conflict of loyalties mentioned above, it must be added that although Tadek was rescued by Christians, he was himself very active in trying to save his life by fighting for food in the ghetto and jumping down from the train on the way to Auschwitz. And last but not least, he could have chosen to remain in the monastery and make a career in the hierarchy of the Church. But his urge to find other survivors of his family was so great that he made contacts and finally left his refuge with his aunt.

The dream where Tadek leaves his wife behind in Auschwitz has also to be understood as a reaction to the actual aggression of his wife at that time. It was *she* who wanted to leave him. So the dream confronted him with his shadow, here the potential murderer.

The remark on early relationships with regard to regeneration is interesting. But according to Simenhauer (1968, p. 306 ff.) it is beyond reasonable doubt that the previous personality plays a relatively small part in the psychic sequelae of ex-prisoners of Nazi camps.

I feel completely at a loss to discuss the most interesting remarks with regard to the persecuted Jew being an eternally suffering Christ figure. May I only state that this seems to me to reflect christological thinking. The survival of the Jewish people after 2,000 years of persecution and the loss of one-third of its members in our century, and the building up in return of an 'old-new country' remain for me a myth where some meaning may only be found in a universal context furthering consciousness.

REFERENCE

Simenhauer, E. (1968). Late psyche sequelae of man-made disasters. *International Journal of Psycho-Analysis* 49:2–3.

CHAPTER SEVENTEEN

Working against Dorian Gray: analysis and the old

Luigi Zoja

The project of Zoja's paper is far wider than its title implies. In addition, there is a salient critique of Freudian theory, in which the psychoanalytic contribution is linked with several problematic features of our culture. Then there is an analysis of the culture's main problem: ignorance and fear of death. This, in its turn, is connected to a radical undercutting of the authentic patterns of life so that all of us, not just the old, suffer from anomie and ontological anxiety.

One other feature of the paper to which I should like to draw attention concerns Zoja's use of puer *and* senex. *These terms, which may be unfamiliar to some readers, refer to differing psychological and emotional outlooks (and are not intended to be restricted to males). They are not developmental concepts, though they can be employed in that vein—for even old women and men*

First published in *The Journal of Analytical Psychology* 28:1, in 1983. Published here by kind permission of the author and the Society of Analytical Psychology.

can be seen to have puer *or* puella *characteristics; similarly, the* senex *can be seen in the character of babies. Clearly, each of us will have both* puer *and* senex *in her or his make-up. The* puer *suggests the possibility of a new beginning, revolution, renewal, and creativity generally. The* senex *refers us to qualities such as wisdom, balance, steadiness, generosity towards others, farsightedness. Each 'position' can become pathological: unmitigated* puer *is redolent of impatience, overspiritualization, lack of realism, naive idealism, tendencies ever to start anew, being untouched by age, and given to flights of imagination. Pure* senex *is excessively cautious and conservative, authoritarian, obsessional, overgrounded, melancholic, and lacking imagination. The injury that our culture has done us concerns the forcible splitting of an archetypal interplay between* puer *and* senex.

A.S.

Youth! Youth! There is absolutely nothing in the world
but youth!
[*The Picture of Dorian Gray*, Oscar Wilde]

Analysis

A nalytical therapy began officially with Freud, and, as we all know, treatment was soon restricted to young patients. 'Never trust any patient over 30' could then have been—and now often is—the slogan of many orthodox Freudians, analogous to the slogan of the student revolt in the 1960s and not in my opinion a coincidence, because we can now see that the Freudian point of view anticipated and paved the way for many radical changes in society, the most obvious among which being the emphasis on sex. But I want to deal here with the youth-centred vision so apparent in our culture today and the accompanying repression of most of the archetypes surrounding old age, and to dare to raise the question of the extent of the contribution of Freudian thought to contemporary gerontophobia. I do not pretend to have the answer, but I suggest that if in fact the Freudian *Weltanschauung* has exerted this influence, it has probably done so indirectly by centring psychic life on and around sexuality, which in its turn is biologically and archetypally linked with youth.

Jungians, on the other hand, seem to me to be better equipped theoretically to work with the old than are Freudians: we are linked more to the archetypes and less to the *Zeitgeist* and are therefore less influenced by the 'juvenilistic' culture of this century. Jungians have often included the elderly among their patients, though generally perhaps this is due more to an absence of negative prejudices than to any specific rules about therapy. Nevertheless, none of us to my knowledge has undertaken any systematic study of the problems of analysis with the old; so, without any claim at being exhaustive, I would like to try to relate our therapeutic practice to a very simple framework and to examine its roots.

In a country like mine, culturally a part of Western Europe but much below it in average income per capita, analysis in general is a natural target for radical intellectuals, who attack it for being too expensive and therefore beyond the reach of most people. At first sight this certainly seems to be a well-founded criticism, but I want to consider it briefly and see if it really is pertinent in the case of the old. The State in modern societies is held to have some responsibility for the welfare of the old, so we might ask if it could not offer them some psychological help. Unfortunately, in recent times State funds have become almost bankrupted by a geometric escalation of costs that cannot be controlled, of which those allocated to the old show the greatest and least controllable increase. Firstly, the direct rate of increase is higher than that of any other social cost: not only does the outlay per person constantly mount, but also the older section of the community forms an ever-growing percentage of the total population. Secondly, assistance to the old moves, economically speaking, in a vicious circle: it indirectly swells other costs such as special housing, hospitals and so on; and, in so far as it is successful, it promotes the growth of an irreversibly dependent category of person in contrast to other social policies which aim at helping dependent people to become independent.

Further study of public assistance for the old also reveals that it consists almost entirely of material aid, decided upon by relatively young bureaucrats or politicians rather than by the recipients themselves, and often resulting in failure to meet their true needs. This is, of course, an enormous issue with prevailingly sociological implications which I do not intend to explore further here, but it is impossible for a depth psychologist to avoid the impression that such contradictions arise because society is often motivated more by unconscious guilt feelings towards the old than by their real needs. Indeed, our society must conceal a great deal of guilt towards old age, if we think that this century has, radically and for the first time in history, expropriated the traditional rôle of the old: by inventing retirement, it has taken away most of their socio-economic rôle, and by inventing the mass media and mass culture it has dispossessed them of their psychological, truly archetypal rôle as guardians and transmitters of wisdom, traditions and collectively accepted values.

Psychotherapy with the old is less costly in my experience than is analysis in general, because they do not usually require such a high frequency of sessions. Once a week is normally sufficient for the elderly person whose psychological as well as biological rhythms have slowed down, and part of the enormous sums already being misused on aid for the old could easily be shifted from material to psychological help. However, to finance psychological assistance for them is to make a choice that is basically socio-political rather than psychological, and that tacitly creates a sociological category of 'the old', which in itself might paradoxically turn out to be psychologically harmful. Our culture already tends to view the old and young, *senex* and *puer,* as socio-political rather than as psychological categories—as polarities of an archetype in Jungian terms—and to pose the problem in economic terms implicitly reinforces this onesidedness. Analytical work is concerned with old/young as intrapersonal and not chronological polarities: when these are emphasized as interpersonal, the individual is inevitably regarded as belonging to either one or the other, and it is worth asking if such a rigid separation does not do even more harm to the in-dividuality (Latin: non-divisibility) of the psyche than in the case of other archetypal polarities. True, a man deals with psychic feminine elements, his anima, all his life and vice versa, but he usually retains his masculine rôle and identity at a conscious level. In the opposition young–old, a rigid identification of the ego with one of the poles is even more damaging because every old person is a young one transformed, and most young people will become old or are, at least, ageing every day. When, however, a sociological split occurs, the inner dynamism of the two poles is devalued, if not totally repressed, and young and old adopt a schematic view of each other at the expense of their individual complexity. We can see from the disappearance of positive archetypal rôles *based* on old age and not carried out *in spite* of it (a distinction to which I shall return later), that this over-simplification has led to youth becoming the representative of value and old age of non-value: the archetype *puer/senex* becomes split, and its vitality in the individual is lost because of the absence, or underestimation at least, of one of the polarities.

To come back to the economic criticism of providing and assisting analysis for the old, we have to recognize that here we come up against obvious material limits. However, looked at theoretically, it is precisely the main objections—public assistance already costs too much and the old form such a relatively large section of the community—which demonstrate that we are talking about the richest societies in history. Furthermore, from this standpoint, we are reinforcing sociological categories to the detriment of psychological realities, and might even unconsciously accept the modern prejudice which tends to view old age as characterized by a basic deficiency of youth—rather than with a specific character—related less to the concept of youth than to concepts such as in-validity, un-employment and so on.

I now want to consider the second, more complicated, controversial and subtle criticism levelled at analysis by the radicals. They maintain that analysis is an instrument of conformity which aims at readjusting people to modern society and its ideology of production. This objection frequently seems valid because very often a student does indeed return successfully to his studies or a worker to his work as a result of analysis. For us analysts, however, this is just 'a' result and not 'the' result and is only the outer and not even inevitable manifestation of the main process of individuation. This point is further clarified by the old distinction between support therapy and analytical therapy: the task of the first is to face difficult outer circumstances, while that of the second is undoubtedly individuation although it may often also indirectly assist the first. It therefore seems to me that psychotherapy for the elderly falls clearly into the category of analysis in spite of the relatively low frequency of sessions more often associated with support therapy than with depth analysis: after all, the distinctive feature of psychological work is its basic aim and not the speed at which it proceeds. The real task and goal of analytical work with old people cannot be to readjust them to life, especially to an efficient and productive one, but is most certainly to help them gradually to detach themselves from life and to cover, without traumas, the archetypal path of life which is the path towards death.

Another distinction familiar to Jungians and leading to a similar conclusion is made by Hillman in the introductory chapters of *Suicide and the Soul* (1964). He gives a clear differential definition of analytical activity, differential in that he superimposes it upon several other activities, including medicine, and then focuses on and identifies their respective elements. This method enables him to show the great difference between analytical and medical work: the basic value, the 'root metaphor' of the first lies in the life of the soul, that of the second in biological life. The analyst can stay with death and work on it without fighting it, since the experience of death is essential for the soul albeit unhealthy for the body; but the physician can only oppose himself to it, because for the body death is not *an* experience but the *end* of experience, and physical dying cannot be valued as an *initiation*—a beginning—as it can psychologically, but only as a *termination*. Hillman uses this distinction in discussing suicide and emphasizes that the analyst, unlike the doctor, should not necessarily fight the idea of it, but should rather work it through. We would do well to recall Hillman's argument here since the geriatrician, whose task is to fight death by constantly delaying it, is in opposition to the analyst whose work with the old searches for a natural, untraumatic 'physiological' link with death even if the topic is not actually mentioned. In short, we can say that the medical model fights against death by trying to exclude it, whereas the analytical model includes it as a major element in psychic life and, in the case of analytical work with the old, as *the* main element and the main problem to be faced. It therefore appears to me that the criticism of analysis as a mere tool of readjustment can only stem from the idea of analysis as an activity based on an old-style medical model, revealing that the criticism itself, which pretends to be progressive, is in fact unconsciously linked to an epistemologically outdated concept.

As I have already said, we often find a student returning to his books and a worker to his work at the end of an analysis. Many parents of depressed students will suggest analysis and pay for it; even though they do not know what analysis really is, they find it natural to do anything in order to reconcile their children to their studies, and many up-to-date social insurances will pay for analytical treatment for someone whose phobias or compulsive ideas keep him away from his work. But let us suppose my father has recently retired, he suddenly feels useless and cannot accept it and becomes moody and depressed. Should I dare to suggest an analysis to him, and will I be generous enough to offer to pay for him? Will I not simply side with those who say 'he's facing a difficult moment, but he has to accept it'? Of course he has to accept it—but is that all?

Few things are more distressing than the deep suffering of a young person facing the sudden loss of his lover: all at once feelings and sexuality are denied their usual expression. An elderly couple has also to face a similar loss since the simultaneous death they may long for is an archetypal need and not a significant statistical reality—a striking analogy, by the way, with the modern myth of simultaneous orgasm. An old person who loses his partner is not less lonely than a young one, but his loneliness has little if any remedy: one can scarcely start being promiscuous in old age, but many recent studies have shown that sexuality knows no age limit, and that it is cultural prejudice that makes old people give up their sex life (cf. de Beauvoir, 1972). In Dostoievsky's *The Adolescent,* when the old prince Sokolski wants to remarry, the whole family ostracizes him and even threatens to send him to the asylum. We may reproach these relatives for their egocentricity, but our culture has not changed much in its prejudices against the elderly who still seek physical and spiritual love, and we have no concern at all for their sexuality, which offends our aesthetic taste. Taboos on sexuality may have fallen, and we can now even watch sex between humans and animals at the movies, but you may have noticed that they are always young and healthy—both the shepherd and the sheep.

Nobody is very drawn to doing psychological work with the old, and although traditionally this has been the field of the clergy, they, like everyone else at present, seem more concerned with the young. If we fail to help an adolescent, someone who is entering upon life, he might reproach us later; but not so if we fail to help someone whose main goal is to enter death—a dimension which is out of reach. If we add this to the economic consideration— psychotherapy with the old is a bad investment because they will not be going back to 'their duty' since they have no productive duty—we can see why so little analysis is undertaken with them. Yet, is it *they* who do not respond to analysis or *we* who do not respond to them? Was not analysis originally meant for everybody, the old as well as the young? Some might answer it was not, because psychoanalysis was born with Freud, and his concern was life and sexuality and his interest in death was bounded by his atheistic ideology. This remains an open question, however, since there are some significant elements in his work which could be seen as pointing in the opposite direction: for example, why did he take Virgil's phrase, *Flectere si nequeo superos Acheronta movebo* ['if heaven be inflexible, hell shall be unleashed'—*Aeneid* vii, 312] as his motto and why did he call his discipline psychoanalysis when ἀνάλυσις means not only melting and dissolution but also death? Simple slips?

However that may be, Freudians today are without doubt less concerned with the elderly than are Jungians, and it may be worthwhile summarizing briefly their respective schools of thought, which have given rise to these differences in practice. First of all, as regards therapeutic technique: Freudians are usually more rigid than Jungians, who adjust more readily to individual needs. This is very important with elderly people, upon whom one cannot impose strict rules and whose long-accustomed ways have to be accepted. Secondly, the Jungian viewpoint, being more teleological than causal, places less emphasis on anamnesis, a feature which is paradoxically a help in analysis with old people. They are, of course, free to speak about their past, but to try to trace the link between their present anxiety and its possible aetiology is not usually so essential for them. They already know—or believe they know—what was wrong in the past, and the relative rigidity of their conscious attitudes makes it difficult for them to accept new explanations. The main cause of their anxiety lies in the future, in the archetypal goal of life which is death, and the aim of 'soul-work' is to create a link between the present and that future even if death is not explicitly touched upon by patient or analyst. This, at least, is the way in which I have dealt with those elderly patients I have worked with. Many of their dreams concerned the future and often contained what seemed to me to be symbolic hints of death, such as the entering of an endless ocean or a kingdom beneath the ground or the sea, or the crossing of a channel and the discovery of a new land; there were relatively few dreams where I felt it necessary or relevant to bring an objective exploration of the actual past into the discussion.

The Jungian approach, with its frequent resort to mythology, prepares the ground for another kind of link with the past. Indeed, the old patient needs to turn back and to build his life-myth; in a way, he must complete the circle begun in his youth, when he strove for individuation: then he fought to differentiate his psychic life from the archetypes, now he must give it back to them, and to create this myth might mean harmonizing and fusing his memories with a mythical pattern. Memory becomes selective in old age, and if we believe in the hypothesis of the unconscious psyche, we assume that such selectivity is not random but follows an unconscious project. The analyst assists the patient in this natural process which is now not remembering but forgetting—a 'selective anamnesis' or an 'ana-amnesis'.

The theoretical differences between Freud and Jung account even more obviously for the wider interest in the old displayed by Jungians. Jung's work is a general psychology, that of Freud is a psychopathology, and, as I have already pointed out, it is quite out of place to approach the psychic suffering of the old by trying to heal them in the traditional sense. It is true that Freud introduced the concept of θάνατος, but thanatos has a negative sense, it is the denial of life, whereas for Jungians death as the last step in the individuation process can become an active presence without automatically pathological implications, a real process in itself; death can be viewed 'not as an event, but as a process' (Gordon, 1978).

Old age

After having considered the criticisms made of the rôle of analysis in our society, I would now like to look briefly at those made of old age. I think we would all agree that the situation of the so-called 'third' age in the Western world today is both striking and unprecedented. Unfortunately, most studies on the subject either approach it from a socio-economic point of view and are only an indirect help to depth psychologists, or those that do take psychological factors into account, do so only from the angle of consciousness. Simone de Beauvoir, for example, in her important book *Old Age* (1972), presents a wealth of sociological, anthropological and historical material most convincingly, but then says: 'Time is carrying the old person towards an end—death—which is not *his* and which is not postulated or laid down by any project' (p. 217). I think that depth psychologists would not be so categorical and would probably distinguish between conscious and unconscious purpose (where de Beauvoir speaks—in translation—of project). Except in the case of suicide, death is certainly not a conscious 'intention' of the old but is, in a way, *the* archetypal intention of life as a whole; even Freud, without of course speaking of archetypes, formulated a similar hypothesis (1920g). For my purpose here, however, it will suffice to single out those main aspects of present-day culture which may be thought to influence the psychological situation of the old.

The first of these is the growing *medicalization of life* (Foucault, 1967; Illich, 1975). Until a few generations ago 'normal' birth and 'normal' death took place at home and were ministered to by the family hierarchy, an arrangement that showed a deep inner respect for the archetypal patterns of life. Today, 'normal' birth and death occur in hospital or a similar institution and are attended by a hierarchy of technicians who are strangers. Looked at from a psychological rather than a sociological point of view, this means that even before he loses his physical life the old person is deprived of his psychological life: he is denied his archetypal rôle of the wise old man. Whereas in times gone by the approach of death enhanced this rôle and the old person became the representative of a wisdom freed from the burden of petty daily needs, now it forces him to give up his autonomy and take on the passive rôle of a patient. The consequences for the old are dramatic, in spite of undeniably better 'health' care; a French study quoted by Simone de Beauvoir (1972) shows that of those sent to a nursing-home, 54% die in the first year, of whom 29% die in the first month (p. 256). Whether we believe it or not, archetypes are indeed an essential part of life, and deprivation of archetypal experience can kill—we know, for example, that to be deprived of dreaming is more intolerable than to be deprived of sleep.

The second transformation in our culture which is critical for the old is the *taboo of death*. In the short span of a couple of generations, our over-optimistic, hypomanic and one-sided society has burdened death with a silence and repression hitherto unknown in the history of man. Our culture is ashamed to speak of death, and our average citizen is ashamed of death and therefore ashamed of dying. Mourning likewise has become something to hide, as if it were, in Gorer's words, 'an analogue of masturbation' (1965, p. 111), and the whole topic of death— according to Ariès (1975) and to most of those who have studied it—has in recent years taken over the rôle of sexuality towards the end of the nineteenth century. Today only a minority of people have seen somebody die, to witness which was the rule in past centuries. Nowadays both doctors and relatives usually consider it their duty to conceal a patient's fatal condition from him. They do this on the 'psychological' ground that the lie has a *placebo* effect and can help the patient to some sort of recovery, but here again the concept of 'psychology' is reductive, and there is no consideration of the unconscious and archetypal element. In earlier times it would have been unthinkable to deprive someone of a gradual preparation for the final moment and of the possibility of harmonizing the conscious and archetypal endings of life, and it was not only in the East but also in the West that people thought their ultimate task was to prepare themselves psychologically for it.

We often read that people used to make a will before going on a journey, to which our usual reaction is: 'How dangerous travelling must once have been!' But this also is a somewhat reductive attitude, and the culturally dramatic change lies not in the safety of travel but in our attitude to death. It is a relatively recent development that a will should be concerned only with money matters; it used to be a witness to an inner preparation for death, an apotropaic act like taking an umbrella so that it will not rain. Sudden, unexpected death was traditionally a most dreaded occurrence, a dread still reflected in popular beliefs about restless ghosts haunting their place of death. These people are usually supposed to have died young or suddenly—more especially to have been murdered—and, their preparation for death not having been completed, they are unable to die completely. The fear of sudden, unritualized death was universal—*a subitanea et improvisa morte libera nos, Domine* [from sudden and unforeseen death, deliver us Lord]—in complete contrast to our attitude today, and how intense it was can be gauged when we think of the enormous amount of physical suffering it would at least have spared in times when medical care was rudimentary and anaesthesia virtually non-existent.

In those days the entire preparation for death was a great happening and an important ritual. The old person was believed already to possess wisdom, and with the approach of death this wisdom reached its climax: no matter how insignificant and lost in the crowd a person had been in life, the words he spoke before dying were considered to contain teaching for everybody. By reason of old age and especially the approach of his death, Mr Nobody finally became Somebody—even more, he became a Teacher. The person who had passively accepted life became active at the last; the person who had nothing to give could now make psychological gifts to others, and for us Jungians it is interesting to note that an essential path of individuation was thus always provided even for the most collective person and that it coincided with old age. This erstwhile function of the last chapter of life is particularly significant if we compare it with what happens nowadays, when nursing homes and hospitals tend to transform it into the most collective and anonymous episode in life. The active rôle which, after a passive life, the old or dying person could once assume has turned into its opposite; modern Western man has, theoretically at least, a series of opportunities to develop his personality and to differentiate himself inwardly and outwardly from the crowd, but these constantly decrease during old age to the point where he is no longer a subject but a patient, a passive object of medicine and its sophisticated technology.

Over the past hundred years the Italian population has doubled, but the number of the old has increased sevenfold. This means that in our society old age is statistically present as never before, while psychologically it is tending to disappear. Current values, which are reflected in the mass media and advertising, have rendered our society both hypomanic and 'juvenilistic'. One has only to turn on the radio or television to notice that the 'Mr Average' advertised and appealed to has to be terribly extrovert, active and healthy—in a word, he is basically young. According to the advertisements, he needs a lot of goods, but goods can be substitutes for individuation and belong to the world of youth; a car or liquor, for instance, are sold to you because you are young or they make you feel young. If the advertisements or the media do address themselves to the older person, it is precisely in order to ask him to disown his age, and if he wants to remain a client—and he usually does, or he will be lost to society—he must betray and repress his archetypal reality.

Furthermore, when we see mass culture extolling the energy of some old man in power such as Reagan or Brezhnev, it is impossible to avoid the impression that such men incarnate the myth of eternal-youth-in-spirit-of-age rather than of dignified ageing. Even if we take into consideration the fact that the old are a disadvantaged group in society, we know that the sociological problems of such a group cannot be solved at the expense of those psychological ones inherent in falling prey to a false ideal or neurotic identity. It is known that black leaders fear the risk of becoming too like the whites and feminists of apeing masculine rôles, but we somehow assume that the old person wants to renounce his identity and at bottom wants to be more healthy and active—in short, younger. Our average man has bowed to some myth of eternal youth, and we are forced to ask if this is pathological and could lead to disaster, as in the story of Dorian Gray; we can certainly see that every old person suffers potentially from psychic injury and that the whole of society is unbalanced when deprived of one of its polarities.

Another aspect of the problem is that it is now considered bad taste to speak about old age and death. There are thousands of specialists studying the misunderstandings between the middle-aged and their children, but I have not seen any studies on the psychological difficulties of communication between the middle-aged and their elderly parents. As a consequence of, and in compensation for, this one-sided attitude, the collective way of dealing with old age usually takes the form of emotionally charged prejudice—the generation gap—or of ambivalent curiosity; in short, of projections. Similarly, we avoid the subject of death in daily conversation; and what was once called the War Ministry is now hypocritically renamed the Ministry of Defence; and then we discover to our surprise that books on death become best-sellers, and a fatal street accident automatically draws a crowd, gathered there not to pray but to comment. Are these people trying unconsciously to reconstruct a collective ritual around death? In any case it is certain that life and death have never been so far asunder as now, unlike every other age in Western culture which provided many rituals in preparation for and surrounding death. According to Ariès (1975), death was once, and especially in the eighteenth and nineteenth centuries, literally a major public ritual. Family and acquaintances would visit the dying person and speak with him about death; children of every age would also be brought in because it was felt that through death they could learn about life, and even the passing traveller on hearing that someone was dying often considered it his duty to attend.

I want now to turn to the so-called primitive societies, where the ritual surrounding ageing and dying is in even greater evidence. In the total absence of mass media or even books, the transmission of culture itself is entrusted to a large extent to the old: in our culture the mass media are infected by gerontophobia, a phenomenon that is probably more than coincidental when we realize that they and old age are engaged in mutually exclusive competition. Since the old are relatively few in number in primitive, underdeveloped societies, the ritual importance of becoming old and of dying is stressed and enhanced. The whole process tends to follow a pattern of initiation and becomes particularly significant in the light of the concept of individuation. For the primitive, every 'correct' death has its initiation aspects, and every initiation corresponds to a psychological death. Myths of the origin of death are quite common in Africa, North America and South-East Asia and are curiously similar to some modern existentialist writings (cf. Eliade, 1976; Gordon, 1978, p. 60f.; Herzog, 1966; Radin, 1952). Looked at from a Jungian standpoint, these myths reveal an extreme effort to grasp why this most intolerable of all events takes place. The need to find a reason is so desperate that some of them even tell us that man deliberately chose death (Gordon, 1978, p. 67). So difficult is it to resign himself to the idea, and so great is the fear of having to acknowledge that he is at the mercy of uncontrollable forces, that man prefers to face it by taking sides with those forces. In every culture man tries to come to terms at least with death and to link it with its psychic life, and by so doing to recognize it as a natural event. The psychological effort, however, is tremendous and does not always succeed, so that it is often a problem to track down a proper archetypal image of death. Some primitives believe that there is no natural death, and every death corresponds to a murder (Freud, 1912–13). Nevertheless, whenever primitive cultures manage to come to terms with death—and most of them do—they link it with life as its final ritual step for which old age is the natural preparation.

The initiatory pattern does not only mean that death is an initiation and every initiation is a symbolic death, but also usually implies a second birth. This birth, unlike the first one, is spiritual and must be ritually created by the active participation of the dying person and his spiritual assistants, as was once the case in Europe (Eliade, 1959). Eliade says that wherever death has the significance of a second birth, it also becomes the paradigm of every momentous change (ibid.). Here I come back to my quotation from Simone de Beauvoir and the distinction between conscious and unconscious intention of dying: if a 'natural' death requires ritually created elements, then it follows that a 'normal' death, especially in old age, involves some intention. Such intention is largely but not wholly unconscious and archetypal; we know, for instance, that often in Eskimo and nomad societies an old person was expected actively to accelerate, while psychologically preparing for, death.

The notion of death as rebirth that has to be actively achieved implies that it cannot be attained automatically and by everyone, and many peoples consider it essential to practice for it in advance throughout the entire lifespan and not only in old age. The prototype for such practice and the most complete anticipation of death is ecstasy, for which the best preparation is shamanic apprenticeship, or at least the assistance of shamans who are experts in ecstatic states. Ecstasy is an anticipation of death in that it follows the same archetypal pattern: it is usually accompanied by initiation rituals and brings about the separation of soul from body (ibid.). Preparation for death is an archetypal need which has been almost totally repressed in Western society. Traces of it, however, can still be found when an outwardly 'normal' and young person daydreams about his own death. Of course this can be viewed reductively as a narcissistic symptom, but why should it not also be an exercise through which he learns to experience 'sympathy' with the whole pattern of his individuation and to recover the unique meaning of his existence and his death?

What has been said about ecstasy is valid for dreams and all psychic states where the ego relinquishes its leading rôle and makes way for unconscious contents. Many cultures believe that the soul literally leaves the body in dreams and travels to all those places that are later remembered, and that if somebody meets in his dream people who are dead, he has obviously visited the kingdom of the dead. The older a person becomes, the more frequently will the people of whom he dreams inevitably be already dead, and if he remembers his dreams and uses them to good advantage in analysis, he will be undergoing what modern terminology calls psychotherapeutic treatment and will at the same time rediscover a long-repressed archetypal ritual. In this way he can recover an archaic pattern in which individuation is sought through a psychic exercise in preparation for death.

Conclusion

In the near future, neither the economically poor nor the peoples of the Third World, but the old, will in many respects be the 'damned of the earth'. Every modernization seems to bring about a growth in their number and a radical alienation of their identity—a striking analogy with Marx's analysis of the working classes in the nineteenth century. This loss of identity is both psychological and sociological, subjective and objective. Once upon a time the old person knew that he concentrated many collectively recognized values in himself, but now the mass media prove to him that he is the prototype of the loss of accepted values.

Public institutions administer gigantic funds to help the old, but this does nothing to restore the lost value of their archetypal rôle: the State seems to think that the ideal assistance is to make them forget their age and their approaching death; there is, in short, no concern for the unconscious psyche. As the producer sells his goods, so the State supplies its aid only if the elderly repudiate their identity, a blackmail that is constantly at work—'Come free of charge to the public holiday resort, and you will feel as lively as you did in your twenties': 'Accept this motorized wheelchair—it's better than a Cadillac.' Thus neither words nor money are spent on the real issue. The old do not need so much to travel physically, for which they are dependent on the guidance of the young, thereby emphasizing their alienation, but to travel inwardly along the path where eventually the young will follow their guidance. The already difficult task of individuation in old age is thus at risk of losing a favourable ambience for its development.

Youth too is affected by the cultural one-sidedness which represses old age, and most of us do not know what to do with our 'old' side. We look around desperately for some sort of archetypal wisdom, and, finding no answer, we try to quench our thirst with handbooks of 'grandmother's recipes'. Already as teenagers, many suffer from a neurotic ambivalence about getting old and do not know how to deal with the images of old age which increasingly populate their dreams. I have encountered in my practice, and in case discussions with colleagues have heard about, several girls who could only reach orgasm when fantasizing being possessed by a very old man.

Analysis has in principle the possibility of healing, and not just the healing of a single patient but of the repressed side of the whole culture. The rediscovery of the sexual drive by Freud, and of the archetypal patterns of the psyche by Jung, were radical revolutions, but as far as the condition of the old person is concerned, the official 'radicals' today seem only to be interested in his outer well-being and to look at his relationship to life against a medical and economic model. We analysts are theoretically in a position to compensate this one-sidedness in both the individual and our culture; dreams and visions in their purest form have traditionally signified a journey of the soul to the underworld, and to communicate constantly with them is the best archetypal preparation not only for life but also for death.

Jungians often speak of νέκυια, the journey to the land of the dead, but only seldom do we guide somebody for whom the 'νέϰυια' is an urgent and concrete task. Why is this so? Analytical treatment involves more than psychological work; it involves the spending of money. To what extent do we analysts yield to present collective values by agreeing that even though expensive, analysis is a good investment if it helps a still relatively young person and thereby saves a lot of future public expenditure? The Health Service in Germany has looked at this financial aspect and has decided on these grounds to pay for treatment. While this is certainly an admirable extension of health care, one wonders none the less whether it will not draw our attention even further away from the soul. To regard healing as an investment could eventually, in Hillman's words, confirm and clinch the 'root metaphor' of economics which pictures old age as a negative investment. Furthermore, to conceive of healing as an exclusively medical matter could convert the whole of old age into a chronic terminal disease. By so doing it would validate the root metaphor of the medical model and at the same time show up its natural limitations, since medicine perhaps provides 'prevention', but certainly not 'preparation', for the most natural of all events.

Summary

The evaluation of old age by a sociologist probably cannot be reconciled with that of a depth psychologist, since the former tends to split the complementarity of the *puer* and the *senex* archetypes and to give them opposed values. Opposition instead of complementarity means the denial of the values of old age as such and transforms it into a pathology. Depth psychologists— Jungians at least—substantially reject such pathologization and, in my opinion, should not confine their rejection to a diagnostic attitude but should try to conceive of analysis for the old as an initiatory rather than a clinical process. This suggested conception of analysis as initiation (*initium,* meaning a beginning) aims at viewing old age not simply as a loss of youth but as a psychological state attained gradually and with difficulty but worth entering into (*initium* in its turn derives from *in-eo,* to enter). At the same time by implication it hopes to reaffirm wisdom as a quality of experience and points to the importance of a psychological preparation for death.

REFERENCES

Ariès, P. (1975). *Essai sur l'Histoire de la Mort en Occident, du Moyen-Age á nos Jours*. Paris: Seuil.

Beauvoir, S. de (1972). *Old Age* (Appendix IV). London: André Deutsch and Weidenfeld & Nicholson.

Eliade, M. (1959). *Naissances Mystiques*. Paris: Gallimard.

———— (1976). *Occultism, Witchcraft and Cultural Fashions*. Chicago, IL: University of Chicago Press.

Foucault, M. (1967). *Origin of the Nursing Home*. London: Tavistock.

Freud, S. (1912–13). Totem and Taboo. *Standard Edition* 13. London: Hogarth.

———— (1920g). Beyond the Pleasure Principle. *Standard Edition* 18. London: Hogarth.

Gordon, R. (1978). *Dying and Creating: a Search for Meaning*. Library of Analytical Psychology, Vol. 4. London: Karnac Books.

Gorer, G. (1965). *Death, Grief and Mourning*. London: Cresset Press.

Herzog, E. (1966). *Psyche and Death*. London: Hodder & Stoughton.

Hillman, J. (1964). *Suicide and the Soul*. London: Hodder & Stoughton.

Illich, I. (1975). *Medical Nemesis*. London: Calder.

Radin, P. (1952). *African Folktales*. New York: Pantheon.

INDEX